WITHDRAWN
UTSA Libraries

Soviet–Third World

Relations

Soviet–Third World Relations

*Carol R. Saivetz
and Sylvia Woodby*

Westview Press / Boulder and London

All rights reserved. No part of this publication may be reproduced or transmitted in any form or by any means, electronic or mechanical, including photocopy, recording, or any information storage and retrieval system, without permission in writing from the publisher.

Copyright © 1985 by Westview Press, Inc.

Published in 1985 in the United States of America by Westview Press, Inc., 5500 Central Avenue, Boulder, Colorado 80301; Frederick A. Praeger, Publisher

Library of Congress Cataloging in Publication Data
Saivetz, Carol R.
    Soviet–Third World relations.
    Bibliography: p.
    Includes index.
    1. Developing countries—Foreign relations—
Soviet Union. 2. Soviet Union—Foreign relations—
Developing countries. 3. Soviet Union—Foreign
relations—1945–   . I. Woodby,
Sylvia. II. Title.
D888.S65S24 1985   327.470172′4   84-21939
ISBN 0-86531-647-3
ISBN 0-86531-648-1 (pbk.)

Printed and bound in the United States of America

10   9   8   7   6   5   4   3   2   1

LIBRARY
The University of Texas
At San Antonio

For
Richard, Michael,
Aliza, and Eric
—and—
our students

Contents

Tables, Figures, and Maps

Preface

Over sixty years ago, Lenin predicted that the fate of mankind's struggle for universal social justice would be vitally affected by political changes in what we now call the Third World. In many respects, his prophecy has proved correct. Our attention is constantly directed to skirmishes and upheavals in the Third World, whether they be in Vietnam, in the Middle East, on the Horn of Africa, or in Central America. Some of these events have been critical to international politics, and Soviet involvement has often been an important part of the drama. Both the USSR and the United States have interpreted the outcomes of Third World political developments as a reflection of their own prospects, and the Third World itself has frequently been an arena for East-West competition. Although much has been said about the Soviet Union's successes and expansion in the Third World, not all of this has been accurate. A careful assessment of Soviet–Third World relations requires examining many aspects of the record of Soviet behavior, including the USSR's expectations, methods, opportunities, and vulnerabilities.

Analyzing and explaining this record is a major undertaking, which includes exploring Soviet actions in nearly every region of the world, as well as examining the developing states of the Middle East, Asia, Africa, and Latin America. We have consciously chosen to exclude China and Korea as countries that have distinctive and special relationships with the USSR. We have also chosen to concentrate on state-to-state relations. Soviet actions in wider fora (such as the United Nations) and Soviet relationships with the international communist movement will be studied only as they affect those state-to-state relations. Thus while the scope of this book is ambitious, it will not satisfy those who seek detailed histories of either Soviet regional relations, or Soviet bilateral relations with individual Third World countries. Yet by asking important questions about Soviet behavior throughout the Third World, we can learn much about Soviet outlook, Soviet aims, and Soviet performance as an international actor that might be missed by narrower studies. Thus we hope to provide a comprehensive framework that complements the many existing works with a regional or country focus.

As a first step, we do not assume that ideology is the source of Soviet actions; however, we do believe it provides important information about Soviet perceptions and expectations. Moreover, Soviet objectives are frequently expresssed in ideological terms. Our detailed survey of Soviet–Third World relations confirms our understanding that Soviet policy reflects the interaction of the Third World environment with Soviet values and aims. While not denying the value of careful study of domestic determinants of Soviet behavior, we have not attempted to unravel the dynamics of the policy-making process within the USSR. Instead we have chosen to focus our attention on foreign policy outcomes, and thereby to highlight the interactive nature of Soviet foreign relations. In the process, we provide a review of a great many factors that, we conclude, become part of the internal and external decision-making context. Thus, we will offer no simple answer to the question of Soviet foreign policy motives. Nonetheless we hope that this study provides insights and evidence that will be helpful in the overall study of Soviet foreign policy.

We will begin with a survey of changing Soviet perspectives on the Third World, which provides a useful context for efforts to assess Soviet policies. A review of the record of Soviet–Third World relations follows. This will proceed chronologically, with separate treatment by regions. The record forms the basis for consideration of the openings and obstacles the USSR has encountered in the Third World. A separate chapter will then review the tools of Soviet involvement, including economic, military, diplomatic, cultural, and political instrumentalities. The next section will explore factors that may account for Soviet behavior in the Third World. We will identify possible Soviet objectives and weigh the impact of the domestic and foreign decision-making environment. Finally, we will evaluate the record, identifying long-term trends and assessing Soviet successes and failures. This provides a basis for some speculation about prospects for the future of Soviet–Third World relations.

We will show that while the Soviet presence in the Third World has expanded, Moscow's activities have not been uniformly skillful or successful. The Third World political terrain presents temptations and dangers, and the Soviets appear to have learned from their experiences. Lacking the ability to control events, and having abandoned apocalyptic visions of favorable political change in the Third World, the Soviets now proceed with caution.

Carol R. Saivetz
Sylvia Woodby

Acknowledgments

We would especially like to thank our colleagues Seth Singleton, Margaret Leahy, Melvin Goodman, and Robert O. Freedman for their comments and suggestions. Barbara Devine, Mary Vancura, and Ginny Boegner provided valuable technical assistance; Genevieve Macomber and Martha Cottam were much-appreciated sources of moral support. We wish to express our gratitude to Professors John N. Hazard, J. C. Hurewitz, Jacob Weintraub, Donald Zagoria, and Uri Ra'anan for their example and encouragement. We also wish to acknowledge support provided to us by the Russian Research Center at Harvard University and by Goucher College.

C.R.S.
S.W.

Chapter One

Changing Soviet Perspectives on the Third World

Ever since the earliest days of the Soviet state, the USSR has conducted multifaceted relations first with the states contiguous to its borders and then more extensively with the whole of the Third World. Today these ties include close political and economic links with so-called progressive* states as well as diplomatic and commercial ties with conservative and even anticommunist countries. Making sense of these sometimes chaotic sets of relations requires, first of all, analyzing how the Soviets see the Third World. Although the Soviet leadership has traditionally justified its relations with the nonindustrial world in terms of both the "world revolutionary process" and Soviet state interests, even a cursory look at Moscow's activities between 1917 and the present reveals that its attitudes and interests toward the Third World have changed and have been modified by its experiences there.

The Soviets' unique slant on Third World politics and on their relations with the less-developed countries (LDCs) emerges from Soviet official statements, academic discussions, and a vast monographic literature. Soviet perspectives on the Third World are an important indicator of Soviet priorities, of the roles the Soviets have designed for themselves, and, therefore, of Soviet objectives.

The evolution in Soviet–Third World relations and consequently in the Soviets' world view reflects and is part of some major shifts in international politics—primarily the changed status of the USSR within the international system. In the more than sixty-seven years of the USSR's existence, Soviet military and economic capabilities have increased substantially. Starting as "the new kid on the block" with a revolutionary political philosophy and an economic and military system in shambles, the Soviet Union emerged from World War II as a superpower, in fact one of two superpowers. However one assesses the contemporary military and economic prowess of the Soviet Union, its growth and power are unquestioned. In terms of Soviet–Third World relations, the Soviets' statements about their interest in and attitudes toward the nonindustrial

---

*The use of the terms *progressive, progress,* and *anti-imperialist* in this work follows common Soviet practice. It should not imply that the authors subscribe to the Soviet view.

world help us to gauge how Soviet leaders intend to use their clout. These pronouncements plus academic studies of Third World politics all facilitate a glimpse of policy discussions and represent attempts to create a fit between ideology and policy.

This chapter will provide an overview of Soviet perspectives on the Third World with particular attention to Soviet ideas about the importance of the Third World, expectations for political change there, and about Soviet roles in and relations with the nonindustrial states.

MARXIST-LENINIST AND RECENT SOVIET VIEWS

The USSR professes to conduct its diplomacy according to the dictates of Marxism-Leninism. In fact, the Soviet leadership claims that its very existence and the existence of the socialist bloc exert a profound influence on international affairs. Ironically, although Karl Marx and Friedrich Engels, the "grandfathers" of Soviet ideology, did comment on diplomatic and military events of their day, there is little international relations theory to be found in their work. Marx's elaborate theory of history and economic development focused on class issues; he presumed that workers' and capitalists' interests would cross national boundaries and render them obsolete. Vladimir Ilich Lenin adapted Marxism to conditions within the tsarist empire and to the tactical exigencies of seizing power. He reconstructed Marxism to emphasize political education and propaganda of the masses by a dedicated and well-trained elite. Lenin argued that political power in appropriate hands could be used to alter economic structures and thus move history along. (As we shall see this has echoes in many prescriptions for Third World political development.) But Lenin, unlike his ideological predecessors, also wrote about international relations. His analysis of world politics blamed imperialism, that is, the exploitation of colonial markets, for the continuing survival of capitalism, and he, therefore, perceived a link between what was happening in Russia, Europe, and the "Orient." As early as 1913, Lenin noted that "hundreds of millions of toilers in Asia have a reliable ally in the proletariat of all the civilized countries."[1]

In fact, the manifesto of the founding conference of the Communist International (Comintern) in 1919 stressed:

> The emancipation of the colonies is possible only in conjunction
> with the emancipation of the metropolitan working class. The
> workers and peasants not only of Annam, Algiers, and Bengal, but
> also of Persia and Armenia will gain their opportunity of

independent existence only in that hour when the workers of
England and France, having overthrown Lloyd George and
Clemenceau, will have taken state power into their own hands. . . .
Colonial slaves of Africa and Asia! The hour of proletarian
dictatorship in Europe will strike for you as the hour of your own
emancipation.[2]

The anticipated revolution in Europe never occurred, leaving Lenin and
his fellow Bolsheviks to conduct their own peculiar brand of diplomacy.
In the years immediately following the October Revolution, Soviet foreign
policy seemed to center on Europe. Not only did the new Soviet
government negotiate its withdrawal from World War I, but it also had
to establish relations, however tenuous at first, with the other European
powers. This was made more difficult by the Allied expeditionary
intervention on the side of anticommunist forces during the civil war.
By 1921, Moscow signed a trade agreement with England, and in 1922,
Germany and Russia concluded a formal treaty that included commercial
and military provisions. Almost simultaneously, the British presence in
Iran and Afghanistan prompted the Soviets to support local anti-British
forces in these contiguous countries.

By 1921, Bolshevik Russia had negotiated treaties with Turkey, Iran,
and Afghanistan. In the Turkish situation, nationalist leader Kemal Pasha
(Ataturk) approached Moscow for assistance in his war for independence.
The Soviet state responded with financial assistance and ultimately
secured a treaty that accepted Soviet dominance in the Caucasus and
promised a Soviet role in any international conference dealing with the
Dardanelles. However, this did not prevent Ataturk either from turning
on the local Turkish communists, or working out friendly relations with
the Western European powers, once his regime was safe. In Afghanistan,
the new Soviet leadership extended diplomatic recognition to the embattled Afghan emir, who won his throne over British opposition. The
Iranian case is more complex: Moscow not only protested the British
occupation of Iran, but also helped a rebel leader to establish a Soviet
republic along the northern borders. In the end, the Soviets abandoned
the local communists in favor of a neutrality treaty with the central
Iranian government. This treaty included a mutual pledge not to join
any military alliance against the other, or to permit hostile forces to
operate from its territory. Should one of the parties be unable to prevent
such use of its territory, the other was entitled to invade in order to
eliminate the aggressive threat.

Lenin's anounced sympathy with liberation struggles everywhere
necessitated a redefined role for the small native communist parties in
many areas. In general, as the Iranian case illustrated, local communists

were to be far less important than "bourgeois nationalist" leaders. Despite objections from some members of the Comintern,[3] Lenin chose to support national liberation movements, which were by definition anticolonial regardless of their noncommunist composition. Lenin went so far as to argue that with the help and guidance of the *Russian* communists, certain of these liberation leaders could skip the capitalist stage of development and take steps toward socialism.

With Lenin's death and Joseph Stalin's accession to power, the Soviet policy of alliances with nationalist movements was refined and reinforced. Stalin wrote:

> Of course this does not mean that the proletariat should support every national movement, always and everywhere, in all separate concrete cases. Rather, this means that the proletariat should support those national movements which are directed at the weakening or destruction of imperialism. . . . The struggle of the Afghan Emir for the independence of Afghanistan is objectively a revolutionary struggle despite the monarchical outlook of the Emir and his colleagues, for it weakens, disintegrates and undermines imperialism. . . . The struggle of the Egyptian merchants and bourgeois intellectuals for the independence of Egypt is for the same reasons a struggle objectively revolutionary.[4]

Stalin sought to mediate between local communists and nationalists so that anticolonial alliances need not damage the fortunes of the local parties. The difficulty inherent in this approach was nowhere more evident than in China; there, the Soviets tried to support nationalists and communists simultaneously. Even prior to Lenin's death, local Chinese communists were urged to join the Kuomintang and in 1923, the Soviets expressed support for Sun Yat-sen, while noting that "conditions for the successful establishment of either communism or Sovietism" did not exist in China.[5] In the mid-twenties, Stalin argued that Chinese communists, waiting for a later chance to take over the government, could best advance their own fortunes by collaborating with the nationalists. Chiang Kai-shek, however, successfully out-maneuvered the communists; in 1927, he nearly annihilated them all. Stung with defeat, Stalin, through the Comintern, urged local parties to fight the local national bourgeoisies.[6]

These early tentative relations with the areas immediately contiguous to the USSR illustrate several features about the importance of Soviet–Third World relations at this time. First, Lenin and his followers were preoccupied with consolidating their hold on power and with establishing a functioning economic system in Russia. Second, the confused Soviet activity of this period reflected multiple approaches to the outside world.

Lenin, as noted above, supported nationalists in their anticolonial struggle, while maintaining relations with ruling governments where appropriate. Simultaneously, the Soviets, through local communist parties and the Comintern, sought to influence the course of the ongoing political struggle. Third, the Soviet Union of the twenties was not the post–World War II USSR: Soviet leaders in this period, lacking the economic and military capabilities now associated with Moscow, could hardly expect to play a more major role in the Third World. Adam Ulam, for example, called Ataturk the Nasir of his day, but both the situation in the LDCs and the limits on Soviet capabilities clearly prevented the kind of assiduous cultivation that occurred thirty years later.[7]

By the late twenties, the Soviet Union seemed to turn inward. Stalin's rapid industrialization drive required a major overhaul of Soviet society. By the same token, the purges of the mid-thirties riveted the Soviets' attention. Yet, in some ways, this period had an outward thrust as well—even if indirectly. The industrialization drive, of course, resulted in a major build-up of Soviet capabilities (which would be needed to fight the coming war). By the end of the war, the Soviets would have demonstrated their military prowess, culminating in the achievement of superpower status. Moreover, the purges themselves had an international relations aspect. By using charges of international espionage against prominent Soviets, the leadership implied a hostility from and toward foreigners. With regard to specific foreign policy issues, Europe was indeed the top priority. The record of Soviet diplomacy of the thirties shows that the Kremlin leadership was preoccupied with Europe and the growing Nazi power on the continent: Policy was directed first at containing and then at working with Hitler's Germany. The USSR signed a nonaggression pact with Poland in 1932; joined the League of Nations in 1934; negotiated treaties with France and Czechoslovakia in 1935; and signed the infamous Nazi-Soviet Pact with Germany in 1939. In Asia, the Soviets were concerned primarily with Japan and China and the conflict between them. The rest of the Third World paled in comparison.

From June 22, 1941, when Nazi Germany attacked the Soviet Union, until the end of World War II, the Soviet goal was survival. In the colonial areas this meant, for example, that the communists in Bolivia supported the pro-U.S. government against striking workers and that Indian communists backed the British against a nationalist noncooperation movement. In China, communists agreed to cooperate with the Kuomintang against the occupying Japanese.

By means of the victory at Stalingrad, the eventual defeat of the Axis Powers, and the occupation of substantial sections of Eastern Europe, the Soviets proved to themselves and the rest of the world that they were a major power that could challenge the United States. At the end of the war, the Soviets demobilized but never to the same extent as the West. They proved capable, as a result, of pressing their new role and image in Eastern Europe (including Berlin), in border regions such as Iran and Turkey and, of course, in Korea. Simultaneously, the USSR developed its nuclear arsenal, thus further enhancing its superpower status. This growth in prestige and capabilities was matched by increasing opportunity created by the era of decolonization. As subsequent chapters will show, the USSR groped its way—sometimes acting cautiously and sometimes adventurously. The remainder of this chapter will present an overview of the Soviets' own attempts to understand Third World dynamics and to interpret their involvement.

The dramatic changes in postwar international politics, Stalin's death in 1953, and the ensuing succession struggle contributed to a rethinking of the international environment in which the Third World would acquire increasing significance. Soviet analyses of the time emphasized the changing international balance of power in favor of socialism; indeed, the espousal of several varieties of home-grown socialism and of vehement anti-Westernism by a growing number of Third World leaders seemed to confirm this trend. At the Twentieth Communist Party Congress in 1956, Nikita S. Khrushchev, the Party secretary, announced that because of the strength of the socialist camp, war was not inevitable and that a vast "peace zone" existed in the awakening Third World. The Congress also provided an arena for criticisms of leaders who argued against dealings with developing states and of the institutes of the Academy of Sciences that had not provided adequate information or devoted enough energies to contemporary issues.

The evolving Soviet world view implicitly permitted the Soviet Union to be active in the Third World: Formal diplomatic relations were conducted with many nonindustrial states and, as they had in the twenties, the Soviets proffered economic and military aid to several others. As part of the change, nationalist leaders who had been reviled under Stalin became honored guests at Kremlin receptions. Nevertheless, Moscow's growing interest in the Third World did not overshadow other foreign policy concerns. Priority has still been accorded to Soviet relations with the United States, China, and Western Europe. These policy spheres are, however, interrelated and decisions and/or events in one area may impinge on policy in another region.

The proliferation of Soviet ties with an ever increasing number of Third World states brought with it ideological problems, intracommunist disputes, and practical concerns. The Kremlin's dealings with the Third World radicals of the late fifties and early sixties infuriated local communists as well as some of the more doctrinaire members of the Politburo.

Critics from both groups challenged policy assumptions and the wisdom of neglecting ideological imperatives. Several Third World leaders who were attractive to the USSR because of their anti-Westernism proved equally anticommunist. While jailing, if not executing, members of the local parties, they also initiated domestic programs that seemed to merit Soviet approval. The series of nationalizations, the establishment of agrarian cooperatives, the curtailment of foreign investment—all without Soviet prompting—forced Moscow to assess how socialistically acceptable these home-grown socialisms truly were. On a pragmatic level, the Soviet leadership was concerned about how the burgeoning investments of the USSR were being used. This worry prompted some of the earliest attempts to sort out and evaluate local development strategies. Thus Soviet involvement in the nonindustrial world carried with it the need to guard the USSR's international prestige as leader of the socialist bloc. Moreover, the Soviets hoped as well that their activities matched their superpower status.

As a result of these problems and pressures, the Soviet leadership and the members of the relevant institutes of the Academy of Sciences attempted, over the years, to define "acceptable" Third World allies and to suggest programs to alleviate some of the apparent troubles. The analyses by politicians and academics combined Marxist-Leninist social science with some empirical observation. Additionally, their prescriptive nature is evident in the suggested strategies for movement from a traditional to a Soviet-type society.

The first significant formulation was the National Democratic State (NDS), which appeared as part of a statement issued in 1960 by the Conference of Communist and Workers' Parties. The statement characterized an NDS as a state that maintains close economic and cultural ties with the socialist bloc and pursues a pro-Soviet foreign policy. Domestically, the state was to raise the people's living standards and to ensure "democratic rights and freedoms." The emphasis on what the Soviets call "democratization" was clearly designed to pave the way for communist admission to decision-making circles. Prescriptively, the economic programs included agrarian reforms, creation of a "state sector," and the nationalization of foreign-owned industry.[8]

As a measure of reliability and "progressiveness," the National Democratic State proved simultaneously too vague and too restrictive. Its vagueness left unclear just how socialist a national democracy might be. The Third World of the early sixties contained few if any national democracies and, therefore, the restrictiveness of the construct could hardly be helpful as an indicator of who deserved Soviet support or as a justification for Soviet policies. The NDS probably represented a compromise formulation that said that any government with a pro-Soviet foreign policy and a combative attitude toward Western business and governments should get the support of its communist party. The wording of the NDS formulation would also seem to imply that the USSR would pressure these quasi-socialist governments to accept communist participation. As Chapter 2 will show, this proved a difficult undertaking.

Because of these inherent weaknesses, the National Democratic State was for all practical purposes replaced by 1963 with a new theoretical construct with a new vocabulary, the Noncapitalist Path (NCP). The noncapitalist formulation combined the socialist prescriptions that inform Soviet development literature with some of the realities of conditions and political processes in the Third World. As compared to the NDS, the NCP represented a more systematic approach to some of the problems raised by Soviet–Third World relations.

As the name implies, the NCP described a means of passage rather than an ideal type. Soviet theorists define it as: "that stage of social [and] economic development . . . in which by noncapitalist means the necessary preconditions for the transition to the construction of socialism are created."[9] Without the jargon, this means a pro-Soviet foreign policy combined with anticapitalist or noncapitalist domestic developmental programs. It also put considerable distance between noncapitalist development and socialism. Precisely because the formulation was a "path" rather than a description of ideal state forms, it directed attention to prescribing strategies that would ensure continuation along the road.

The logic of the rhetorical and ideological debate singled out four areas of concern: class issues, economic tasks, agrarian reform, and foreign policy. Considerable discussion, with the aim of deciding how effective and how socialist specific development strategies were, surrounded the first three categories. But it was probably the foreign policy issues that were the most significant. In this aspect, especially, the ideological discussions paralleled policy concerns. Observers not only urged closer ties with the Soviet bloc, but also recognized the connections between foreign policy and the willingness to accept foreign investment. For that reason, Soviet experts, while acknowledging the huge investment requirements of development, voiced alarm at Western assistance programs. Because foreign assistance was a tool of cultivation for the Soviets as well as for the West, the USSR charged that Western aid would subvert the independent (anti-imperialist) positions of the nonindustrial states. Of course, the Soviets claimed that their economic largesse would be provided with no strings attached. The fact that foreign policy and foreign aid were always discussed together highlights the interrelationship between the domestic and foreign policy prescriptions. It is implicit in the Soviet world view that the domestic transformations, as the Soviets call them, reinforce the foreign policy orientations and vice versa.

The flexibility inherent in looking at direction rather than ideals helped explain dealings with many Third World states to domestic and foreign critics. Aid to Egypt, Algeria, and Ghana could be justified as helping them achieve progressive development en route to socialism. Incremental steps, however small, signified progress in that direction. The message contained within public pronouncements and academic writings was that these self-proclaimed anti-Western socialists were acceptable to the USSR.

However, considerable ideological controversy arose over how forward thinking these states and their leaders actually were. Apparently, those who opposed dispensing political and economic support questioned the class origins—a measure of progress—of the Third World leadership. To bolster his argument, Khrushchev in 1963 dusted off an old term, "revolutionary democrat," to refer to noncommunist nationalists who, because of their experience with imperialism, shared the Marxists' hostility toward capitalism. Members of the Soviet leadership and the academic community theorized that revolutionary democrats would gradually become full-fledged Marxist-Leninists and that radical Third World leaders would eventually convert their states into members of the socialist camp. In the end, the Khrushchev faction, backed by political analyses from selected orientalists, appears to have won out. Nasir, Ben Bella, Nkrumah, and others received the accolades of the Soviet Union for their policies.[10] In fact, the awarding of Lenin prizes became part of the cultivation process. The Soviets, both implicitly and explicitly, arrogated to themselves the roles of supervisor and mentor.

The Soviets thus accepted radical but noncommunist leaders as friends and urged them to implement further social, economic, and political changes. However, the inherent limitations of this mentor role became obvious when a number of radical leaders were overthrown between 1965 and 1968. These coups were a dramatic reminder that pro-Soviet behavior by nationalist leaders, or their commitment to some kind of socialism, did not necessarily create lasting alignments. The disappointments and setbacks of the mid- to late sixties produced a noticeable shift in the focus and tenor of Soviet development studies. Both the NDS and the NCP proved inadequate as measures of self-styled radicals or as sets of prescriptions it was hoped many of these would follow. One can find within the Soviet pronouncements on Third World problems frank admissions that Marxism-Leninism had not produced correct analyses. With official prompting, the Soviet academic community devised new approaches to the study of the often contradictory processes in the Third World and to the assessment of socialist fortunes there.

The introduction of these sophisticated approaches coincided with change in the Soviet leadership, détente, and the acquisition of additional military capabilities that could influence the course of events in the Third World. The Brezhnev era brought with it a more sober approach to the nonindustrial world, with Khrushchev blamed for many ill-advised schemes at home and abroad. From the Soviet point of view, détente enshrined the achievement of parity with the United States; but of equal importance, Moscow's responsibilities did not prevent it from actively supporting radical Third World forces. The build-up of the Soviet navy facilitated a more global reach and Soviet power projection capabilities proceeded commensurately. As Soviet capabilities increased, the leadership and the military revised military doctrine to fit the new circumstances. New categories of wars specific to the Third World were invented and the Soviets debated the escalation factor in local conflicts. The weakening of the link between local wars and a world war permitted the possibility of Soviet intervention either directly or by arms transshipments. As Chapter 2 will show, beginning in 1969, the USSR manifested an enhanced willingness to participate directly in the Third World. Moreover, from the perspective of the Kremlin, these actions befitted a coequal of the United States.

Increased direct involvement necessitated accurate assessments and ideological justifications. In addition, Soviet policy concerns were reflected in a renewed emphasis on prescriptions geared to keeping pro-Soviet leaders in power and to reinforcing pro-Soviet progressive development strategies. By the early seventies, ideological and prescriptive statements indicated an awareness of the inherent difficulties in the Third World terrain and implied that earlier optimism was not justified. The pressures for accurate portrayals of Third World politics and for better prescriptions generated new models and added new topics to the research agenda.

One attempt to explain politics in the nonindustrial states resulted in the adoption of a model called *mnogoukladnost'*. The concept is a significant development in the Soviet literature in that it focuses not on the socialist blueprint but on the conflict within nonindustrial societies. The term *mnogoukladnost'* means multistructured or multisectored. Theorists derived the concept from Lenin's writings about the various levels of societal development; it is axiomatic that these levels coexist to varying degrees in the Third World. As a dynamic model, *mnogoukladnost'* explained failures in prescribed programs and highlighted the complexities of Third World politics.

Most analyses of the reassessment period contained two principal concerns: leadership and programs. The fragility of the commitment to progressive ideas and indeed the inherent instability of all Third World regimes seemed interconnected with the personalized politics of most of these states. Consequently, many theorists directed their attention to issues of depersonalization and of institutional development. In particular, scholars studied the role of the military and of political parties in the Third World environment.

Although initially hostile to military regimes, these observers became convinced by their experiences with Nasir and some other Middle East leaders that under specific conditions military establishments could be useful instruments of change. The revised assessments of military regimes were clearly linked to Soviet foreign policy concerns. The dynamics of military intervention affects and is affected by Soviet (and Western) arms transfers. Although military assistance provided entree into several Third World areas, such aid alone has not been sufficient to perpetuate either Soviet or U.S. positions. Despite the number of progressive military regimes, experience has taught the Soviets not to ignore the possibility of reversals.

With this in mind, Soviet experts on the Third World have devised new prescriptions designed to ensure the progressive orientation of the army. Observers stress that military aid and the presence of military advisors must be complemented by purges of untrustworthy military personnel, reorganization, and indoctrination. This last prescription most often entails political education programs, frequently under Soviet direction.[11] Moreover, scholars urge the radical military leaders to demilitarize, that is, to create civilian political organizations.

Since their own political system and ideology confirm the pivotal role of a committed and controlling political party, it is not surprising that Soviet analysts recommend "party building" as the way to institutionalize progressive development. Marxist-Leninists stress political parties not only as a framework in which to unite and mobilize like-minded individuals, but also as an agent of further social change. Since most Third World countries lack a communist party, Soviet theorists recommended that their allies imitate communist party organization forms by creating "vanguard" parties. As one scholar noted, "The experiences of Ghana, Mali, Egypt and others bears witness to the fact that without this type of party it is impossible to resolve completely the tasks of the national democratic revolution, or to guarantee the stability of revolutionary democratic regimes."[12] Vanguard parties are supposed to be highly disciplined organizations that carefully screen members and organize party cells at places of work. Their existence and proper functioning, even though they are not considered communist parties, would ensure continuity in domestic and foreign policies in the event of leadership change.

The growing sophistication of Soviet assessments of Third World politics clearly required a parallel effort to develop new criteria of acceptability. Just as the NCP superceded the NDS, the State of Socialist Orientation concept, supplanted the NCP by the early to mid-seventies. Soviet academics describe a socialist-oriented state as one completing the noncapitalist transition to socialism; that is, a state whose pro-Soviet foreign policy is complemented by an explicit commitment to Marxism-Leninism and to Soviet-style institutions. The characteristics of a socialist-oriented policy include consolidation and expansion of the public sector on an "anticapitalist" basis, agrarian reforms, and the creation of a vanguard party. Essentially, a state of socialist orientation is a Third World imitation of the Soviet party-state, differing in the transitional character of the economy and the absence of an explicitly communist party.[13]

The construct of a socialist-oriented polity is similar to the NCP in that it measures trends or directions, but it is also more narrowly defined. In the sixties, the list of states on the NCP included Mali, Algeria, Egypt, and several others. By the late seventies, the primary examples of socialist-oriented societies were Angola, Mozambique, Ethiopia, and the People's Democratic Republic of Yemen (South Yemen, PDRY).

With so few states belonging to this exclusive club, Soviet–Third World experts appear to concede that the socialist-oriented option is not a feasible choice for most countries. Furthermore, the academic discussions make it clear that even those states that do choose to become states of socialist orientation are far removed from the ideal of a Soviet-style state. Implicitly, the mentor/supervisor role is reconfirmed. Third World realities leave the Soviets in a position to comment extensively on how far most states are from the ideal and to offer detailed prescriptions to close the gap. Additional implications of this most recent construct are less clear. As with the other constructs, the state of socialist orientation explains and justifies Soviet relations with radical Third World states. The label, an accolade, is no guarantee of direct Soviet support. Of the socialist-oriented states, for example, Angola and Ethiopia are recipients of direct Soviet aid in the form of Soviet military equipment and Cuban troops. In the PDRY, the Soviets provide military aid, while the East Germans train security forces. Yet others receive no such aid. Thus, in terms of defining Soviet activity, the construct justifies in ideological terms a range of policies up to possible military intervention but does not necessarily ensure such actions.

REALISM AND PRAGMATISM

This survey of Soviet perspectives on the Third World is intended as background to what follows. Study of the evolution of Soviet development theory reveals that Moscow continues to seek explanations for events and problems that affect the success or failure of Soviet policy. This drive may be seen in the increasing number of Soviet experts on the Third World and in their studies. The various constructs adopted illustrate the categories of thought used by the Soviets and the types of analyses that are ideological rationales for aspects of Soviet–Third World relations.

In the almost thirty years since the Soviets began to revise their views of international politics and in particular of the dynamics of Third World political processes, we have seen them try to clarify their own thinking about the less-developed countries. Behind the constructs lie patience and flexibility, which derives from the Soviets' decision to take what they can get. There can be no doubt that revolutionary priorities have been abandoned. Moscow will accept a pro-Soviet foreign policy alone or together with acceptable domestic programs. At different times, each construct represented a tentative fit between ideology and pragmatic politics. And the patience is inherent in the admission that ill-conceived and ill-timed programs may cost the radicals dearly, economically and politically. Moreover, those within decision-making circles who might have preferred more progressive policy changes on the part of Soviet Third World allies were cautioned that such setbacks potentially hurt Soviet policy. The time frame for progressive development has been significantly elongated: In fact, the Soviets, especially in the aftermath of Afghanistan, now urge caution upon their friends. Perhaps most striking is the recognition that full-fledged Marxist-Leninist states are not about to spring up across the Third World.

If the Soviets are more realistic about radical prospects in the Third World, then why do they continue to describe and prescribe socialist development strategies? There are two primary reasons for these prolonged efforts. First, the Kremlin continues to stress what it calls the "correlation of forces" or balance of power in the world, and the existence of radical pro-Soviet states in the Third World adds weight on the Soviet side of the scale. Therefore, it is incumbent upon the leadership to encourage and to appear to be associated with progressive development so as to prove that the balance is continuing to shift in their favor. Second, unlike radicals of the sixties, who adopted self-styled socialisms, the radicals of the late seventies and eighties espouse Marxism-Leninism. The Soviets, as leaders of the socialist bloc, can hardly ignore their claims; instead, the Kremlin has had to accommodate and recognize them.

In all, the newer prescriptions, with the emphasis on the pitfalls of rapid development, the tumultuous nature of Third World political processes, and the political directives to ensure leadership continuity all complement the Soviet role as superpower and leader of socialist-oriented states. The changes in rhetoric and theory as they parallel Soviet roles and capabilities imply a major intrusion of practicality.

NOTES

1. V. I. Lenin, "Backward Europe and Advanced Asia," *Pravda*, May 19, 1913, as cited in *The National Liberation Movement in the East* (Moscow: Foreign Languages Publishing House, 1957), p. 63.

2. The Manifesto appears in Leon Trotsky, *The First Five Years of the Comintern*, vol. 1 (New York: Pioneer Press, 1945), p. 25.

3. At the second Comintern congress (July 1921), a fascinating dispute about communist-nationalist relations erupted when Lenin's draft theses on the topic were challenged by Indian revolutionary Manabendra Nath Roy. Roy objected to Lenin's recommendation that communists seek alliances with colonial nationalist movements that were naturally middle class. His alternate proposal urged communists to organize their own independence movements. Both sets of theses were adopted after being amended to endorse communist-nationalist alliances provided that revolutionary possibilities were not compromised. Debate has continued among communists about the proper interpretation of the Comintern document, the language of which has been corrected by Soviet historians to downplay the importance of Third World communist parties. See Sylvia Woodby, "Leninism Revisited: The Fate of the Lenin-Roy Debate" (unpublished manuscript).

4. I. V. Stalin, "Ob osnovakh Leninizma" (1924), *Sochineneiia*, vol. 6 (Moscow: Gospolitizdat, 1947), pp. 142–144.

5. The Sun-Joffe Declaration of January 1923 may be found in Jane Degras, ed., *Soviet Documents on Foreign Policy*, vol. 1 (London: Oxford University Press, 1951), p. 370.

6. Joseph L. Nogee and Robert H. Donaldson, *Soviet Foreign Policy Since World War II* (New York: Pergamon Press, 1981), p. 131.

7. Adam B. Ulam, *Expansion and Coexistence: Soviet Foreign Policy, 1917–1973*, 2d ed., (New York: Praeger Publishers, 1974), p. 123.

8. The statement, after detailing the acceptable policies, concludes: "The formation and consolidation of national democratic states ensures for these states the possibility of rapidly developing along the path of social progress and playing an active role in the struggle of the peoples for peace, against the aggressive policy of the imperialist camp and for complete abolition of the colonial yoke." The full statement may be found in "Statement of Conference of World Communist Parties—II," *Current Digest of the Soviet Press*, vol. 12, no. 49 (January 4, 1961), p. 4.

9. R. A. Ul'ianovskii, *Sotsializm i osvobodivshiesia strany* (Moscow: iz. Nauka, 1972), p. 445.

10. Oded Eran makes an effective argument that factions of the leadership enlist the aid of various scholars to support their respective positions. See his

The Mezhdunarodniki, An Assessment of Professional Expertise in the Making of Soviet Foreign Policy (Ramat Gan, Israel: Turtle Dove Press, 1979).

11. Soviet officials, including A. A. Yepishev, the head of the Soviet army's Main Political Administration, frequently travel to Third World countries that have received Soviet military assistance. Yepishev, in charge of indoctrination and political education, presumably advises radical states on similar issues in the Third World military establishments.

12. Iu. V. Irkhin, "Avangardnye revoliutsionnye partii trudiashchikhsia v osvobodivshikhsia stranakh," *Voprosy Istorii,* no. 4 (April 1982), p. 58.

13. Sylvia Woodby Edgington, "The State of Socialist Orientation: A Soviet Model for Political Development," *Soviet Union,* no. 8, pt. 2 (1981), pp. 235–237. See also her "Leninism for the Third World: Recent Trends and Tensions" (Paper presented at the American Association for the Advancement of Slavic Studies, Kansas City, Mo., October 1983).

Chapter Two

The Record

The international political system has been fundamentally transformed in our century by the application of the principle of self-determination on a global basis. As the number of independent states has grown, so has their visibility in world politics. The USSR was ideologically poised to welcome and seek to benefit from these changes, and has in fact become a significant actor throughout the Third World. However, this was accomplished gradually, with mixed results. This chapter will review the record of Soviet relations with the Third World from 1946 to the present, in order to provide a foundation for judgments about sources and trends in Soviet behavior.

A full history of Soviet activity in the Middle East, Asia, Africa, and Latin America is beyond the scope of this book. However, we have attempted to include significant highlights that combine to present an accurate general picture. Our information is presented in five parts, corresponding to identifiable periods in Soviet foreign policy. Within each period, the four major geographical subdivisions of the Third World are treated separately. Although we recognize that this plan may obscure patterns or trends that do not fit our periodization scheme and may promote a fragmented image of Soviet actions, the mass of detail requires some systematic organization. The phases we have selected reflect major events of Soviet foreign policy and political history that marked a change in leadership or policy mood. Each section begins with a brief summary of the nature of these events in order to outline the larger context in which Soviet–Third World relations occurred.

THE END OF THE STALIN ERA: 1946–1953

Soviet foreign policy in the immediate postwar period reflected a number of contradictory themes that evolved in response to a dramatically changing, challenging, and often promising new political environment. As one of the victor states, the Soviet Union achieved a tremendous boost in status. Yet the role the Soviets were to play in the postwar world would depend on the relationships with the wartime Western allies and on the way in which the Soviets would handle the many opportunities and problems that presented themselves.

The most important feature of the postwar international situation, which must have dominated Soviet perceptions, was the pervasive and organizing presence of the United States in Europe. The willingness of the United States to take responsibility for European economic reconstruction and defense and its emerging interest in containment of the USSR were indeed serious threats. The Soviets gradually, despite Western objections, consolidated their hold on Eastern Europe, began rebuilding their war-damaged economy, and acquired atomic weapons.

It soon became obvious that East-West tension would prevent the conclusion of a general peace treaty. Germany was left divided, with Berlin under British, French, U.S., and Soviet occupation. At times in the early phases of the cold war, the Soviets tried hard to present themselves as sincerely interested in continued cooperation with the Western countries. Then, between 1947 and 1949, Soviet foreign policy rhetoric became highly inflammatory and bellicose. U.S. interest in economic and military assistance to Europe was denounced as an indication that the United States was preparing for a new world war. Communists were called upon to lead an "active struggle" against governments that cooperated with the United States. Western reaction to Soviet actions in Europe and the Far East helped to formalize the cold war in the establishment of the North Atlantic Treaty Organization (NATO) and the Warsaw Treaty Organization (WTO).

Although the consolidation of the Soviet hold on Eastern Europe proceeded successfully, probes elsewhere generally did not succeed, but only served to encourage the West to unite. Yugoslavia successfully asserted its independence from Moscow, and the attempt to unify Korea by force was rebuffed. By 1950 it must have been clear that acquisitive policies and belligerent rhetoric were counterproductive. New approaches that emphasized the desirability of "peaceful coexistence" and diplomatic agreements with the Western countries emerged. Moreover, in 1950 and 1951 European communists were being directed not to try to overthrow their governments, but to try to pressure existing ones to be anti-American. This more opportunistic approach was officially endorsed at the 1952 Soviet Party Congress. Amid references to a possible non-aggression pact with the Western states, Georgy Malenkov stated that countries with "independent peaceful policies" would enjoy the USSR's "complete understanding."[1] In this period, the dismantling of colonial empires was just beginning. Although many Western studies have given an impression that the USSR did not show any interest in colonial nationalism until after Stalin's death and that at first the Soviets were hostile toward nationalists who were willing to negotiate independence,[2] careful examination of the sources reveals a more subtle and complex picture.

Themes in Soviet Approaches to the Third World

The record of Soviet relations with the Third World for the 1946–1953 period includes much that is really verbal behavior: positions, statements, and interpretations. It is difficult to see general trends. Rather, a mixture of cooperative and confrontational themes is present, although Soviet direct and indirect policy in these areas reflects the moods and character of policy in Europe: Soviet actions and declarations with reference to the decolonization process were initially receptive, then militantly hostile, then more actively friendly.

In the immediate postwar period, the Soviets endorsed the idea of United Nations trusteeships, a system Soviet commentators said would give the colonies "concrete possibilities for progressive development."[3] Nationalist movements seeking negotiated independence were generally applauded. This approach was in line with the restrained position of British, French, and Dutch communists, who were responsible for guidance of their colonial counterparts. While Soviet commentators made it clear that imperialists would always try to delude their colonial subjects with minor concessions and "prophylactic reforms," the very fact negotiations occurred was taken as evidence that the old days were over.[4] The Soviet media recalled that the Soviet Union had assisted independence struggles in Afghanistan, Turkey, Iran, Mongolia, and China in the twenties because of the "well-defined historically progressive significance" of their conflicts with imperialism.[5] This seemed to indicate that the Soviets would welcome good relations with the postwar nationalist movements.

By 1947, as East-West tension escalated, commentaries on independence movements in the colonies became notably more suspicious of concessions granted by former rulers. Many of the factors that had made collaboration between communists and other local political forces possible or desirable were disappearing. The USSR lost its ally image; governments everywhere began to ban communist parties; the schism with Yugoslavia was quickly beginning to give all "nationalists" a bad name within the communist movement; and hardliners were gaining ascendancy within Soviet society and government.

The founding of the Cominform in September 1947 articulated these trends and contributed to the bipolar image of a world at near-war. This was paralleled by a shift of tone and direction in Soviet recommendations and the tactics of those who followed them. The keynote speech by Andrei Zhdanov (fresh from launching a xenophobic cultural campaign within the USSR) described the world as increasingly divided into two hostile camps, but it put nationalist movements on the Soviet side.

> The basis of the [democratic] camp is the USSR and the countries of new democracy. It also includes countries which have broken with imperialism and firmly set foot on the path of democratic development, such as Rumania, Hungary, and Finland. *Indonesia and Vietnam are associated with it, and it has the sympathy of India, Egypt, and Syria.* The anti-imperialist camp is backed by the labor and democratic movement and by the fraternal Communist parties in all countries, by *the fighters for national liberation in the colonies and dependencies,* by all progressive and democratic forces in every country.[6]

This optimistic formulation identified regimes established through ne-gotiations (coerced more than granted in the case of Indonesia and Indochina) as sympathizers and associates of the Soviet state in its global struggle with imperialism. What would this mean for Soviet relations with these emerging ex-colonies? Once anti-Americanism was accepted as a priority, the Soviets could welcome statesmen like Indian Prime Minister Jawaharlal Nehru, who had declared an interest in an inde-pendent foreign policy.

However, in an atmosphere of high confrontation, anything less than clear support of the Soviet side might not be enough. Indications that this was the trend in Soviet thinking were available soon after Zhdanov's speech, as leading Soviet scholars heaped praise on those fighters "actively undermining imperialism," and claimed (generally without foundation) that communists were an important political force in the colonies.[7] Certainly, the rhetoric heated up considerably. The international communist press soon filled with attacks on European socialists and criticized "neutralists" as de facto servants of imperialism. Whereas in 1946, Soviet aid to the independence struggles of Iran, Turkey, and China in the twenties had been recalled, the nationalism of these movements was now attacked. "Bourgeois nationalism," it was claimed, had eventually led to the transformation of these countries into "appendages of Anglo-American imperialism."[8]

But as the confrontational tone in Soviet policy in Europe changed during the Korean war, the attitude toward ex-colonial regimes also began to improve. The opposition of many of the new states to the war and to U.S. plans for military alliances and bases stimulated Soviet optimism about the potential utility of these states as international political actors. At first, such behavior was attributed by the communist press to "popular pressure," then to genuine aspirations for independence. In November 1951, Soviet spokesman Lavrenti Beria's revolutionary anniversary speech complimented India for its foreign policy positions. In 1952, the Soviet press editorially proclaimed that the "struggle for national independence is inseparable from the struggle for peace," which was explained as a struggle against military pacts, foreign military bases, and foreign control over natural resources.[9] Signals that emphasized taking up nationalism were sent to foreign communists. In January 1953, a key Soviet journal recalled that both Lenin and Stalin had stressed the necessity of supporting truly revolutionary nationalist movements; it cited Stalin's statement of 1924 that one could be a revolutionary nationalist without being either democratic or proletarian![10]

Overall, the context of Soviet approaches to the colonies in this period varied widely. However, except for a brief period of tactical and doctrinal militance, it sems clear that the Soviets accepted the decolonization process as beneficial from their point of view. Moreover, they did not expect rapid changes, and were receptive to friendly relations with the dominant political forces in the ex-colonies.

Although the USSR was preoccupied with Europe during this period, a number of important initiatives were directed at the Third World. This Soviet activity in colonial or formerly colonial areas was acquisitive, but not foolhardy, and can be seen as attempts to maximize opportunities presented by wartime occupation or postwar disruption. These probes did not persist when opposed strongly by the West.

The Middle East

The Kremlin took an active interest in the Middle East. The war left the political future of a number of areas uncertain, and in many ways the USSR sought to take advantage of highly fluid circumstances. When V. M. Molotov requested a trusteeship over Libya during the London Foreign Ministers' conference in September 1945, the Western participants apparently did not take him too seriously. In any case, they strongly resisted his suggestion, even when it was later reformulated as a request for a joint great power trusteeship over the former Italian possessions.

In 1945, Soviet troops moved into northern Iran and assisted in the organization of a separatist regional government along their border. When these forces did not withdraw as had been agreed with the Allies, the Iranian government brought a complaint to the United Nations. In fact, the presence of Soviet troops in Iran was the very first item on the agenda when the United Nations Security Council met in January 1946. In the debate that ensued, the Soviets attempted to justify their actions by noting allegedly similar occupations by Great Britain in Indonesia, and by France in Syria and Lebanon. Ultimately, an agreement was reached with the Iranian government, and the Soviets were forced to withdraw their troops by May 1946. At almost the same time, Moscow sought to pressure the shaky Turkish regime to concede military bases and a voice in the administration of the Dardanelles. This was a continuation of a centuries-old Russian interest in free access to the Mediterranean through the straits at the Bosporus. Simultaneous communist activity in Greece galvanized the Americans to assume responsibility for political stability in this area. The "Truman Doctrine," proclaimed in 1947, identified the spread of communist totalitarianism as a threat to U.S. interests, and justified U.S. military and economic commitments to Turkey and Greece. The Greek insurgency ended shortly after the Soviet schism with Yugoslavia, and the closing of the Greek-Yugoslav border in 1948. The demands on Turkey came to naught with the signing of a United States–Turkey military pact.

Soviet activity was even bolder with respect to the tumultuous situation in Palestine. In the debates at the United Nations, the USSR took a strong pro-Zionist position in favor of a partition of Palestine that would create a Jewish state. Although the United States wavered in its willingness to endorse this idea, the Soviets were steadfast. Eventually both the United States and the USSR supported partition and recognized the state of Israel, which declared its independence in May 1948. War followed between the Israelis and a multinational Arab force. Soviet military assistance to the Zionists (in the form of small arms shipped into Palestine through Czechoslovakia in 1947 and 1948) was critical to the survival of the Jewish state. The Soviets may have seen this as an easy chance to score a victory over British imperialism (perceived at this time to be at least mildly pro-Arab). In this instance, an intrusion of Soviet military aid was not greeted with much alarm, since the United States was doing the same.

The Soviet Union was the first country to extend formal recognition to the Israeli state and supported it regularly in the UN debates. Israeli gratitude was expressed, for example, by voting with the Soviets for admission of the People's Republic of China to the United Nations. As Israel developed a close association with the United States, however, the Soviet stance altered. In 1951, the Israeli Knesset rejected a proposal for closer ties with the USSR. After the Tripartite Declaration of 1950, in which the United States, Britain, and France promised not to alter the military balance of the region, the Soviet press began calling Israel a base of U.S. imperialism. Although Arabs took offense when a Soviet ambassador presented his credentials in Jerusalem in December 1953, a shift to support of the patronless Arabs was already under way.[11]

Asia

The victory of the Chinese communists and the establishment of the People's Republic of China in 1949 transformed East Asia. The Soviets apparently provided considerable indirect matériel assistance to the victorious Chinese Red Army during their final campaigns in 1948 and 1949. However, later Soviet claims of generosity notwithstanding, the actions of Soviet forces in the field were less than magnanimous. Eyewitnesses say the Soviets stripped factories in former Japanese-held Manchuria without regard to possible needs or prerogatives of the fraternal cousins. Moreover, the USSR was extremely cautious about its diplomatic posture and went to considerable lengths to maintain correct relations with Chiang Kai-shek's rival government until after the actual establishment of the People's Republic in October 1949.

Allied agreements included shared U.S.-Soviet responsibility for disarming the Japanese in Korea. But efforts to arrange unification were quickly frustrated, and separate regimes were established in the North and South. When the North Koreans launched their invasion of the South in 1950 (undoubtedly with Soviet approval), almost all U.S. forces had been withdrawn. The North Koreans were initially victorious, sweeping easily down the peninsula. But the gamble that the United States would not react was lost. When U.S. intervention, sanctioned by the United Nations as a police action against aggression, nearly effected conquest of North Korea, it was the Chinese who stepped in to rescue the Soviets' Korean client. By the end of 1951, the fighting had produced a stalemate, although skirmishes continued intermittently until 1953, with the opposing armies confronting each other along the original dividing line. Although the USSR carefully distanced itself from this adventure, Western perceptions interpreted this war as a product of communist expansionism. The conflict contributed significantly to U.S. rearmament and the consolidation of NATO and other military alliances, and helped justify U.S. assistance to France in its war against communists in Indochina.

Soviet activity was very limited elsewhere in Asia. In Indochina, interests in both communists and nationalists were subordinated for a time to European priorities. The French Communist Party was a member of the government from 1945 to 1947 and did not endorse independence for France's colonial territories. In fact, the French Communist Party even went along with the military campaign against the independent state that Ho Chi Minh declared in 1945. By 1949, the Vietnamese began to receive active assistance from the Chinese communists. Accordingly, the level of Soviet support for the Vietnamese war for independence intensified. (Simultaneously, the United States began to assist the French military forces fighting there.) The Soviet government extended diplomatic recognition to Ho Chi Minh's government in 1950 (perhaps spurred by conversations between Stalin and Mao). Like the Vietnamese themselves, however, the Soviets supported the concept of negotiations with the French, who were fighting to regain control over the entire peninsula. The fighting continued inconclusively into 1953.

Indonesian nationalists, like the Vietnamese, proclaimed independence in 1945, before their former colonial rulers could return. Communists and leftists of all types generally cooperated with Achmed Sukarno and the other nationalists attempting to negotiate with the Dutch. The communist party was legal in Indonesia, and in 1947 was participating in the government. The USSR defended this government's right to exist at the United Nations, and volunteered to be part of a multinational fact-finding mission to visit the archipelago in 1946. When the Dutch invaded Indonesia and sought to restore their rule by force, the Soviets supported efforts in the United Nations to secure Dutch withdrawal and to supervise a cease-fire. In 1947, the Soviets signed a consular agreement with the Indonesian Republic.

The Indonesian communists found themselves increasingly at odds with their government over conduct of the negotiations with the Dutch. In 1948 the communists apparently determined to try to take over the government themselves. When their revolt was sparked prematurely, Sukarno declared a state of emergency, suppressed the uprising by force, and executed several of its leaders. These events interrupted Soviet-Indonesian relations, and Moscow criticized the Indonesian government for its willingness to settle for independence within a Netherlands-Indonesia Union in November 1949. However, by 1951 the Indonesian government attracted Soviet attention, since it was beginning to pursue a foreign policy that was critical of the United States. Opposition by both Indonesia and Burma to U.S. proposals for a Pacific security pact paved the way for the Soviets to establish diplomatic relations with these governments in 1951 and to praise their foreign policy "independence."

Nehru's startling statement in 1946 that he intended to lead India on an "independent course" in foreign policy and that India would "not be a satellite of Great Britain" was happily reported in the USSR. Diplomatic relations were established between India and the USSR in April 1947, and Nehru was described as a "revolutionary democrat" reminiscent of Sun Yat-sen, the nationalist leader who had developed friendly relations with the Soviets in the twenties. However, the course of Soviet-Indian relations in this period was affected at several points by the outlook and actions of the Communist Party of India (CPI).

At first, the British communists had supported negotiations for independence, and welcomed the establishment of the Dominion governments in India and Pakistan in 1947. Communists within India had also pledged their support to the new regime's democratic aspirations. In the aftermath of the formation of the Cominform, communist attitudes inside and outside India became very hostile to Nehru, and Soviet-Indian relations cooled temporarily. Much of this seems to be a case of a self-fulfilling prophecy. That is, communist criticism of Nehru led to campaigns against his government. The arrests of communists that followed appeared to confirm and justify labeling Nehru as an enemy. In December 1947, the CPI interpreted Zhdanov's Cominform speech to mean that the party should denounce the Nehru government as collaborationist and attempt to replace it with a people's democracy. A CPI congress in February and March 1948 outlined the new strategy for members and guests from Southeast Asian parties. (Communists in Malaya, the Philippines, Burma, and Indonesia shifted to insurrection shortly afterwards.) When Nehru's government cracked down on communists for pursuing these tactics, the CPI denounced him in a letter that was carried in the Soviet paper *Pravda* in 1949. Nehru subsequently became a target for extremely harsh criticism as an "imperialist agent."[12]

By 1951, Nehru's offer to act as a mediator in Korea and criticism of U.S. policies revived favorable Soviet comment about his nationalism. In November 1951, a revolutionary anniversary speech by Beria complimented India for its foreign policy positions. The Soviet press then gave considerable favorable publicity to a shift of tactics by the Indian communists, who were once again ready to support Nehru's "anti-imperialist" foreign policy initiatives.

Africa

Soviet commentaries on Africa during this period did not predict rapid success for nationalist movements. Promises of political reforms and eventual self-government had been made to the colonies in Africa during the war. However, political activity surrounding discussions about such changes had not yet reached the point where there was much reason for optimism about the emergence of new states. The kinds of gradual transitions and incremental reforms being proposed hardly justified expectations of rapid changes in the status of African colonies. The Soviets were suspicious of British and French intentions toward their colonies, and of U.S. strategic designs on the continent. Press accounts, which were critical of nationalist leaders, echoed the positions of British and French communists, who at this time were in favor of gradual moves toward colonial self-government, rather than immediate independence.

Latin America

In Latin America, the Soviet Union's wartime alliance with the United States had facilitated friendly relations with a number of states. However, as the cold war intensified, many Latin American regimes banned their communist parties, and almost all states that had previously maintained diplomatic relations with the Soviet Union broke them. In a few countries, the collaborationist tactics of the late forties assisted political growth of fairly broad leftist coalitions. One of the most successful cases was in Guatemala, where the Guatemala Labor Party was legalized in 1952. It became part of the political base for a leftist government under Jacobo Arbenz Guzman, which moved to establish friendly relations with the USSR.

ACTIVE DIPLOMACY: 1953–1964

Stalin's death was announced to the world on March 5, 1953. Ensuing power struggles among Stalin's heirs involved both foreign and domestic policy issues, and therefore complicate attempts to find coherence in Soviet behavior during this period. In the immediate post-Stalin period, Soviet leaders moved to set aside cold war tensions but also began to explore opportunities for enhancing the USSR's global status. Nikita S. Khrushchev emerged as the dominant Soviet leader in 1957. In the years of his relatively undisputed stewardship, Soviet foreign policy was characterized by an almost chaotic succession of crises and confrontations.

The division of Europe, and of Germany, was institutionalized with the admission into NATO of the Federal Republic of Germany, while its counterpart, the German Democratic Republic, joined the WTO. This division became increasingly accepted as a permanent one, despite political crises that threatened Soviet control in East Europe in 1953 and 1956. In the two years following Stalin's death, the new leadership took a number of steps to reduce the sense of confrontation with the West. In 1953 the Soviets were apparently responsible for breaking the deadlock at the Korean armistice talks that ended the fighting in July. The Soviet leaders also agreed to summit conferences on Germany, Indochina, and Korea, and set up bilateral talks with the United States. Meanwhile, Soviet leaders intensified diplomatic activity designed to project a nonaggressive image. These initiatives included proposals at the United Nations on disarmament, suggestions for trade ties with Western countries, the return of an old military base to Finland, invitations to leaders of many smaller countries to visit the USSR and establish "friendly relations of mutual benefit," and the like.

Khrushchev compiled an uneven record of accomplishments. Major Soviet gains in weaponry and missile technology were reflected in the acquisition of fusion weapons, the successful launch of the orbiting satellite "Sputnik" in 1957, and the first manned space shot in 1961. These were offset by West German rearmament, steps taken toward nuclearization of NATO, and an accelerated U.S. arms program. The USSR was doubtless pleased with the disarray that developed in the Western alliance. (De Gaulle removed the French Mediterranean fleet from NATO in 1960 and proceeded to build an independent nuclear force.) However, severe management problems developed within the socialist camp as well. The Sino-Soviet dispute, which revolved around issues of revolutionary zeal and politics, became a public diplomatic quarrel in 1960 and seriously challenged perceptions of communist power. Because it split the international communist movement, the dispute seriously weakened Soviet ability to speak with authority in ideological matters and exposed every policy initiative to intensive criticism.

Adam Ulam has suggested that Soviet foreign policy in this phase of Khrushchev's dominance reflected a "grand design" to negotiate a settlement with the West that would trade a nuclear-free Germany for a nuclear-free Pacific—a goal that he pursued frantically as the ability to control China became ever more questonable.[13] After the Cuban missile crisis of October 1962 had displayed the dangers of brinkmanship, the emphasis in Soviet policy became more accommodationist, and a number of concrete agreements that helped to reduce tension and lay a foundation for détente were reached with the United States.

Most fascinating for our purposes, an ambitious effort to court Third World states, giving Soviet relations with them an unprecedented visibility and importance, was launched. This effort included offers of economic aid, trade agreements, cultural exchanges, high-level visits, and even military aid. At the Twentieth Soviet Party Congress in 1956, Khrushchev officially proclaimed his priority for a foreign policy of "peaceful co-existence" with the West. He also endorsed the idea that the newly independent states, together with the socialist countries, formed a "zone of peace," which was changing world politics. Khrushchev was an active diplomat and became personally associated with attempts to win new friends and allies in the Third World. Soviet cultivation of Third World states proceeded on several levels. Public diplomacy continued to be an important aspect of Soviet activity. The USSR sought to associate itself with the Afro-Asian solidarity movement, to win over the nonaligned states, and to emerge as the champion of the oppressed countries at the United Nations. More dramatic was the establishment of close ties with regimes on almost every continent and Soviet involvement in several Third World conflicts.

This diplomatic campaign to extend Soviet relations with Third World countries was complemented by major revisions of Soviet ideology and outlook. This had two aspects: On the one hand, the theme of peaceful coexistence was interpreted to mean that cooperation with Third World countries was necessary for peace and would help to promote socialism's final victory over capitalism. On the other hand, Leninism was redefined to emphasize the necessity for supporting anti-Western nationalism.

The Middle East

By the mid-fifties, Soviet policy in this region had shifted toward support of Arab positions. This process was encouraged by Israel's move toward strong ties with the West, together with the appearance of Arab nationalist regimes eager to defy the former colonial powers. Gamal Abd al-Nasir, who emerged as the new leader in Egypt after a 1952 military coup, was eager to demonstrate independence from the West and find an important international role for the Arabs. Nasir declined to join the Western-sponsored Baghdad Pact, later called the Central Treaty Organization (CENTO), an act of defiance that he compounded by seeking Soviet military assistance. Soviet arms were delivered to Egypt in 1955, via Czechoslovakia.

The introduction of Soviet-bloc arms into the Middle East created a diplomatic sensation at the time. Western reaction to this move into the Middle East was intensely hostile, but unavailing. In July 1956, U.S. leaders publicly cancelled an offer to finance the Aswan Dam. In defiance, Nasir nationalized the Suez Canal, and a major diplomatic crisis erupted. The British and French, with Israeli assistance, invaded the Sinai in an effort to recapture the canal. However, the United States refused to support this attempted invasion, and joined with the USSR in demanding withdrawal. As the crisis dissipated, and it was clear that the invaders would have to withdraw, Khrushchev even indulged in a threat to protect Egypt with Soviet missiles, if necessary. Thus he was able to claim credit for Egypt's victory over its former masters.

With Egypt as an important starting point, the Soviets offered military and political support to other emergent Middle Eastern regimes. In 1956, the Ba'ath (Arab socialist renaissance) party took power in Syria. The new government received Soviet arms; President Shukri al-Quwatli visited the USSR; and generous credits were extended in 1957. The Syrian regime at first identified itself with Nasir's pan-Arabism, and pledged itself to his brand of locally messianic socialism. In fact, in 1958 Syria joined with Egypt to form the United Arab Republic (UAR). While the Soviets applauded the merger, the inspiration for this union was to some extent anti-Soviet. Soviet aid had both symbolic and practical value for this regime's commitment to end "neocolonial" ties with the Western powers.

In Iraq, the pro-Western monarchy joined CENTO and made Baghdad its headquarters. But in 1958, this regime was overthrown by a Ba'ath group headed by Abdul Karim Qasim. The new military government under Qasim proceeded to legalize the communist party (this proved to be a brief phenomenon), withdraw from the Baghdad Pact, request Soviet military aid, and demand revisions of oil contracts with Western companies. The Soviets praised these actions and restored diplomatic relations, which had been broken in 1955. Soviet-Iraqi relations developed very smoothly at first. Moscow provided military aid, large credits, and technical assistance (most notably for the development of nuclear energy facilities). But problems developed due to Qasim's increasingly hostile attitude toward the Iraqi communists, and to his repression of the Kurds (a large domestic minority that enjoyed Soviet support). In 1963 Qasim was overthrown, but better Soviet-Iraqi relations were not reestablished until General Abdul Salam Aref, who had seized power in 1964, traveled to the Soviet Union seeking additional military aid.

Overall, the effect of Soviet association with anti-American Arab nationalism was to reinforce Western commitments to the more conservative regimes that remained. Anxieties about potential "Nasirite" subversion in Jordan and Lebanon provoked the U.S. administration to issue in January 1957 the "Eisenhower Doctrine," which proclaimed that the purpose of the United States was to assist militarily any country threatened by aggression from "a country controlled by international communism." In 1958, the political climate became so tense that both Jordan and Lebanon invited Western troops to help assure domestic order.

This situation in the Middle East gave the USSR additional opportunities to act like a champion of the oppressed. The Soviets became involved in 1957 by warning Turkey (a member of NATO) to stop threatening Syria, and in 1958 by denouncing the Western "neocolonial" intervention and calling for a summit meeting (including themselves) to discuss Middle Eastern problems.[14] Although this diplomatic initiative failed, the Soviets subsequently expanded their military aid to Syria, Iraq, and Egypt. They also finally committed themselves to finance the Aswan Dam in Egypt.

Soviet attention was also directed toward other parts of the Middle East. During the Algerian war for independence, 1954–1962, the USSR was careful not to become openly involved. The Soviets extended de facto recognition to the Provisional Government in exile only in 1960. (The Chinese had recognized it de jure in 1958.) However, once Algeria became independent in 1962, the Soviets set about cultivating friendly ties with its self-declared socialist leader, Ahmed Ben Bella. Not only were the properties left behind by the fleeing French nationalized, but the new government also established state control of trade and banking, and introduced agrarian reform. In foreign policy, Algeria took a vocally militant posture, helping to organize the Casablanca grouping of African states, and pledging itself to aid the liberation struggle in Africa. Ben Bella willingly expanded trade with the Soviet Union, and accepted Soviet economic assistance in constructing textile, steel, and fertilizer plants. By 1963 the Soviets were providing substantial military assistance to the Ben Bella government.

While Soviet military assistance and commitments of large amounts of economic aid to these Arab states was no doubt appreciated, difficulties arose. Demonstrative anticommunism on the part of its new allies was embarrassing to the Soviet offensive in the Third World, and provoked some bitter complaints by Khrushchev and in the world communist press. This was a problem in Egypt, Syria, and Iraq. No matter how much the Soviets may have valued the ties with these new nationalist governments, their attacks on local communists were unsettling. In 1962, Khrushchev delivered an angry speech in Sofia, Bulgaria, in which he criticized self-styled socialists who had not mastered Marxism and warned that those who did not understand the need to rely on the working class would be succeeded by "others who do." But in 1963 a compromise was reached, in which local communist parties agreed to dissolve themselves and join the ruling party or front, in return for amnesty and jobs in the civil service. Egyptian communists did do this, and joined the Arab Socialist Union as individuals. Accordingly, Soviet-Egyptian differences were patched up and Khrushchev, during his visit in 1964, announced that confusion about socialism was "a thing of the past" in Egypt. In Algeria, the communists did attempt to convert to membership in the only official party, the National Liberation Front (FLN), but were never enthusiastically accepted. Eventually, they reconstituted themselves as the Socialist Vanguard Party of Algeria. An Algerian party and government delegation visited the USSR in 1963, and Ben Bella followed in 1964. He was warmly welcomed as a comrade and awarded an Order of Lenin and Gold Star of Hero of the Soviet Union. Such compromises were not really relevant with regard to the successive military regimes in Syria and Iraq, where the communists were banned for many more years.

Not all of Soviet relationships were with progressive regimes. The Moroccan monarchy was hardly socialist, but proved interested in establishing trade with the USSR. A trade agreement was signed in 1958, and diplomatic relations were established in 1959. Exchanges of military delegations and state visits followed, including one by Brezhnev in 1961. An arms deal was apparently concluded in 1960, and Soviet arms began arriving in 1962. Soviet statements praised "positive" elements in Moroccan foreign policy. In 1963, for example, Soviet observers applauded King Hassan's demand that the United States evacuate its military bases in Morocco. However, when Algeria and Morocco fought a brief border war in 1963, the Soviets claimed that "imperialist-backed Morocco" was seeking to weaken Algeria's commitment to an anti-Western orientation and to socialism. The Soviets supported the Algerian position in the dispute, and stepped up their military assistance. (Fidel Castro sent Cuban troops to aid Ben Bella.) Elsewhere in North Africa, the Soviets were less successful. Moscow extended credits to Tunisia and published commentary sympathetic to President Habib Bourghiba's position in a dispute with France in 1961. King Idris of Libya, in comparison, refused an offer of friendly relations.

The crown prince of (North) Yemen visited the Soviet Union in 1956 and 1957, and announcements of agreements for Soviet assistance in constructing an airport, canals, and port facilities and in geological explorations followed. In 1956, Yemen, like Egypt, also received shipments of military equipment via Czechoslovakia. However, when the monarchy was overthrown in 1962 and civil war broke out, the USSR joined Nasir's Egypt in siding with the republicans. Soviet military assistance, both direct and indirect, was critical to the republican struggle against the royalists, who were supported by Saudi Arabia and the United States. Yemeni President Abdallah al-Salal visited the USSR early in 1964, and renewed an old friendship treaty.

In 1953 Iran experienced a major internal political crisis. Muhammed Mossadeq, a leftist, was elected prime minister, and the government under his control moved to nationalize the Anglo-Iranian Oil Company. Shah Reza Pahlevi fled the country, but with the help of the U.S. Central Intelligence Agency, soon regained his throne in a military coup. Iran formally joined the Baghdad Pact a few months later. The shah took severe reprisals against the Tudeh (communist) Party in 1953–1954, for its role in helping Mossadeq. Yet despite Iran's close ties with the United States, in 1956 the shah accepted a Soviet trade agreement and some technical assistance. However, in 1958 the shah rejected an offer to sign a nonaggression pact with the USSR, choosing instead to conclude a defense agreement with the United States. After the Cuban missile crisis, Soviet efforts to improve relations met with greater success. The Soviets, seeking assurance from the shah that foreign states would not be permitted to base missiles on Iranian territory, made several generous offers. Trade was expanded and Soviet credits were extended for construction of power plants and irrigation facilities. In 1962 Brezhnev visited Teheran.

Asia

Asian states were important objects of Soviet attention in this period. The USSR offered economic assistance to Afghanistan in 1954 and, subsequently, to other states in the region. Indian President Nehru visited Moscow in June 1955, and U Nu of Burma made the trip in October. The new Soviet effort to cultivate friendly relations with Third World governments was dramatically and vividly demonstrated in Asia, when in the fall of 1955, Khrushchev and Premier Nikolai Bulganin embarked on an unprecedented and highly publicized tour of Afghanistan, India, and Burma. Then in June 1956, Indonesian President Sukarno traveled to Moscow, followed in July by Prince Norodom Sihanouk of Cambodia and in August by Afghan Prime Minister Muhammed Daoud. Generous economic and trade agreements were offered to each of these countries: The Soviets offered US$250 million to India, and US$1 million each to Indonesia and Afghanistan.

During their visit to India, Khrushchev and Bulganin announced they would finance construction of a steel mill, endorsed the Indian position in the Kashmir dispute with Pakistan, and supported India's forcible incorporation of former Portuguese enclaves into their state. Moreover, Khrushchev publicly described India as a "great power" and declared that professions of neutrality by the new states "meet with the full understanding and support" of the USSR. In effect, the Soviets endorsed the ruling Congress Party as the appropriate government for India and advised the Indian communists to act as a loyal opposition. Moscow took India's side in local issues and provided increasing amounts of military aid. By 1960, credits offered to India were nearly double the total extended to China. Significant credits for military purchases were extended as well.

Soviet support for India in its quarrels with Pakistan (militarily allied with the United States) and with China confirmed the sincerity of Moscow's commitment to India's desire to find its own way in international politics. When a border dispute erupted between India and China in 1959, Soviet professions of neutrality apparently enraged the Chinese. Even worse, just prior to the armed clashes that occurred on the Sino-Indian border in 1962, the Soviets actually stepped up arms deliveries to augment India's fighting capability. At the same time the Soviets agreed to set up a MiG-21 plant in India—representing a type of weapon not then available to the USSR's own Eastern satellites or to China. However, during the war itself, Moscow urged China to desist, and adopted an officially neutral position.

There is no doubt that the USSR valued India's role as a self-assertive neutral inclined to trust the USSR and often vote with it or speak in its behalf at the United Nations or the nonaligned meetings. While hardly a pliant tool, the Indians did not condemn Soviet action in Hungary or in Cuba and supported major Soviet initiatives on European security. On some questions, the Indians were critical of Soviet actions. For example, in 1961 Nehru, Nasir, and Tito criticized the USSR's resumption of atmospheric nuclear testing. Nonetheless, Soviet-Indian relations continued to develop along multiple lines, with extensive trade, cultural, and diplomatic links.

Carefully cultivated relations with neighboring Afghanistan became considerably warmer during this period. Afghan-Pakistani relations had often been acrimonious because of a longstanding dispute over borders and the treatment of the Pushtunis (an ethnic group divided between the two countries). The 1954 U.S. military alliance with Pakistan embittered Afghan-U.S. relations, encouraged a turn toward the Soviets, and particularly stimulated the expansion of Soviet-Afghan trade. During their 1955 visit, Khrushchev and Bulganin reaffirmed the 1931 neutrality treaty, supported the Afghan position on Pushtunistan, and agreed to finance Afghanistan's purchase of Soviet and Czech military equipment. An arms agreement was officially announced in 1956.

The situation in Indochina at this time was complex. After their military defeat at Dienbienphu in 1954, the French ended their attempt to regain control over Indochina. Soviet representatives at the subsequent Geneva conference supported a negotiated settlement. Agreement on both a cease-fire and a plan for unification of Vietnam through elections was worked out, but not signed. The Soviets apparently pressured the Vietnamese communists and their Chinese allies to accept these agreements, although the communists under Ho Chi Minh could probably have won militarily. The Soviets may have been attempting to avoid provoking the United States, which had already become deeply involved in supporting France's effort to resist a communist victory. It has also been claimed that the USSR urged a negotiated settlement in hopes of influencing France's position on European rearmament. In any case, the scheduled elections were never held in Vietnam. Instead, the United States moved to assist the regime of Ngo Dinh Diem, who replaced Emperor Bao Dai in 1956.

In 1957, the USSR attempted, without success, to secure the admission of both Vietnamese states to the United Nations. And Moscow offered credits to North Vietnam for economic development assistance in 1957 and again in 1960. It was apparently the Soviet view that the North

Vietnamese should concentrate on national consolidation, rather than renewing attempts to conquer all of Vietnam. This attitude eventually alienated the North Vietnamese, who in 1963 took up a pro-Chinese position in the Sino-Soviet split and turned toward more and more direct involvement with the liberation struggle in South Vietnam.

At the same time that the Vietnamese were being encouraged to accept the division of Vietnam, the Soviets were displaying considerable interest in the neutral status of the two other Indochinese states, Laos and Cambodia. The Geneva agreements of 1954 had called for a neutral government in Laos that would include representatives of all three major political groupings. Although the various Laotian parties agreed in 1956 to a coalition, pro-Western groups managed to retain political power between 1957 and 1960, when leftists finally seized control.

The Soviets established diplomatic relations with this regime, but fighting among communist forces (the Pathet Lao) and neutralist and CIA-supported groups soon brought serious civil war. The Soviets sent military assistance transport aircraft to support the ruling group. However, at their Vienna summit meeting in June 1961, Khrushchev and U.S. President John F. Kennedy endorsed the idea of another Geneva conference on Laos. The negotiations were lengthy and tedious but resulted in an agreement to establish a coalition government under Prince Souvanna Phouma in 1962. However, the three political groupings in Laos found it difficult to cooperate, and continuing civil strife provided numerous occasions for the USSR, in its role as co-chair of the Geneva conference, to represent itself as an advocate of moderation and neutrality. The Soviet Union established diplomatic relations with Cambodia in 1956. It also praised Prince Sihanouk's neutrality and his defiance of U.S.-sponsored security pacts. However, Sihanouk's development of close ties to China limited Soviet-Cambodian relations.

Indonesia under Sukarno offered a different kind of relationship. The Soviet Union agreed to establish diplomatic relations with Indonesia in 1953, but the exchange of ambassadors was delayed until 1954 because the step was not at first politically acceptable. Indonesia's President Sukarno was a volatile nationalist who heaped criticism on "neo-colonialism," criticized U.S. military security pacts, and emerged as a major sponsor of Afro-Asian solidarity. He pledged a socialist future for Indonesia, and he set up a "Guided Democracy," which included the participation of the Indonesian Communist Party (PKI). Soviet analysts were never really sure what to say about Indonesia's domestic system. As the years passed, they were increasingly derisive of poor administration and high levels of corruption, which helped to frustrate economic development plans. Praise was generally limited to Indonesia's foreign policy and to its leaders' aspirations for social justice.

When Sukarno visited the USSR in 1956, he received the Order of Lenin. The first major loan from the USSR to Indonesia, offered in 1956, was not accepted until 1957. The Soviet aid program in Indonesia was slow getting under way and was criticized both within and without the country for involving too many "showy" projects (including a large stadium, for instance). Nonetheless, military aid was extensive, including deliveries of some of the latest equipment: MiG-21 aircraft, naval vessels, including two submarines, and surface-to-air missiles. Soviet support for Indonesia's nonalignment encompassed its demand for the annexation of West Irian, a primitive territory retained by the Dutch, as well as Sukarno's irredentist claims against Malaysia.

Soviet-Burmese relations began in 1955 with a similar pattern of state visits and offers of credits. Although never so close as the relations with India or Indonesia, significant Soviet-Burmese trade began in 1956, and modest amounts of credits were extended. Once General Ne Win had secured control of the government in 1962, the Soviets developed a habit of citing Burma as an example of a Third World country committed to a socialist course. Ne Win announced a foreign policy posture of positive neutrality and set out to nationalize foreign assets. The fact that Burma had already signed a nonaggression treaty with China (in 1960) and was plagued by active armed rebellions by two feuding comunist groups complicated development of Soviet-Burmese relations much beyond this.

Ceylon (now Sri Lanka) provided for the Soviet press and leadership another confirmation of Third World countries' proclivity for nonalignment and serious desire to break away from economic as well as political control by their former imperial masters. Diplomatic relations between the USSR and Ceylon date from 1957, and an agreement on trade and Soviet credits for industrial projects was concluded in 1958. During the administration of Mrs. Sirimavo Bandaranaike (1960–1965), Ceylon took a socialist and neutralist course and laid the groundwork for the nationalization of foreign-owned oil companies. As a result, the United States suspended its aid program in 1963. The Soviets were quick to applaud this defiance and to step forward with offers of credits, technical assistance for industrial development, and agreements to trade in rubber and oil. Although Soviet assistance was not massive, it had important symbolic significance.

Africa

Decolonization in Africa proceeded steadily in the late fifties and early sixties. Yet at the time, the gradual sequence of steps leading to self-government appears to have obscured an appreciation of the magnitude of the political changes taking place. Soviet relations with African states, in the pattern of the Khrushchev-Bulganin tour of South Asia, began with friendly approaches (in 1956) to the oldest independent African state, Ethiopia. Diplomatic relations (broken during World War II) were reestablished at the ambassadorial level in 1959, and Emperor Haile Selassie was invited to the Soviet Union for a state visit. Moreover, the Soviets offered Ethiopia a generous credit (about half the size of initial offers made to Afghanistan and India, but about the same as that offered to Indonesia).

The most extensive and dramatic Soviet involvement in Africa, however, centered on certain key radical states that were cultivated and welcomed as "comradely" allies. Guinea, an anomaly in the gradual decolonization process, proved an attractive and logical target of Soviet interest. Ahmed Sékou Touré was the only leader of a French colony to reject association with de Gaulle's French Community in the 1958 referendum. By voting "no," Guinea chose full independence. The French then withdrew completely, leaving the new state to fend for itself. Touré quickly established diplomatic relations with both the USSR and China and adopted a militant anti-imperialist foreign policy. He concluded trade agreements with a number of socialist states. In September 1959, a Communist Party of the Soviet Union (CPSU) delegation attended a meeting of the vaguely Marxist Democratic Party of Guinea (PDG). The Soviets subsequently identified this party as a "revolutionary democratic" one, entitled to maintain regular ties with the CPSU. Touré visited the Soviet Union in 1959 and again in 1960. Soviet press and leadership were enthusiastic about Guinea's militant anti-imperialism, as expressed in nationalization of foreign property, involvement in the Afro-Asian Peoples Solidarity Organization, and encouragement to liberation movements elsewhere in Africa. In 1961 during Brezhnev's visit to Guinea, Touré was awarded a Lenin Peace Prize.

Relations did not proceed completely smoothly, however. Guinea also developed ties with the United States and France, and when Touré's plans for socialist development fell into difficulty in the early sixties, he chose to encourage foreign and private investment. In December 1961, Touré angrily accused the Soviets of involvement with opponents of his regime and ordered the Soviet ambassador expelled. Despite this incident, new Soviet credits were extended the following year, and government and party relations continued to develop. Soviet analysts recognized Guinea as a progressive state, and the up-to-date vocabulary of acceptable Marxist categories was applied to this country.

Ghana (formerly the, Gold Coast), which gained independence under an increasingly radical leadership, proved to be another favored client. Diplomatic relations were established and a trade agreement concluded in 1959. In 1960 and 1961 the Soviets offered credits amounting to about half the sum offered to Ethiopia. Soviet assistance programs, included training for Kwame Nkrumah's security force. Many Ghanaians traveled to the USSR and the Eastern bloc for programs of study. Nkrumah adopted favored Soviet foreign policy positions as his own (on the German question, for instance). Soviet-Ghanaian foreign policy cooperation in the Congo crisis, at the United Nations, and other international organizations was extensive enough to provoke Western charges that Ghana had become a "satellite." In 1963 Nkrumah stated his belief in "scientific socialism," which was then duly incorporated into the program of his Convention People's Party (CPP). The development of party relations between the CPSU and the CPP encouraged public Soviet enthusiasm about Ghana's political prospects.

Mali (formerly the French Sudan) attracted Soviet attention soon after independence when it chose a radical path in close contact with Guinea and Ghana. Mali's leader Modibo Keita proclaimed himself in favor of a truly neutral foreign policy and pledged himself to socialist economic planning. At the same time, he requested that the French withdraw their military bases, and Mali left the franc zone. Diplomatic realtions were quickly established with China and the USSR. Soviet credits were promised in 1961 and 1962, and visits were exchanged by government and military delegations. Keita's ruling party, the Sudanese Union–African Democratic Rally, announced the adoption of scientific socialism in 1962. Subsequently, the Sudanese Union was invited to attend Soviet party functions, while its youth group attended Komsomol conferences. Along with Ghana and Guinea, Mali was regularly listed with pride in Soviet reviews of the progressive changes in Africa, which pointed to the inevitable triumph of socialism.

In the Belgian Congo, independence was granted with very little preparation. As the announced date for independence (June 1960) approached, aspiring Congolese political leaders maneuvered frantically for places in the new government. Joseph Kasavubu, who became the first president, represented a federalist and pro-Western approach to Congo's future. Patrice Lumumba, who became prime minister, urged a strongly centralized government structure. A leftist friend of Nkrumah, Lumumba became the Soviet favorite. Within a few weeks of independence, the fragile Congolese government was beset with mutinies and public disorder. Most serious, the mineral-rich province of Katanga seceded. When Belgian forces intervened in apparent sympathy with the secessionists, the new government appealed to the United Nations for help.

Although the USSR followed the lead of the majority of African states in endorsing the dispatch of a UN peacekeeping force, the Soviets remained skeptical about the motives of the Western powers in the Congo. Prime Minister Lumumba shared these apprehensions. He concluded that the UN forces were too cautious about removing the Belgians, and appealed to the USSR directly for help. In August, the Soviet government issued a warning that it would "not hesitate to take decisive measures aimed at repelling the aggressors." On request from Premier Lumumba, the Soviets actually airlifted some supplies, delivered trucks, and ferried Ghanaian troops to the combat zone. UN commanders considered the actions to be unilateral interference, in violation of UN directives, and closed Congolese airports to Soviet supply missions. The Soviets angrily charged partisanship, and proceeded to denounce the UN's activities and officials. Ultimately, United Nations forces did restore order in the Congo and helped to subdue two rebellious provinces.

At the same time, internal political conflict intensified within the Congo. At one point in 1960, Kasavubu and Lumumba attempted to dismiss each other. They sent rival delegations to the United Nations, each claiming to represent the legitimate government of the Congo. U.S. pressure helped ensure victory of the Kasavubu group in the credentials fight at the United Nations, and Western support helped him remain in control in the Congo. When Lumumba was assassinated early in 1961, the Soviets blamed the West for his death and withdrew their ambassador from the Congo temporarily. The pro-Western character of the Congo operations and their political results brought continued Soviet complaints and demands that the office of the UN secretary general be redesigned. Khrushchev himself went to the United Nations session in 1961 to argue in favor of a "troika" proposal, to replace the secretary general with a threesome of Western, Eastern, and "neutral" representatives. Soviet refusal to pay for military operations in the Congo produced a serious crisis at the United Nations in 1964, once arrears had reached the point where the USSR should have lost its General Assembly vote.

Thus what began as participation in multinational assistance to a new African regime degenerated into a frustrating battle for control over the political future and alignment of the Congo. Lumumba's death left the USSR without an ally. At the end of 1961 diplomatic relations were reestablished with the central government, but they were not particularly friendly ones. In 1963, two Soviet diplomats were charged with helping to prepare an aborted coup and expelled. The Soviets were also apparently involved in 1964 in a regional rebellion, which was put down with U.S. and Belgian assistance. The ensuing government was not only pro-Western, but was headed by Moise Tshombe, the secessionist leader of Katanga province who had invited in the Belgians and had fought against his countrymen with South African mercenaries.

The regime that emerged in the Congo (renamed Zaire) from this tumultuous beginning was to remain firmly anti-Soviet.

As the decolonization process continued, other states were courted by the Soviets. The Kremlin appeared to be very pleased with the "positive neutrality" aspirations of the new Sudanese government. During his 1962 trip to Africa and the Middle East, Brezhnev, then chairman of the Presidium of the Supreme Soviet, stopped in Sudan, where he offered Soviet credits and a trade pact. After a number of changes of leadership, a 1964 coup left communists included in the government, and Soviet reaction was appropriately approving. When Somalia gained its independence in 1960, the Soviets established diplomatic ties almost immediately and apparently offered military aid in 1963. In 1964 the USSR, with warnings against British naval interference, moved naval vessels into the vicinity of the newly independent leftist regime in Zanzibar. At the same time, a limited amount of Soviet assistance seems to have reached African liberation movements, particularly through aid to Nkrumah and Touré, whose territories were host to a number of training camps for rebel groups.

Latin America

Leftist, anti-American nationalism presented tempting opportunities in certain Latin American countries. In Guatemala, the leftist government headed by Jacobo Arbenz Guzman initiated sweeping economic reforms aimed at both local vested interests and U.S. companies. In 1954, reports circulated that a shipment of Czech weapons was en route by sea. U.S. reaction to this hint of Soviet involvement was swift and punitive. "International communist subversion" in the Western hemisphere was denounced, and the CIA coordinated a coup that replaced Arbenz with a more pliant government under Castillio Armas.

In Cuba, the regime of Fulgencio Batista collapsed when he fled in the face of growing political and guerrilla opposition. The new regime, headed by the guerrilla leader Fidel Castro, inexorably moved toward an anti-American posture, which made seeking Soviet assistance a logical and attractive option. U.S. efforts to coerce Castro's regime into less hostile policies proved futile and probably accelerated the Cuban-Soviet alliance. In 1961, Castro announced that he was a lifelong Marxist-Leninist and formed a new political organization that included the local communists. Then, in a somewhat breathtaking sequence of events, Cuba became the site of first, a major U.S. humiliation (the Bay of Pigs invasion attempt, 1961), and then, a tense Soviet-U.S. showdown (the Cuban missile crisis, 1962). The resolution of the Cuban missile crisis provided for the removal of Soviet offensive missiles from Cuba, and a U.S. pledge never to attempt another invasion. Eventually, Cuba was identified as a "socialist state."

The acquisition of a Soviet client so close to the United States was a dramatic achievement, but an expensive one. Soviet credits and military assistance soon were pouring into Cuba, and the USSR took responsibility for the regime's financial survival. However, Castro's attempts to help spread the guerrilla struggle against "American imperialist lackeys," was not in tune with Soviet approaches to the hemisphere. Moreover, Castro's revolutionary activities represented a challenge to established Latin American communist parties. These had generally been pursuing electoral respectability, based on constituencies in urban labor unions. The Soviets and Cubans quarreled repeatedly about appropriate political tactics. In 1964, the dispute was temporarily settled by a Soviet acknowledgment of the value of armed struggle in certain conditions, and by an apparent Cuban promise to moderate its activities in support of guerrillas.[15]

Elsewhere in Latin America, some progress was made in an effort to establish or reestablish commercial relations with many states, in line with Khrushchev's view of peaceful coexistence. Trade agreements and improved diplomatic contacts were achieved with Brazil, Mexico, and Argentina, but these were marred by occasional disputes over Soviet political or commercial activity. Relations with Chile, Colombia, and Bolivia were somewhat more hostile. The activities of a Cuban-backed guerrilla movement in Venezuela made that government resistant to Soviet offers of renewed diplomatic relations.

CAUTIOUS DÉTENTE: 1965–1973

Khrushchev, under fire for both domestic and foreign policy failures, was removed from office in October 1964. A period of retrenchment and reordering of priorities followed. His successors, Leonid Brezhnev and Aleksei Kosygin, appear to have worked hard to present a new image to the world—that of a responsible and cautious but powerful and critically important superpower. Just before his ouster, Khrushchev had acknowledged that the USSR's first international duty was to build up its own economic system, and this principle was reaffirmed and elaborated by the new leadership at the 1966 Soviet Party Congress.

The 1965–1973 period presented the USSR with problems of communist alliance management: the liberalization in Czechoslovakia in 1968, to which they responded with armed intervention; and numerous border incidents with the Chinese, including a brief war scare set off by serious armed clashes in 1969 along the Ussuri River. The new leaders also intensified efforts to catch up militarily with the United States, and attempted to restore harmony and some degree of solidarity to international communism.

The Soviets resumed the efforts begun by Khrushchev toward accommodation with the United States. Brehzhnev's leadership group managed to avoid problems over the escalating war in Vietnam by respecting the obvious U.S. desire to keep the war limited and by not becoming directly involved in the fighting. At the same time, the new leadership was able to reach a series of important agreements that signaled the end of the cold war: the nonproliferation treaty in 1968, a nonaggression pact with West Germany in 1970, and a four-power agreement on Berlin in 1971. These agreements became part of a new climate in East-West relations. Arms control negotiations, which had begun in 1969, culminated in the Strategic Arms Limitation Treaty (SALT I), signed along with several other agreements by Nixon and Brezhnev at the Moscow summit in 1972. Soviet accounts of these developments gave most attention not to the arms restrictions, but to the Agreement on Basic Principles, which in effect constituted a statement that both superpowers would adhere to peaceful coexistence. The agreement further stated:

> The USA and the USSR attach major importance to preventing the
> development of situations capable of causing a dangerous
> exacerbation of their relations. Therefore, they will do their utmost
> to avoid military confrontations and to prevent the outbreak of
> nuclear war. They will always exercise restraint in their mutual
> relations, and will be prepared to negotiate and settle differences by
> peaceful means. . . . Both sides recognize that efforts to obtain
> unilateral advantages at the expense of the other, directly or
> indirectly, are inconsistent with these objectives.[16]

A statement that peaceful coexistence required mutual respect for security interests "based on the principle of equality" was generally interpreted by the Soviet press as a Western acknowledgment of Soviet power.

Soviet–Third World relations in this period reflected a marked change of style and tone, although the basic elements of Khrushchev's approach were retained. The general effort to cultivate friendly relations based on common values continued, and the geographic scope of Soviet presence continued to grow. However, a mood of care and retrenchment was visible here too. With the explosive period of decolonization largely over, Soviet commentary became less apocalyptic, and interchanges with the new states less generous. Although the Soviet aid program continued, few new credits were extended at first. Whereas Khrushchev had sought to appear lavish, the new leadership was frugal. (The word they used was "businesslike.") At the same time some Third World producer countries became part of an enlarged Soviet trade offensive, which sought to establish commercial relationships with a variety of capitalist trade partners.

The sudden fall from power of some notable Soviet friends in the late sixties undoubtedly reinforced a mood of caution. The flamboyant aspects of Khrushchev's courting of Third World nationalist leaders, the Peace Prizes and lavish state visits, were largely discarded. For a time, the new Soviet leadership appeared to take up the defense of foreign communist parties more emphatically, perhaps reflecting a desire for more reliable allies or disillusionment with pseudosocialist radicals. However, the ideological tolerance of the Khrushchev years was reaffirmed, and concern for communist causes was not allowed to take priority over development of friendly state relations with regimes willing to align themselves with the USSR.

Middle East

Between 1964 and 1973, the Middle East presented the Soviet leadership with numerous difficulties and crises. First, a series of regime changes in several countries affected the state of Soviet ties. Second, the Soviets, as armorer to the Arabs, became embroiled in two major Arab-Israeli wars and the 1969–1970 War of Attrition along the Suez Canal.

Algerian politics presented a brief dilemma. Ahmed Ben Bella, a self-proclaimed socialist with an anti-Western foreign policy whom the Soviets had assiduously and successfully cultivated, was overthrown in 1965 by Houari Boumedienne, his military commander. Initially the Soviets were suspicious of this new regime, which set out to restore friendly relations with France and to eliminate foreign influence. Moscow began to court the new government, and in December 1965, Boumedienne visited the USSR. The Soviets found him receptive, but stubbornly opposed to open Soviet support for Algerian communists. Nonetheless, Soviet-Algerian exchanges, trade, technical assistance, and military cooperation continued to develop extensively.

In Syria, a coup by the radical left wing of the Ba'ath party in February 1966 was a more promising development. The Soviets quickly moved in with an offer for a huge loan and military aid. Among other things, this was to finance a Euphrates River hydroelectric project, which would be compared by Syrians to the Aswan Dam on the Nile. Soviet arms began to flow to the Syrians almost immediately, although the regime was troubled by factional rivalries and opposition from Islamic groups hostile to its outspoken socialist secularism. In 1966 a more radical regime also took power in Iraq, and for a time Iraqi-Syrian cooperation seemed possible. The Soviet Union apparently made efforts during 1966 and 1967 to promote some kind of union among all the radical Arab states. Instead, radical and conservative Arab states alike put aside their political differences in spring 1967 to construct a joint command (built primarily around a dramatic Egyptian-Jordanian rapprochement) to confront Israel.

The Soviets have been accused of forwarding misleading intelligence reports to Nasir about an impending Israeli attack on Syria, thus contributing to the sequence of events that led to the war. It is probably more accurate to note that the Soviets feared that the Syrian government was about to fall and may have hoped to secure Egyptian help for it through these scare tactics. But it is also true that border provocations and anger over the scale of Israeli retaliatory raids (which included mock bombing runs over Damascus) were serious enough to raise tensions to the point where all Arab leaders felt tremendous pressure to do something about the Israeli military threat. Nasir's demand for the withdrawal of UN forces from border zones, restrictions on Israeli shipping through the Gulf of Aqaba, and a pan-Arab defense agreement finally so alarmed the Israelis that they launched a preemptive attack on June 6.

Many observers agree that the Soviets sought to restrain the Egyptians and warned them that Soviet assistance in case of war would be limited. As the conflict progressed, and the totality of the Arab military collapse become apparent, Soviet-U.S. discussions on the hot line helped to clarify Soviet concern lest the Arabs actually be overrun. When the Israelis ignored the first cease-fire of June 9, obviously attempting to improve their strategic position, the Soviets reportedly did threaten a possibility of military action unless the United States could convince the Israelis to stop. A Warsaw Pact meeting also declared a determination to do "everything necessary" to repel Israeli aggression. On June 10, the Soviets made good on an earlier threat and broke diplomatic relations with Israel. Soviet panic about the Arab defeat was evident in rumors that Soviet pilots were attempting to fly undamaged planes out of Egypt to the Sudan.

Analyses of Soviet behavior after the war vary, but it is quite clear that the Soviets were more willing than the Arabs to accept a settlement that involved recognition of Israel. Indeed, the Soviet leadership has consistently upheld Israel's right to exist. At the United Nations, the USSR supported Security Council Resolution 242, which called for Israeli return of territories seized from its neighbors, but also promised secure borders to Israel and guaranteed freedom of navigation. At various times

Soviet leaders promoted an internationally supervised Middle East settlement—an arrangement not popular with the United States, or with the radical Arab states, who suspected a sellout. As for Egyptian-Soviet relations after the war, the USSR agreed to help rebuild the Egyptian army. Nasir also appeared to be taking some steps in line with Soviet ideas for his economy and political system, including professions that the ruling party, the Arab Socialist Union (ASU), was becoming a "socialist vanguard." Party ties between the ASU and the Soviet party proceeded apace. Soviet military assistance included the presence of several thousand advisors and training specialists in Egypt. Moreover, the Soviet navy was granted basing rights—a significant strategic asset, and the first for the USSR in the Third World.

The decision to rearm not only Egypt, but also the other Arab belligerents, inevitably involved the USSR increasingly in the anti-Israeli cause. But Soviet military matériel did not afford Moscow the opportunity to control the course of events. The humiliation the Arabs had endured on the battlefield encouraged heated rhetoric on a "no peace, no recognition" platform (reached at the Arab summit in Khartoum, in September 1967), which inhibited efforts to find a negotiated solution. Nasir gave up supporting the republican partisans in Yemen in return for Saudi financial assistance to help rescue the Egyptian economy from damage of the war, loss of Sinai oil fields, and loss of the canal revenues. And U.S. diplomats were active in attempts to engineer withdrawal agreements between Israel and the defeated Arab powers.

Nasir began in March 1969, apparently without Soviet approval, the artillery and air battles with Israeli forces along the Suez Canal that became known as the "War of Attrition." This war has generally been viewed as an effort to intensify pressure on Israel to resolve the situation by which it occupied so much Arab territory. The fighting soon became serious. When Israeli air reprisals put the Egyptian capital in jeopardy, Nasir pleaded with the Soviets, who agreed to extend direct military assistance. Soviet soldiers reportedly flew combat missions, manned surface-to-air missile installations, and assisted in construction of defensive positions in what was supposed to be a demilitarized zone around the canal. These measures were effective in protecting Eygpt from the Israeli air force and also in stimulating the peace negotiations. Soviet-U.S. and Soviet-Egyptian discussions continued during the fighting, and a cease-fire was finally arranged by U.S. Secretary of State William Rogers in August 1970.

Almost as soon as the cease-fire around the Suez Canal had been arranged, trouble erupted on the other side of Israel, involving the increasingly active Palestine Liberation Organization (PLO), Syria, and Jordan. The PLO went on record in 1968 as fundamentally opposed to

UN Security Council Resolution 242, which had been accepted by the USSR. By 1969 PLO fighters in territories adjacent to Israel were a disruptive and potentially explosive force. In August 1970, the PLO hijacked and held four airliners, complete with hundreds of hostages, on a deserted Jordanian airstrip. The king of Jordan ordered the Palestinians disarmed and sent his army to attack them in September 1970. Syria and Iraq protested and moved tank units toward Jordan in support of the Palestinians. Although at the time some U.S. officials were convinced the Soviets encouraged the Syrian move, most observers do not think this was the case. In any event, the United States and Israel apparently promised to back up Jordan in its campaign against the PLO should military assistance be required. In the end, the fact that the Syrians and their allies did not join the fighting left the Jordanian army free to defeat the Palestinians. Remnants fled into Syria or Lebanon, where they were to remain a destabilizing force, embittered about the failure of their friends to prevent the loss of their bases in Jordan.

Nasir died in September 1970, and was replaced by Anwar Sadat. Although never so pro-Soviet as his predecessor, he signed a treaty of friendship and cooperation with the Soviet Union in June 1971. Nevertheless, he soon found himself at odds with the USSR over the pace and size of Soviet arms deliveries. Impatient to secure some return of Egyptian territory, and convinced the Soviets were more interested in détente than in Arab causes, he expressed his frustrations in July 1972 by summarily ordering all Soviet advisors out of the country. (Only naval base rights were retained.) The Soviets resumed arms shipments a few months later, although apparently in return for cash supplied by the Saudis, who had long expressed their displeasure with the Soviet presence in Egypt. Sadat's distaste for the Soviets extended to domestic politics as well, for he purged the ASU of pro-Soviet elements and moved to arrest Egyptian communists (reconstituted as a party in 1972), whom he blamed for disruptive demonstrations and criticized as hostile to the ideals of Islamic society.

The Soviets continued to cultivate friendly political relationships with all the Arab regimes that espoused socialism, although Soviet commentators emphasized that social progress would be very slow in these countries. Of course, as regimes changed, attitudes toward socialism varied too. Soviet relations with Syria and Iraq were troubled not only by disagreements over strategy on what was now being called the "Palestinian problem," but also by serious political rivalries, and by anticommunism. Soviet economic and military support to these regimes was considerable. The relationship with Iraq was formalized by a treaty of friendship and cooperation in 1972. Although Syria was apparently not interested in a treaty, a long-term military aid agreement was reached about the same time.

Where it was possible, the Soviets welcomed direct relations between the CPSU and the Ba'ath socialist parties, which they encouraged to coexist peacefully with their local communist parties. Despite considerable restlessness among Syrian and Iraqi communists, they did accept the Soviet point of view in favor of political support to these military regimes. In return (probably with Soviet pressure), political agreements were concluded in Syria (1972) and Iraq (1973) on formal establishment of "national fronts." These deals granted the communist parties a guaranteed, permanent minority position in the government, but put certain restrictions on their political activities. Disputes about accepting these conditions produced a split in the Syrian communist party, which the Soviets tried hard to mend. These developments were highly praised in Soviet commentaries as vindications of the "loyal opposition" tactic.[17] However, neither the Iraqi nor the Syrian regime had completely abandoned their suspicions about the communists and their political ambitions. The loyal parties were both visible and vulnerable under these arrangements.

The problems of bilateral relations and the issues of local communist participation were overshadowed by the eruption of another major Middle East war in October 1973. This was a dramatic event with widespread repercussions for the Soviet role in the region. When Brezhnev and Richard Nixon met in June 1973, the Soviets warned that the danger of war was increasing. They also evacuated their diplomatic personnel from Egypt and Syria a few days before the war broke out. The attack, spearheaded by Egypt, brought initial Arab military success and enthusiastic support and at least token participation from a great many other Arab states. A part of the Sinai was recaptured, and the Syrians regained some territory on the Golan Heights. Both the United States and the USSR appear to have assumed another Israeli military miracle would occur, and adjusted their counsel and their aid policies accordingly. When the extent of Israeli difficulties became clear, U.S. resupply shipments fueled a counteroffensive that recovered much of the territory originally lost to Egypt and Syria.

The Egyptians at first resisted Soviet advice to seek an early cease-fire but finally accepted one worked out during a visit by U.S. Secretary of State Henry Kissinger to Moscow, on October 20, 1973. At this time, President Nixon further proposed that the United States and the Soviet Union together impose a settlement on the parties. However, a daring Israeli drive across the Canal in defiance of the cease-fire surrounded a large Egyptian force. This brought angry protests from the USSR, and warnings that the United States should restrain Israel. Brezhnev proposed an intervention by U.S. and Soviet joint forces, and warned that the Soviets might have to act unilaterally, if Israel could not be stopped: "I will say it straight that if you find it impossible to act together with us in this matter, we should be faced with the necessity urgently to consider the question of taking appropriate steps unilaterally."[18] Sadat also suggested joint U.S.-USSR intervention to enforce a peace. However, the Nixon administration opposed this idea and responded with a military alert apparently designed to deter any Soviet action. Strong U.S. pressure was applied to Israel, and the cease-fire was finally achieved.

In the aftermath of the war, there were several moves on the diplomatic front. The Arabs successfully used an oil embargo against Israel's supporters, an impressive demonstration of economic power applauded by the Soviets. Meanwhile, a plan to reconvene a Geneva conference, which the United States and USSR would co-chair, to discuss a Middle East peace settlement promised continued Soviet involvement on behalf of its Arab clients. Although the Arabs had failed to win a complete military solution of the Arab-Israeli dispute, the military successes that had been achieved would effect progress in negotiations.

If the Soviets were reluctant to become involved in the Arab-Israeli conflict too directly, or in ways that could provoke a Soviet-U.S. confrontation, there were other areas in the Middle East in these years where the risks of U.S. reaction were less serious, and where the Soviets did seem more adventurous. In Yemen, the Soviets stepped into the civil war after Egypt withdrew in 1967. Soviet assistance to the republicans apparently included not just supplies, but some direct involvement in military operations. By 1969, these Soviet friends defeated the Saudi-supported royalists and established the Yemen Arab Republic, which has continued to receive modest amounts of Soviet aid on a regular basis.

The Soviets were able to develop even closer relations with Aden (to become generally known as South Yemen). After the British departure from Aden in 1968, a radical regime was set up calling itself the People's Democratic Republic of Yemen (PDRY). Although the Soviets had to compete with the Chinese in the PDRY and the regime has been beset with seemingly unending factional strife, Soviet commentators enthusiastically endorsed the vanguard party structure that was allegedly formed there in 1969. From a strategic point of view, the Soviets gained when they were offered access to a major Persian Gulf [hereafter called the Gulf] port (whose improvement the Soviets have been more than ready to finance). The PDRY also became the conduit for Soviet military aid to the Dhofari rebellion against the sultan of Oman. Marxist leaders of this movement formed a Popular Front for the Liberation of Oman and the Arabian Gulf (PFLOAG), which sought both Soviet and Chinese aid. By 1970 the PFLOAG controlled approximately two-thirds of Dhofar. However, they were effectively defeated by 1973 with help from Britain and Iran.

Asia

Soviet activities in South Asia were shaped by the Indo-Pakistani conflict, which erupted into two wars during this period: a border war over the Rann of Kutch and Kashmir in 1965 and a war over the secession of East Pakistan in 1971. The USSR, of course, had already provided substantial military aid to India while Pakistan received military aid from the United States and then from China. Nonetheless, the Brezhnev-Kosygin leadership wanted to improve its relations with Pakistan: They quietly dropped Soviet support for India's claim to Kashmir and then extended offers of substantial credits to the Pakistani government. A trade agreement was concluded with President Ayub Khan during his visit to Moscow in the spring of 1965. This process of rapprochement was disrupted by the outbreak of war between India and Pakistan in late spring 1965. The Soviets took up a neutral stance, proclaiming their interest in a peaceful settlement. While the Indians objected, they had to take comfort from Soviet threats to China not to become involved, and from the fact that when the United States cut off military aid to both parties, the Soviets continued theirs to India. The Soviet Union offered to serve as mediator, and in January 1966 representatives of the two states met with Premier Kosygin in Tashkent, USSR. The Soviet mediation effort was successful, in that India and Pakistan pledged to settle future disputes peacefully. However, the Kashmir issue remained unresolved.

Following the war, and building on their role as peacemaker, the Soviets resumed their efforts to develop relations with Pakistan. In fact, Ayub's government soon found itself the target of diplomatic attention by all three major powers. Over the next few years, the United States, China, and the USSR courted Pakistan with aid offers and high-ranking diplomatic visits. However, the Soviet effort to establish friendly relations with both India and Pakistan ran into difficulties. News of Soviet military aid arriving in Pakistan in 1968 caused a furor in India. Indian diplomats immediately scheduled a series of visits to the United States and to China. These had the desired effect of stimulating further Soviet offers of economic and military assistance to India.

In 1971, when Pakistan's eastern province rebelled and attempted to secede, the army moved in to restore order. During the civil war that followed, large numbers of refugees moved across the border into

India, creating major problems for the New Delhi government. The Indians, who sided with the East Bengalis, approached the USSR to finalize negotiations for a treaty. In August 1971 India and the USSR signed a twenty-year friendship and cooperation treaty, which was followed by greatly accelerated military deliveries. This may have been intended as a concrete gesture to deter the Chinese from becoming involved in the impending war over the secession of East Pakistan. Officially, the Soviets supported a peaceful settlement and apparently tried hard to discourage the Indian government from using force. However, in practice, the treaty freed the Indians to enter the fighting in December 1971. Once India had joined the war on the side of the secessionists, the USSR took up a plainly partisan position at the UN and vetoed cease-fire resolutions until the position of the East Bengalis was relatively secure. Moreover, Soviet ships moved into the Bay of Bengal to offset the presence of U.S. naval forces. The Soviets extended recognition to the new government of Bangladesh almost immediately and soon offered economic aid.

As India, Pakistan, and Bangladesh moved to normalize their relationships in 1972 and 1973, it appeared as if the USSR could emerge as the benevolent patron with controlling interests in all three states. But the Indian government was cautious about appearing to have joined a military alliance with the USSR. Despite a program of regular Soviet naval visits to Indian ports, frequent reports that the Soviets would soon have navy or air bases in India did not prove accurate. The Indians refused to go along with Soviet proposals for an Asian collective security system, did not sign the Non-Proliferation Treaty (which most observers feel is a Soviet priority), and proceeded with its own mini nuclear weapons program.

Soviet relations with neighboring Iran and Afghanistan during this period continued to emphasize cooperative, but not intimate, relations. The shah and the king both made several state visits to the USSR, and there was every reason to expect that the record of technical assistance, cordiality, and political noninterference with regard to both countries would continue. The volume of trade between the USSR and Iran increased very rapidly in the early Brezhnev years, and until Iran's oil wealth made such steps superfluous, Soviet credits were generous (exceeded in amount only by those to India). The most important area of cooperation was in the development of Iran's natural gas resources, as plans were made for a Soviet-Iranian pipeline that would eventually help to supply Eastern Europe. In 1972 a fifteen-year Soviet-Iranian treaty of cooperation was signed. In Afghanistan, King Zahir was overthrown in a July 1973 coup, led by Prime Minister Muhammed Daoud. The new president had visited the Soviet Union and was considered friendly to the USSR. His declaration that Afghanistan would attempt to follow a socialist path was greeted warmly in Moscow and by the Afghan communists.

In this period, Indonesia under Sukarno was a favored Third World client and recipient of large amounts of Soviet aid and military equipment. By 1964, however, the mercurial Sukarno had become more closely associated with the Chinese. When he launched a "confrontation campaign" against the new federation of Malaysia, the large and well-organized Indonesian Communist Party (PKI) supported him. In September 1965, the PKI attempted a coup—or more accurately, were provoked into launching one prematurely. The abortive coup precipitated a bloody countercoup by the military in which, by some estimates, half-a-million suspected communist sympathizers (mostly ethnic Chinese) were killed. For a time, Sukarno remained as titular head of state, but Indonesia's foreign policy shifted in a pro-Western direction. Soviet aid programs were suspended and debt repayment interrupted. The fact that Sukarno had drawn increasingly close to China and had even joined in Chinese criticism of the Soviet role in the Third World reduced the Soviet sense of loss. By 1972 correct relations were resumed with the new Indonesian government, but close ties were never restored.

The conflict that pitted U.S.-backed South Vietnam against Soviet- and Chinese-supported North Vietnam dominated politics in Southeast Asia. Soviet support for a negotiated settlement was evident in statements made after Khrushchev's ouster in October 1964 and during Kosygin's trip to Hanoi in February 1965. This position was maintained despite the coincidence of this visit with the beginning of U.S. bombing of North Vietnam, a "fraternal socialist country."

As the fighting intensified, both communist powers supplied the North Vietnamese regime with military equipment; however, they quarreled over the transshipment of Soviet supplies to Vietnam through Chinese territory. Vietnam in fact did become an issue in Sino-Soviet polemics, which harshened during the Cultural Revolution (1966–1969). The Chinese accused the Soviets of cowardice: Fear of the United States, they said, was inhibiting Soviet aid to Vietnam. However, Vietnam became more and more dependent on Soviet military assistance as U.S. involvement escalated from 1965 to 1968. Despite the disagreements between its benefactors, North Vietnam persisted in its military confrontation, which seemed the best guarantee of political victory in all of Vietnam. Although the USSR became Vietnam's primary supplier, Soviet conduct during the war did not alarm the United States enough to impede progress toward Soviet-U.S. détente. In the end some U.S. analysts even gave credit to Soviet pressures for successful conclusion of the Paris peace agreements in January 1973.[19]

Elsewhere in Southeast Asia the war in Vietnam intensified anti-Soviet policies. In 1967 the Association of Southeast Asian Nations (ASEAN) was formed by Thailand, Philippines, Indonesia, Singapore, and Malaysia. This group, which was dedicated to cooperation in economic and foreign policy, aroused Soviet suspicions. However, by 1972 Soviet commentators were willing to extend limited praise to ASEAN statements in favor of a neutral zone in Southeast Asia—to the extent that this conflicted with U.S. aims.

Africa

Soviet relations with Africa in this period were shaped by military coups, which were becoming a regular feature of Third World politics. The Soviets lost several carefully cultivated nationalist leaders (Nkrumah in Ghana, Keita in Mali), and the replacement military regimes were not always so interested in close relations with the USSR, or in socialism. But the USSR also gained through military regimes that did profess an interest in Soviet assistance, in Somalia, the Sudan, and Uganda.

In Mali, although the new regime maintained a fairly close relationship, and military and economic aid continued, sources of aid were diversified, and the ruling party the Soviets had praised was dissolved. At intervals the Malian government became critical of Soviet policies in Africa, and even expelled some Soviet diplomats. The new Ghanaian government that ousted Nkrumah claimed that the Soviet role in their country was harmful. Soviet advisors were sent home and the number of diplomatic personnel permitted was cut. The deposed Nkrumah took up residence in Guinea, and there the Soviets allegedly provided aid to his supporters, who hoped to regain power. In October 1968, a nasty incident developed when the Ghanaian government protested Soviet activities in Guinea by seizing two Soviet fishing vessels. The ships and their crews were held for five months and charged with subversive activity. In March 1969, four Soviet warships sailed into the area, and the sailors were eventually released. Subsequently, Soviet journalists and diplomats were expelled, and it was many years before relations could be described as cordial.

African regimes in general, both military and civilian, increasingly were single-party or highly personalistic governments. Almost all were troubled by separatist movements or were plagued by serious internal tribal divisions. In a few cases, the Soviets became associated with unsuccessful leftist dissenters. In Kenya, for example, they apparently extended some aid to Oginga Odinga, a Luo rival to Jomo Kenyatta's ruling group. In the Congo (Zaire), the Kinshasa government expelled several Soviet diplomats for affiliation with leftist rebels. It should be noted that attempts by the USSR to supply or associate with these groups were in part stimulated by the competing presence of the Chinese, who were less inhibited about arming rebel groups. Through their bases in Guinea, the Soviets became involved in aiding liberation movements in Guinea-Bissau and in Cape Verde.

In 1970 the Soviets made much of their role in helping to repel a Portuguese attack on Guinea. The Portuguese were annoyed over the refuge Guinea provided for colonial rebels. Guinean leader Sékou Touré appealed for aid to both the United States and the USSR, but it was the Soviets who provided small arms to the Guinean armed forces and sent naval vessels to Guinean ports. In exchange, the Soviets were permitted to use Guinea's airport facilities for reconnaissance flights over the Atlantic and arranged to buy Guinean bauxite at favorable prices. However, although Soviet ships were allowed to refuel and make use of Guinea's shore facilities, Touré refused Soviet requests for permission to construct a naval base. An important reason for Soviet protection of Guinea was an interest in securing a sanctuary for the national liberation forces operating against the Portuguese in Guinea-Bissau. The African Party for the Independence of Guinea-Bissau and Cape Verde (PAIGC) was a principal target of Portuguese military raids. In January 1973, the PAIGC leader Amilcar Cabral was assassinated in the Guinean capital, and a number of his supporters were seized for return to Portuguese Guinea. Although the Soviets did not claim public credit for it, these PAIGC members were rescued by nearby Soviet ships.[20]

By the late sixties, it appeared the Soviets had shifted to a more cautious orientation that would associate Moscow with the position of the Organization of African Unity (OAU) in favor of strict observance of existing borders. This approach proved increasingly necessary in order to cultivate new allies among the independent African states. When civil war broke out in Nigeria in 1967, the Soviets decided to support the central government in its battle with separatists, who declared their independence as the state of Biafra. The Soviet shipments of military assistance helped the government's campaign to restore its authority. Moreover, Soviet policy was in harmony with the position of the OAU and the majority of Third World states. Soviet willingness to come to the assistance of the Nigerians in this emergency contrasted with U.S. equivocation. The British were supplying the central Nigerian government with some military aid, but they had been reluctant to supply aircraft. Soviet willingness to step in with both fighters and bombers did much to improve the Soviet image in West Africa at the time. The Soviets were also approving when the Nigerian government took steps to control the oil industry, and in the years following the civil war offered generous credits (designed in particular to help with development of Nigeria's oil resources) and an active program of educational and cultural exchange. Soviet attention to the Nigerian Marxist party (the Nigerian Socialist Workers and Farmers Party) was not appreciated however, and a delegate who attended the international communist meeting in Moscow in 1969 was arrested on his return home.

In Sudan, the leftist government that came to power in October 1964 was replaced in 1965 by a new regime, which banned the communist party. Soviet relations with this new government improved by 1968 so that trade, military, and technical assistance agreements were concluded. Then, in 1969 a military coup produced a government that was much more pro-Soviet. The new leader, Colonel Gafar Numayri, was a nationalist who was prepared to conduct an anti-imperialist foreign policy and eager to receive Soviet military aid. Soviet efforts to cultivate Numayri's regime were fruitful until trouble occurred between the Khartoum government and the Sudanese Communist Party. After severe disagreements, military groups with communist backing staged an unsuccessful coup attempt in 1971. Both Egypt and Libya helped President Numayri recover his post, and were not sympathetic when the Soviets apparently asked them to intercede on behalf of the arrested conspirators. Despite a personal appeal by Kosygin, Sudan's leading communists were executed. Moreover, the Sudanese president accused the Soviets of involvement in this coup, and Soviet-Sudanese relations remained frosty for some time.

Developments in Somalia offered another prospective client. The regime of General Siyad Barre, which took power in a 1969 coup, proclaimed a devotion to socialism that attracted favorable Soviet commentary. Aid and trade agreements were forthcoming, and party relations were successfully cultivated. Soviet military aid, including tanks and aircraft, was increased. In 1972 construction started on extensive port facilities at Berbera. Soviet naval visits began on a regular basis, leading to speculation that the Soviets would eventually have a secure naval base in this important country at the Horn of Africa.

In East Africa, the Soviet record in this period was uneven. Idi Amin Dada, who replaced Milton Obote as head of state in Uganda in 1971, carried out a shift of policy that eventually included pro-Arab positions. Amin also displayed an interest in Soviet military assistance, and a number of trade agreements and assistance pacts were concluded in 1972 and 1973. Elsewhere in East Africa, Soviet efforts to extend their presence were not notably successful. Tanzania did accept a very small Soviet credit in 1966, as did Zambia in 1967. The pro-Soviet record of the Kenyan president's political opposition restricted possibilities of improved relations with that government.

Despite the political ferment associated with the attempts to organize resistance to Rhodesia's Unilateral Declaration of Independence in 1965, the states of the area preferred to work for a negotiated settlement if possible. Moreover, the "frontline states" (Tanzania, Kenya, Zambia, and Botswana) also preferred multilateral approaches to aid for Zimbabwean liberation fighters. None of these states was particularly hospitable to a Soviet role in the Zimbabwe independence struggle. Tanzania, Kenya, and Zambia had supported Biafra during the Nigerian civil war, which had already put them in opposition to Soviet activities in Africa.

Latin America

Soviet relations with Latin America in the post-Khrushchev years emphasized expansion of trade and friendly state relations, including the establishment of diplomatic relations where possible. Nevertheless, in their efforts to expand relations with Latin American states, the Soviets had to be concerned first of all with possible U.S. reactions to their involvement in the hemisphere. In 1965 U.S. marines were sent to the Dominican Republic in response to an alleged communist threat. And in 1970 the USSR was warned that U.S. tolerance of the regime in Cuba did not mean the Soviets could establish a submarine base there.

Diplomatic relations were reestablished with Chile (1964), Peru, Equador, and Bolivia (1969), Venezuela and Guyana (1970), and Costa Rica (1971). Credits were offered to Chile, Argentina, Uruguay, and Colombia. The Soviets greatly expanded trade with Brazil, which became a leading customer for Soviet oil, and with Argentina, a major source of grain. The Eduardo Frei government of Chile resumed diplomatic relations with the USSR in 1964 and moved to conclude a variety of commercial and technical assistance agreements in the next few years. In some cases, as in Bolivia, this was related to a change in government. In Peru, a radical anti-American military government, which emerged in 1969, proved unusually receptive to Soviet approaches. This government adopted confrontational policies with U.S. oil companies, and in 1971 became the first Latin American country other than Cuba to purchase Soviet military equipment.

A number of problems emerged with regard to Cuba. While the acquisition of this client state in the U.S. backyard was a major coup, the USSR did not support Castro's radical foreign policy orientation, which included a commitment to insurrectionary movements. In the first place, the revolutionary tactics of rural guerrilla movements that Castro and his associates attempted to project into Latin America were not in harmony with accepted Soviet prescriptions. The Soviet line of support for electoral alliances and the pursuit of political acceptability by communists on a broad anti-imperialist platform was too mild for the Cubans, who sought a more provocative and violent orientation. The Soviets not only found themselves in a three-sided debate over appropriate tactics with both the Chinese and the Cubans, but also were blamed for Cuban agitation. The Uruguayan government, for example, troubled with a number of active guerrilla movements in the late sixties, expelled several Soviets for alleged connections with radical labor groups.

Following the agreement of 1964 between Khrushchev and Castro, the Cubans proceeded to set up a Cuban Communist Party within which old-line communists and Castro's associates collaborated. Cuba also abandoned its ambitious rapid industrialization schemes and lined up behind the Soviets in their dispute with the Chinese. However, Soviet-Cuban relations deteriorated rather seriously from 1966 to about 1970. Intent on building his Third World image, Castro advocated more decisive help for Vietnam, criticized the nonrevolutionary approaches of established communist parties in Latin America, and chided the Soviets for their aid to capitalist or moderate Latin governments like the Frei regime in Chile. At the Tricontinental Conference in January 1966 in Havana, Castro proclaimed his belief that Latin America as a whole was ripe for armed struggle and issued a general summons to revolutionary activity. A Soviet delegate, in contrast, called for "fraternal solidarity" with armed struggle in countries where it was appropriate. (Colombia, Venezuela, Peru, and Guatemala were mentioned.) The OAS, along with several individual Latin American countries, protested quickly to the United Nations about the "subversive" impact of the meeting and its declarations. The Soviet Union then officially disavowed the conference, claiming that the Soviet delegate had represented only "a social organization." (The head delegate Sharaf Rashidov was a candidate member of the Central Committee of the Soviet party and first secretary of the party organization in Uzbekistan.)

Castro's commitment to his more revolutionary line and his sponsorship of radical splinter groups in opposition to established Latin American communist parties provoked some sharp polemics in the international communist press in 1966 and 1967. He even instigated the establishment of an organization for cooperation among "true anti-imperialists," defined as those pursuing armed struggle. Castro defied Soviet authority by snubbing the Soviet anniversary centennial in November 1967, sent no delegation to the international communist preparatory meeting in January 1968, purged a pro-Soviet faction from his government, and refused to sign the Non-Proliferation Treaty. All the while, Castro proclaimed the necessity to struggle boldly for "maximum independence."

While the Soviets continued to supply economic aid to Cuba during this period, military shipments were apparently halted, trade negotiations slowed, diplomatic visits curtailed, and oil shipments cut back significantly. The pressure eventually produced a reconciliation of sorts. At the end of 1968, Castro announced his support of the invasion of Czechoslovakia as "absolutely necessary," although illegal, and asked in a public address whether this meant that the Warsaw Pact would send its troops to Cuba if the United States attacked it.[21] Castro also reoriented his foreign policy in ways that brought it more in line with Soviet preferences.

Military shipments resumed accordingly in late 1969, and new longer-term trade and economic assistance arrangements were concluded. The Soviet pressure also had domestic repercussions. In what Carmela Mesa-Lago calls the "fifth phase" of the Cuban revolution, bilateral Soviet-Cuban commissions began to oversee reorganization of the country's economic planning and financial management, which paved the way for eventual incorporation of Cuba into the Council of Mutual Economic Assistance (COMECON) in 1972.[22] Moreover, Castro specifically declared that Cubans respected each country's choices about its own path, and proclaimed his willingness to develop friendly relations with many of Cuba's neighbors.

The election of Salvador Allende in Chile in November 1970 presented more delicate problems. A Marxist, Allende was the candidate of a coalition of leftist parties, including communists. But he served as a minority president at the pleasure of a loose coalition of democratic groups in the Congress. Whether out of concern for his safety, or for fear of U.S. reaction, the Soviets were not generous with Chile and proceeded cautiously with aid. Nonetheless, the Soviets offered low-interest rates on import financing, and some outright grants. Offers of credits nearly doubled those promised to the Frei regime, and important technical assistance was obtained for the newly nationalized copper mines and for the fishing industry.

The Soviets did not treat Allende's victory in Chile as a victory for the socialist camp. Indeed, in view of Allende's internal struggles with radical left and a suspicious right, such treatment would have been unwarranted. Allende had the support of Chilean communists, who were active proponents of negotiations with other political parties that could help keep him in office. By 1973 the political situation had become sharply polarized. Amidst economic crises and political conflicts, the military seized power in September, killing Allende in the process. Initially the Soviets claimed that Chile had demonstrated the validity of the peaceful path to socialism they had been recommending. After Allende's murder, Soviet theorists had to defend this view by showing that Allende had been right, but that he had perhaps underestimated his unscrupulous enemies and should have done more to make the revolution "irreversible."

ASSERTIVE OPPORTUNISM: 1974-1979

In spite of the near-confrontation during the 1973 Middle East war, Soviet-U.S. relations seemed to continue to improve in this period. The Conference on Security and Cooperation in Europe met from 1973 to 1975, putting together a package of agreements that would clarify the expectations and commitments of both sides. The final agreement, signed in Helsinki in 1975, included a number of elements: First, all signatories agreed to respect the existing borders and governments in Europe (a matter left in doubt by the absence of a World War II general peace treaty). Second, increases in commerical contacts between Eastern and Western Europe were linked with improved treatment of journalists, tourists, and potential emigrants and with pledges of respect for human and civic rights. At the same time, negotiations began on a U.S.-USSR trade treaty that would have finally given the Soviet Union most-favored-nation status and better access to U.S. markets. Soviet commentators praised these developments as evidence that peaceful coexistence was now "an accepted norm" of international life, and that the "balance of forces" had irrevocably shifted to accept the existence and importance of the socialist camp.

At the same time there were some developments hinting that the commitment to détente would not last. Rumblings of discontent within the Soviet elite, on the pages of the international communist press, and among Soviet clients and allies indicated that détente was not universally applauded within the communist camp. Brezhnev and others took pains to explain that détente, like peaceful coexistence, did not mean that the struggle for social progress had ended. At the same time, the Soviet-U.S. trade treaty became caught up in a debate in the U.S. Congress about the treatment of Soviet Jews. In the end, the USSR refused to adopt the treaty, since it had been amended to include provisions regarding Soviet Jewish emigration. These problems in Soviet-U.S. relations were aggravated by the progress toward a Sino-U.S. rapprochement. Ironically, U.S. diplomatic recognition of the People's Republic in 1978 was followed by an agreement to extend most-favored-nation status to China.

The final defeat of South Vietnam in 1975, the brief ascendance of the Portuguese communists, and Soviet sponsorship of Cuban intervention in Angola's civil war in 1975-1976 helped to convince Westerners that Soviet behavior had not become more restrained. By 1979, a second Soviet-Cuban intervention, this time in Ethiopia, the Vietnamese invasion of Kampuchea (formerly Cambodia), and the Soviet invasion of Afghanistan put an end to expectations of harmonious great-power relations. Instead, Soviet-U.S. relations became increasingly tense.

The Soviet Union encountered and took advantage of a number of opportunities in the Third World during this period. A series of new radical regimes in many locations announced their preference for socialist solutions and sought Soviet help in rejecting Western ties. Yet this was not exclusively a period of gains. In the Middle East, the Soviets found themselves effectively excluded from the peacemaking process that led to the Egypt-Israel treaty of March 1979. On the Horn of Africa, the Soviet Union was forced to take sides in a fight between two clients, eventually losing Somalia and its port at Berbera. Moreover, Soviet behavior in the Third World was to become a central part of the controversy over the value of détente.

The Middle East

In the aftermath of the Yom Kippur War, U.S. officials proceeded with their own diplomatic efforts to resolve the Arab-Israeli conflict. They negotiated successive disengagement agreements in 1974 and 1975, which returned part of the Sinai to Egypt, separated Syrian and Israeli troops, and included provisions for U.S. observers in the Sinai. The Soviets, despite the massive assistance they provided to the Arabs, wound up on the diplomatic sidelines. Egyptian-Soviet tensions had, of course, preceded the war, and did not cease afterwards. Sadat's willingness to cooperate with the United States in bilateral negotiations with Israel infuriated the Soviets. The relationship became particularly acrimonious in 1975 over the issue of the Egyptian debt. Although the Soviets agreed to reschedule Syria's debt, they refused to do so for Egypt. Sadat complained publicly about the quality and speed of Soviet arms deliveries, and he turned to Saudi Arabia as well as Algeria and Kuwait for aid in purchasing arms from both Eastern and Western suppliers. He also ordered a reorientation of the Egyptian economy, away from socialist measures and toward the encouragement of foreign private investment. In March 1976, an angry Sadat announced abrogation of the Soviet-Egyptian friendship treaty. Soviet access to naval facilities was terminated shortly thereafter. Not only did Egyptian-U.S. relations become closer, but Sadat also signed a three-way treaty with Saudi Arabia and Sudan in 1976.

The disengagement agreements paved the way for the Camp David talks in 1978 and the Egyptian-Israeli peace treaty of March 1979.

Without Egypt, further Arab military contests with Israel just did not appear feasible. The peace agreements enraged those Arabs who believed that fighting would be necessary to defeat Israel and win back Palestine. The USSR probably considered it a victory when Egypt was expelled from the Arab League and lost its diplomatic and economic ties with most of the Arab states in 1979. A "Steadfastness Front" formed by radical Arab states issued a statement that condemned the peace treaty and specifically referred to the importance to the Arab cause of good relations with the USSR. But by this time, the Arab world was divided by a number of serious conflicts. Inevitably, the Soviets were involved too.

The USSR upgraded its treatment of the PLO after the October War. Two years after the Rabat Arab summit of 1974 recognized the PLO as the legitimate spokesman for the Palestinians, the Soviets permitted it to open an office in Moscow. Soviet military assistance to the PLO increased substantially, and support for Palestinian national rights was soon a key phrase in all Soviet public pronouncements. Although the USSR continued to back Israel's right to exist, Moscow stressed that a PLO presence at peace negotiations was mandatory. Support for the Palestinians might have seemed the logical cause on which all Arab states could cooperate with the Soviet Union, but other quarrels swiftly prevented any but the most superficial Arab unity.

In 1975 a civil war erupted in Lebanon, involving Syria, the apparent new Soviet favorite. Although Syria had agreed to the 1974 disengagement with Israel, its opposition to any peace that excluded the Palestinians helped make Syria a leader among the most radically anti-Israel states. Nonetheless, it became clear as the Lebanese civil war unfolded that Syria has its own ideas about the proper Palestinian political role in the region. In January 1976, as the communal fighting in Lebanon became serious, Syrian-trained Palestinian units intervened. At first Syria acted to rescue the Palestinians and the Arab left, but later, Syria switched to support the Christian minority. In the summer of 1976, Syrian army regulars were sent in to control the Palestinians and to prevent partition of Lebanon.

The Soviets opposed the Syrian intervention and withheld arms deliveries in an attempt to restrain President Hafez al-Assad. Although other Arab radical states (Libya, Iraq, and Algeria) also protested the Syrian actions, neither they nor the Soviets were able to do much about it. Eventually, the Saudis succeeded in arranging a settlement in Lebanon in late 1976 that made Syrian forces the major component of an Arab peacekeeping force. Relations seemed to remain on hold until the signing of the Camp David Accords in September 1978 impelled Assad to seek better ties to Moscow. Syria's participation in the Steadfastness Front and its opposition to the Egyptian-Israeli peace treaty paralleled the Soviet position and met with Moscow's support.

Soviet relations with the states of the Gulf reflect the same on-again, off-again pattern as those with other Middle Eastern states during this period. Ties were threatened by diverging interests, subregional conflicts, and the domestic politics of key states such as Iran and Iraq. At the same time, Moscow gained cordial relations with the Emirate of Kuwait and succeeded by the end of the decade in consolidating its relations with the People's Democratic Republic of Yemen (PDRY).

The economic and military connections between the USSR and Iraq, as formalized in the 1972 friendship and cooperation treaty, deteriorated by the middle of the decade. The two allies disagreed over the proper role of the Iraqi Communist Party, and about Iraq's regional policies. In 1973, the Iraqi leadership had legalized the communist party and offered it a minority position in the government, provided the party restricted its political activities. Following Soviet instructions, the party accepted this arrangement and pledged its support to the regime. The government, which never fully trusted the party, periodically harassed the communists, and in 1978 executed some forty party members on charges they had been attempting to subvert the military. Beginning in 1976, the Iraqi government moved to pursue a foreign policy more independent of Soviet wishes. Newly acquired oil wealth was used to purchase weapons from other suppliers. Simultaneously, Baghdad sought to reduce its isolation in the Arab world. A quarrel developed with the Soviets in 1978, when the Iraqis criticized the Soviet decision to abandon the Islamic Eritrean rebellion against Ethiopia's central government. While the Soviets began to help Colonel Mengistu Haile-Meriam's efforts to suppress the rebels, Iraq continued to support the Eritreans.

Elsewhere in the Gulf, the Soviets fared rather better. Kuwait, which pursued a traditionally independent policy, established relations with both China and the USSR, as well as with several Eastern European countries. In the middle of the decade, the Kuwaitis extended loans to both Hungary and Rumania. Most significant for our purposes, Kuwait concluded two arms agreements with the Soviet Union, one in 1974 and another in 1976. These included weapons sales, as well as agreements for military training assistance and construction of a naval port and air base.

Toward the end of this period, the Soviet position in South Yemen (PDRY) improved dramatically, but not without considerable turmoil and a bizarre series of events. In the mid-seventies, PDRY President Salim Ali improved ties with North Yemen and Saudi Arabia, possibly indicating a desire to move away from the USSR. In June 1978, the president of North Yemen was assassinated by persons reputed to be agents of the PDRY. The pro-Soviet faction of the South Yemeni leadership then accused President Ali of masterminding the assassination. During the factional fighting that followed, Ali was killed, and the pro-Soviet Abdul Fatah Ismail took over, assisted by Cuban troops. Within a few days, Ismail proclaimed Marxism-Leninism. A year later, the PDRY signed a friendship and cooperation treaty with Moscow. A number of analyses conclude that the USSR helped to plan the coup in order to forestall a sharp deterioration in its relations with South Yemen.

The most important event in the Gulf region was of course the demise of the Iranian monarchy in 1979. The USSR and the shah's regime had developed a close economic relationship, highlighted by cooperation in transshipment of Iranian natural gas. By 1977 the political position of the shah had begun to deteriorate. Opposition to his regime had a strong religious base and was led from abroad by the Ayatollah Khomeini. In 1978 periodic rioting further weakened the shah's position, and he finally fled the country on January 16, 1979. Khomeini returned to Iran on February 1, and within six weeks the Islamic Republic of Iran was proclaimed. Khomeini's anti-Americanism earned Soviet applause. When U.S. diplomatic personnel were seized as hostages in November, the Soviets excused Iran, claiming that its actions were understandable in light of the years of U.S. exploitation. Despite the Islamic content of the revolution, the Soviets were clearly pleased by the upheaval in Iran. The new republic withdrew from CENTO, cancelled U.S. base rights, and reversed the shah's policy of aid to Israel.

Asia

Dramatic events occurred in Indochina in this period. The Vietnamese peace treaty of January 1973 and the subsequent U.S. withdrawal from Indochina were described by the Soviet press as a "major setback to imperialism," and a stunning victory for the forces of "progress." Although the peace treaty left two Vietnams, arrangements for participation in the Southern government by Vietcong elements proceeded very slowly. It may well be that the Vietnamese were eager to complete their military victory and were restrained by the Soviets until 1975. In any case, by that time it was evident that the United States was no longer prepared to commit itself to preventing the defeat of South Vietnam. The Vietnamese communists launched their final offensive early in 1975; by April, Saigon had fallen and the process of unifying the two halves of the country began. Large amounts of Soviet aid began to arrive to assist in the restructuring and recovery. Vietnam joined COMECON in 1978 and signed a friendship and cooperation treaty with the Soviet Union a few months later.

Elsewhere in Indochina, the Laotian communists proclaimed a Lao People's Democratic Republic under close Vietnamese supervision in December 1975. According to Soviet scholars, both countries have experienced a particular form of genuine socialist revolution in which communist leadership at an early stage assured the necessary social change. A Vietnam-Laos friendship treaty was signed in 1977. Cambodia did not fall under Vietnamese tutelage so easily. Almost simultaneously with the collapse of South Vietnam, the pro-American Lon Nol government of Cambodia fled, and was replaced by a Khmer Rouge–dominated democratic Kampuchean regime, with Pol Pot as premier. These Khmers harbored ancient grievances against the Vietnamese, and recent experiences had not increased their receptivity to Vietnamese attempts to control their country. Vietnamese-Kampuchean border clashes became increasingly serious in 1976 and 1977. For a time, the Khmers fought back effectively with Chinese military assistance. Kampuchea's ability to resist the Vietnamese was weakened, however, by internal disruption. The Pol Pot regime sought to implement a kind of socialism that involved the forcible removal of most of the urban populace to rural areas. Comprehensive purges of those associated with the previous regime and cruelties in administration produced devastating loss of life.

The Vietnamese successfully invaded Kampuchea in 1978 and installed Heng Samrin as the new head of a pro-Vietnamese government. However, whatever Pol Pot's reputation, this invasion was widely condemned. The USSR vetoed a UN Security Council resolution in January 1979 that called for the withdrawal of all foreign forces from Kampuchea, only to see a similar resolution pass the General Assembly a few months later. The credentials of the new Heng Samrin government were not accepted at the UN, leaving representatives of the exiled Pol Pot regime with Kampuchea's seat. Criticism of the Vietnamese invasion was so prevalent that at the Sixth Nonaligned Summit held in Havana in 1979, an "empty seat" formula was adopted, whereby neither Kampuchean regime was admitted.

The threat of Vietnamese expansionism drove leaders of the ASEAN countries (Thailand, Malaysia, Singapore, and the Philippines) not only to take their own security arrangements more seriously, but also to begin improving relations with China. In response, the Soviets undertook a vigorous diplomatic offensive in 1978 designed to improve relations with the ASEAN countries collectively and individually. These efforts resulted in increased levels of Soviet trade with some of these countries, including the Philippines. There is some speculation that this was a deliberate ploy on the part of the Ferdinand Marcos regime to gain U.S. attention. However, other Soviet initiatives were rebuffed. Indonesia specifically rejected a Soviet aid offer in 1978, and Burma refused to sign a cultural exchange agreement. Nor did the ASEAN countries respond to projects for an enlarged regional organization that would include the three new communist Indochinese states.

The Vietnamese actions in Kampuchea precipitated a serious conflict with China. The China-Vietnam relationship was already extremely tense in 1977 when the Vietnamese government launched an anticapitalist campaign directed primarily against ethnic Chinese. The Kampuchean takeover was the last straw. In February 1979, Chinese troops crossed the Vietnamese border in a "punitive incursion." Although the Chinese were defeated and suffered major losses, their willingness to use force seemed to ensure continued Soviet entanglement with its combative Vietnamese ally.

Soviet relations with South Asian countries also experienced some difficulties associated with regional political changes. Military coups in Bangladesh (1975) and Pakistan (1977) and a shift to the right in Sri Lanka altered the context of Soviet diplomacy in the area. The overall volume of Soviet assistance and trade with these countries declined, while their relations with China improved. Even Soviet ties to India were strained. New Delhi's determination to acquire nuclear weapons capability and refusal to sign the Non-Proliferation Treaty were an irritant. Nonetheless, it appears that the Soviet Union continued to provide the Indians with the necessary heavy water supplies for its nuclear program even after the explosion of a nuclear device in 1974. The Soviets were apparently quite disturbed in 1976 when diplomatic relations were restored between India and China. The Indian government was also hostile to Soviet proposals to create a zone of peace in the Indian Ocean and to the scheme for an Asian collective security pact. When a right-wing Janata government under Morarji Desai replaced Indira Gandhi in 1977, India initiated many steps that improved India's economic, commercial, and military relationships with Western states at Soviet expense. However, the general tenor of Indian-Soviet relations was not damaged.

The 1973 regime change in Afghanistan did not at first hinder Soviet-Afghan relations. In fact, the new Afghan republic proclaimed its intention to continue the long-standing friendship with the USSR. Moscow was pleased to reciprocate with new military and economic aid commitments. Trade nearly doubled, and Prime Minister Muhammed Daoud made a highly publicized state visit to the Soviet Union. Problems within the country, however, took their toll in relations between Moscow and Kabul. Daoud had to contend with a number of domestic adversaries, including pro-Soviet military factions and communist agitation. In 1975 he appeared to move to the right when he banned political opposition and purged military officers suspected of disloyalty. Internationally, he accepted a long-term aid agreement from the shah of Iran and made peace overtures to Pakistan.

As resistance to his policies grew, long-feuding Afghan communist groups joined forces and thus became a target of Daoud's security drive. In April 1978, as Daoud moved to arrest key communists, the Khalq and Parcham factions staged a coup. In the fighting, Daoud was killed. The new government, the Democratic Republic of Afghanistan, was headed by former communist rivals Nur Muhammed Taraki (as prime minister) and Hafizullah Amin (as deputy prime minister and foreign minister). In December this fragile Marxist government signed a friendship and cooperation treaty with the USSR. While the Soviets could applaud the declared intent of this regime to reform Afghan society radically, the assault on traditional ways alienated much of the tribal Muslim population. A series of mutinies and popular revolts prompted the Soviets to provide even larger quantities of military aid, including increasing numbers of advisors and training groups. Despite apparent Soviet advice to moderate what were later termed "ultraleft and premature social policies," Afghan government activities continued to generate popular disaffection.

In September 1979, the feud between Taraki and Amin was resolved forcibly. Taraki, newly returned from Moscow, tried unsuccessfully to oust Amin. Instead, Taraki was killed, and Amin secured his hold on power. Thus the Soviet favorite was eliminated, and Amin continued to pursue his radical revolutionary programs. Internal armed resistance to the government intensified. As the situation inside Afghanistan continued to deteriorate, the Soviet leadership apparently concluded that something needed to be done to save the Marxist-Leninist government from defeat. That is, the decision to invade and install a more pliant government seems to have been provoked by a desire to prevent the imminent collapse of a regime to which Moscow was already heavily committed.

On December 24, 1979, Soviet troops crossed the border into Afghanistan. For the next two days, transport planes brought soldiers to Kabul as rifle divisions moved on the ground. Amin, killed on December 27 during an attack on the palace, was replaced by Babrak Karmal, a former foe of Amin who had been in exile in Czechoslovakia. The Soviets claimed that Karmal had invited their assistance in order to meet a threat of "external aggression," although the invitation was issued after Soviet forces had arrived. Apparently Karmal himself did not appear in Kabul until January 1. By the end of January, some 80,000 Soviet troops were reported to be in Afghanistan, with Soviet citizens virtually in charge of the government.[23]

Africa

The USSR gained some new allies and sympathizers in Africa, although by the end of the decade it had also lost ground. The People's Republic of Congo remained a close friend, linked militarily and politically. Relatively cordial relations were maintained until 1977 with Guinea and with the military government of Nigeria. Political shifts to socialism brought into being some new regimes sympathetic to Soviet foreign policy posture and willing to expand ties with the USSR. These included the establishment of a "people's republic" in Benin (formerly Dahomey), which adopted Marxism-Leninism, nationalized banks and foreign businesses, and attached itself to the radical group within the nonaligned movement. Ties with France remained close, however, and the Soviets did not develop extensive political or commercial links with Benin. In Madagascar, political turmoil brought a series of leftist governments in the mid-seventies. In 1975, a new government formed by Fichie Ratsiraka announced a commitment to socialism and a "soviet revolution." The U.S. ambassador's credentials were not accepted, foreign businesses were nationalized, and talks on trade and aid with Soviet representatives began. Madagascar then joined the ranks of the radical Third World regimes at the United Nations and at meetings of the nonaligned states.

The most dramatic events of this period were Soviet-sponsored Cuban military operations in Angola and Ethiopia that helped Marxist-Leninist groups retain political power. The military coup toppling the Antonio Salazar regime in Portugal was specifically dedicated to ending the costly and ineffective colonial warfare that had dragged on in its African possessions, and the new government soon set about granting independence to Guinea-Bissau (1974) and to Mozambique, Cape Verde, São Tomé and Principe (1975). The former guerrilla leaders who became the political elite in these new states were avowedly socialist, and long years of commitment to struggle against the U.S.-backed Portuguese government had confirmed a general world view sympathetic to the USSR (and China). The conversion of these guerrilla organizations into states in the Portuguese territories was "warmly welcome" to the USSR. Brezhnev said at the Twenty-Fifth CPSU Congress: "The CPSU has always shown solidarity with these peoples and has given every kind of support to the embattled patriots. Today we rejoice that our inter-governmental relations with these countries are being shaped in a spirit of sincere friendship and mutual understanding."[24]

The first Soviet-sponsored Cuban military intervention in Africa occurred in Angola. In January 1975, three contending liberation groups, each with its own outside patron, accepted a plan for independence under a coalition government. But by summer civil war broke out, with each group vying for dominance. In this triangular competition, the Soviets backed the Marxist Popular Movement for the Liberation of Angola (MPLA), which had set up bases and guerrilla training camps in Congo and Zambia. The MPLA had two opponents: the National Front for the Liberation of Angola (FNLA), which was supported by Zaire, operated in the northern regions, and received U.S. and Chinese assistance; and the Union for the Total Liberation of Angola (UNITA), which was a weaker southern Angolan organization that received some Chinese and eventually also some U.S. financial aid. When the fighting began, the MPLA was bolstered by direct shipments of Soviet military hardware and by the arrival of Cuban advisors. As the MPLA became more successful militarily, the United States, Zaire, and Zambia increased their support to both the FNLA and UNITA. South African support also proved crucial. In August power plants along the border were occupied by South African troops; in October the troops crossed into Angola at the joint request of UNITA-FNLA, and spearheaded an effective offensive toward the capital in anticipation of the projected date of independence (November 11, 1975). In response, Agostinho Neto, the leader of the MPLA, urgently requested more help from the USSR and Cuba. Perhaps emboldened by African criticism of the South African role and the absence of clear commitments by other foreign patrons, the Soviets rushed ahead with transport of additional equipment and Cuban troops. A Cuban-led counteroffensive then helped secure MPLA control of the capital in time for the MPLA to declare itself the new government of independent Angola in November. In December the U.S. Congress voted against any further covert assistance to the opposition movements. Cuban mop-up operations helped to consolidate the MPLA's hold on the country while the South Africans withdrew.

Although African countries were at first split on the issue, the new government was recognized by the OAU in March 1976. In October the USSR and Angola signed a treaty of friendship and cooperation, followed by a series of economic and technical assistance agreements. The country has never been completely pacified. Cuban forces remain in Angola, where they operate against South African and UNITA forces, train the Angolan army, and assist South West Africa People's Organization (SWAPO) guerrillas.

Mozambique had been the site of the bloodiest colonial wars, and independence in July 1975 followed a series of mutinies, popular disturbances, and major military operations. Power was handed over directly to Samoro Machel, and the leaders of the Front for the Liberation of Mozambique (FRELIMO) set about creating a People's Republic. Diplomatic relations were established with the USSR, China, and the United States. Significant aid agreements were signed with Sweden and the

United States, and trade continued with South Africa. Nonetheless it was clear that Mozambique would align itself with the socialist camp. When Machel visited the USSR in May 1976, a joint statement was issued on the desirability of establishing party ties between the CPSU and FRELIMO. A number of economic and technical assistance agreements were signed. In 1977 a party congress in Mozambique proclaimed Marxism-Leninism the official ideology, and announced FRELIMO's intent to become a vanguard party. A friendship and cooperation treaty was signed with the USSR in March 1977 and a similar one with Cuba in October.

In a less popular effort in March 1977 and again in May 1978, Angolans apparently assisted Katangese separatists to invade the Shaba province of neighboring Zaire. Relations had been extremely hostile between Angola and Zaire, whose government had aided the MPLA's rivals during the civil war. The incursions were serious enough to require that Zaire request outside help from France, Morocco, Belgium, and the United States in repelling these rebels and rescuing Europeans. Mobutu Sese Seko, the president of Zaire, defended himself for inviting ex-colonial powers into Africa by blaming the raids on Angola's communist patrons. However, the Soviets and Cubans rejected charges that they were involved in these events.[25]

The Horn of Africa was also a subject of vigorous Soviet activity. Somalia's relations with the Soviet Union strengthened, as expressed in a treaty of friendship and cooperation in 1974. Construction of port facilities and other military installations appeared to entrench the Soviets on the Indian Ocean littoral, a development that brought sharp criticism from the United States and from conservative Arab states. It is reported that the Saudis offered Somalia substantial economic aid in 1974 in return for a commitment to reduce the Soviet presence, but were refused.

Meanwhile the replacement of Haile Selassie's imperial Ethiopian government in 1974 by a revolutionary socialist military regime soon attracted Soviet attention. The close ties that had long existed between Ethiopia and the United States began to weaken. Although some arms sales were approved in 1975 and 1976, in 1977 the administration of President Jimmy Carter cut off any further military aid because of human rights violations. The new Ethiopian regime, which was becoming increasingly radical, was troubled with factional wrangling and civil strife. Shortly after Mengistu Haile Meriam emerged as the dominant leader in February 1977, the regime announced its commitment to socialism. In May 1977 Mengistu visited the USSR, where a declaration of intent to develop cooperative relations was published. Mengistu apparently requested Soviet military assistance to protect his fragile regime from a multitude of threats, including the Eritrean separatists and Somali irredentists. Soviet military aid to Ethiopia may have begun even in 1976; in any case, it was evident that the Soviets were supporting Mengistu by mid-1977.

The Somalis were extremely unhappy about increasing Soviet-Ethiopian ties. Cuban and Soviet attempts to make peace between the two states proved fruitless, and in July 1977 the Somalis began a thinly disguised invasion of the Ogaden region of Ethiopia, which was initially very successful. The USSR halted arms deliveries to Somalia, and as the Somali advance slowed, undertook an enormous air and sea lift of armaments designed to rebuild completely the Ethiopian military and to prevent a Somali victory. (Western estimates suggest the USSR invested about US$2 billion in rearming Ethiopia.) In retaliation, Somali President Siyad Barre expelled Soviet military advisors and abrogated the friendship treaty (just three years old).

In the winter of 1977-1978, the Soviets transported large numbers of Cubans to Ethiopia. With Soviet logistic support and allegedly also with Soviet field commanders, Ethiopians drove out the Somalis. As the tide of battle turned, the United States and others feared that Somalia might be invaded. However, the Soviets quickly signalled that they did not intend to aid Ethiopians in crossing into Somalia. The situation inside Ethiopia was unstable, both because of internal factionalism and because the government was challenged by active and tenacious Eritrean liberation movements. A substantial Soviet, Cuban, and Eastern-bloc military presence remained in the country to train the Ethiopians and help achieve internal order. Although the Soviets had supported the Eritrean guerrillas against Selassie, their new relationship with Mengistu meant that they were now supporting the central government against the rebels. Apparently, revolutionary scruples induced the Cubans to refuse to fight against the Eritreans, and the Ethiopian army has been unable to end this insurrection alone.

In November 1978, Mengistu signed a friendship and cooperation treaty with the USSR during a visit to Moscow. Mengistu and other leading members of the military government repeatedly promised that they would begin to set up a vanguard Marxist-Leninist political party. In 1979 a preparatory commission was established. The Soviets chose to treat this commission as if it were a party until the Ethiopian Workers' Party was actually created in September 1984. The Ethiopian government has signed a number of treaties and agreements with various East European regimes, as well as with Cuba. Ethiopia (along with Mozam-bique and Angola) has also sent observers to COMECON meetings.

The association with Ethiopia had unhappy consequences for Soviet relations with Sudan, whose President Numayri was inclined to be suspicious about Soviet intentions. In 1976 when Libyan-backed forces unsuccessfully attempted to overthrow him, Numayri used the occasion to denounce the Soviet role in Africa. In May 1977 anxieties about Ethiopian subversion along the Sudan-Ethiopia border provoked Numayri to expel Soviet military advisors remaining in his country. Close ties between Sudan and Egypt inhibited restoration of good relations with the USSR. However, OAU mediation in 1979 did reduce Sudanese-Ethiopian antagonism.

A number of other relationships with African states suffered reverses. The president of Mali, Moussa Traoré, complained in 1978 that the Soviets had been behind an abortive military coup against his regime and moved to reduce its contacts with the USSR. The Soviets had established a rather bizarre relationship with the tyrannical ruler of Equatorial Guinea, President Macias Nguema. This relationship was ruptured when Nguema was overthrown in 1979 and fled the country.

The USSR had begun to develop trade and aid relations with Idi Amin's regime in Uganda. Soviet military aid apparently began reaching his forces in 1974. A dispute developed with Amin over Angola in 1976, when Amin sided with Zaire's President Mobutu and favored the FNLA. Apparently angered at Soviet pressure to support recognition of the MPLA in the OAU, Amin briefly expelled the Soviet ambassador. Aid deliveries soon resumed; however, Amin's excessively brutal domestic regime and an armed invasion of neighboring Tanzania in 1978 finally provoked a break with the Soviets, who withdrew their military training team.

The Soviets had long been enthusiastic vocal supporters of liberation movements in Southern Africa. The continuing political, military, and diplomatic struggles for independence of Zimbabwe and Namibia appeared to offer fruitful fields for Soviet demonstrations of their anti-imperialism. The demise of Portuguese colonialism and the end of white rule in Angola and Mozambique greatly increased pressure for majority rule in Rhodesia. The Soviet and Cuban role in the Angolan civil war also stimulated greater Western interest in helping to achieve a negotiated settlement there.

The "frontline states" (initially Zambia, Tanzania, Kenya, and Botswana; later also Mozambique, Angola, and Swaziland) at first endorsed the idea of negotiations and accepted the involvement of Western states to help work out a settlement with Ian Smith's white minority government in Rhodesia. The neighboring states were divided in ideology and in their preferences among the various independence groups and leaders, but united in their desire to promote unity among the nationalist groups and a peaceful settlement if possible. However, in February 1976, lack of progress drove the frontline states to endorse armed struggle and to attempt to enforce economic sanctions against Rhodesia. In 1976 Kissinger traveled to Africa, endorsed the principle of majority rule, and warned the USSR and Cuba to stay out of Rhodesia. A new series of diplomatic initiatives appeared to make progress when the Smith government finally agreed in principle to majority rule, and a new round of negotiations among the Rhodesian protagonists began. The Soviets did not participate in these diplomatic efforts, which they criticized, and they continued to supply arms to the various guerrilla groups.

The Zimbabwe liberation groups were split along tribal and personal lines. The two major guerrilla groups each developed different foreign affiliations as well. Joshua Nkomo, leader of the Zimbabwe African People's Union (ZAPU), first traveled to the USSR in 1976; on subsequent trips in 1977 and 1978 he declared himself in favor of Marxism-Leninism. ZAPU's military bases were primarily in Zambia, and some of its members had been trained in Eastern Europe. Robert Mugabe, the leader of the major rival group, the Zimbabwe African National Union (ZANU), was also sympathetic to Marxism, but had close ties with China. Mugabe's ZANU guerrilla forces were largely based in Mozambique. These managed to form a patriotic front in 1976 to coordinate their activities, but were not always enthusiastic about cooperating with each other. Both were sensitive to the disadvantages of obvious international partisanship during the intensive and frustrating negotiations on transitional arrangements, which began seriously late in 1976. In March 1977, Soviet Premier Kosygin traveled to Africa, where he visited the frontline state capitals and met with leaders of Namibian, Zimbabwean, and South African liberation groups. In a formal statement issued in Zambia, Kosygin pledged Soviet assistance to the liberation forces. All these groups eventually received some Soviet assistance, much of it funneled through the frontline states.

The Soviets were approving when the patriotic front resolved to keep fighting and rejected an internal settlement offered by the Smith government in 1978. However, Soviet comments were highly skeptical when the front accepted a settlement agreement, which was worked out with British mediation in December 1979. The agreement included arrangements for a transitional government in which whites and blacks would share power, to be followed by elections that would introduce majority rule.

The Namibian situation proved more resistant to diplomatic initiatives. In 1978 South Africa did agree on negotiations on the devolution of power to the inhabitants of that region, after considerable pressure from the "contact group" of the United States, Britain, France, Canada, and West Germany. However, the South Africans have not hesitated to use force against the guerrillas, wherever based, and against regimes that harbor them. The Soviets regularly expressed skepticism about negotiations with the South Africans. Soviet weapons and training assistance were provided to the Namibian and South African guerrillas, although most of them profess a desire to remain nonaligned. Faced with energetic South African military activities against the guerrillas and their friends, even Zambia (which had been hostile to the Soviet role in Angola) concluded an arms deal with the USSR in 1979.

The cumulative effect of Soviet-Cuban interventions in Africa did arouse considerable opposition. By 1978 Barre of Somalia, Numayri of Sudan, Sadat of Egypt, and Mobutu of Zaire were all highly vocal in criticizing Soviet imperial aspirations in Africa. Zaire's solicitation of French and U.S. assistance to protect itself in 1977 and 1978 was an extreme case of a resurgence of security concerns among the moderate and especially the francophone African states. Even some of the more radical states displayed some sensitivity to fears that an enhanced Soviet presence in Africa might be menacing, and moved to display a more nonaligned posture. Guinea, which had supplied refueling stopovers to Soviet aircraft during the Angolan war, refused such facilities in 1977 during the Ethiopian intervention. As part of a general political reorientation, relations were resumed with France. (President Valéry Giscard d'Estaing visited Guinea in December 1978.) Touré subsequently toured Western Europe and the United States, offering public criticism of Soviet aid. The Maldives, upon independence, reportedly also refused to grant the Soviets a base.

Soviet associations with a number of local conflicts on the continent raised additional problems. One complication was their association with Libya, a much less attractive proxy than Cuba. The radicalization of Libya under Colonel Muammar Qaddafi offered an ally committed to Arab socialism and liberation causes. Libya's enormous oil wealth was also of interest: By 1977, Libya had become a major purchaser of Soviet arms. But Qaddafi's enormous arsenal, his "Greater Sahara" expansionism in Chad, alleged subversion of the governments in Sudan, Somalia, and Egypt, and the conversion of Libyan embassies into "people's revolutionary centers" in 1979 made him a troublesome partner for the USSR in Africa. Idi Amin was another unpopular recipient of Soviet aid. Soviet military assistance to Uganda backfired in 1978 when Amin invaded Tanzania. Disavowals of this action did not alter the fact that Soviet arms had made this action possible.

In the dispute over the Western Sahara that developed after 1975, the USSR found itself trying to be friendly with both sides. Longtime ally Algeria supported the Popular Front for the Liberation of Saquia-el-Hamra and Rio de Oro (POLISARIO) liberation forces, and aided their fight with Morocco, whose king claimed sovereignty over the former Spanish territory. In 1978 the Soviets concluded a very important agreement with King Hassan's government for development of phosphates. As the controversy—and the fighting—raged, the Soviets kept virtually silent, except for occasional expressions of interest in a "just" solution.

Latin America

Although the September 1973 military coup in Chile put an end to the Allende presidency, subsequent developments elsewhere in Latin America—particularly in Central America and the Caribbean—reflected radical trends that benefited the USSR. By 1979, governments sympathetic to good relations with the USSR had emerged in several countries. While Soviet activities in this hemisphere have always reflected caution, there were significant changes in the degree of U.S. dominance that must have been encouraging.

Cuba's relationship with the Soviet Union moved onto a new plane in this period. Now a full member of COMECON, Cuba increasingly integrated its economic planning with that of its fellow socialist states. Ideologically and politically, Cuban communists had absorbed the Soviet line that regimes willing to challenge U.S. dominance of the region should be encouraged and supported. The more moderate Cuban posture and the positive and helpful role it was attempting to play through its aid and technical assistance programs were rewarded in 1975 when the OAS voted to remove diplomatic and economic sanctions originally imposed on Cuba in 1964. Maintaining this "fraternal socialist state" remained extremely expensive. However, Cuban diplomatic activity, technical assistance, and cooperation in Latin America became an important adjunct to Soviet diplomacy in the region. In 1979, Castro was host and rotating chairman of the sixth summit of the Nonaligned Movement, a position he used to great advantage in trumpeting favorite Soviet positions in world politics. When criticized for seeming to shift the meaning of nonalignment, he declared that the USSR was the "natural ally" of all developing states.

At about the same time as the nonaligned summit, it was reported in the United States that a brigade of Soviet troops was stationed in Cuba. President Carter eventually accepted Soviet assurances that the men were not a combat force, but not before considerable public controversy had been raised about the implications of Cuba's alignment and a large group of U.S. Marines had landed at Guantanamo.

The Soviet Union continued to develop trade ties with a number of Latin American countries, especially those (e.g., Argentina and Brazil) that produced grain for export. In fact the USSR steadily ran a trade deficit in its dealings with Latin America. Diplomatic relations were cultivated with an increasing number of Latin American states less likely than in the past to regard the Soviets as an immediate political threat.

One significant military assistance effort was launched—with the revolutionary military government of Peru. This government won extensive Soviet praise for its progressive aspirations, including its nationalization of U.S.-owned oil resources and facilities. Some highly sophisticated Soviet military equipment arrived in Peru beginning in 1973. In 1978 the USSR agreed to reschedule the Peruvian debt for these weapons.

There were some fairly dramatic political changes in Central America and the Caribbean. Three new regimes took pro-Soviet positions, established friendly relations with Cuba, and attacked the U.S. role in the region. Michael Manley, in Jamaica, headed a regime that joined the nonaligned movement, and expanded trade with the Soviet Union and the Eastern-bloc countries. Forbes Burnham, in Guyana, not only joined the nonaligned movement, but hosted one of its foreign ministers' meetings in 1974. Burnham supported Cuba's activity in Angola and permitted use of Guyanese facilities in the military transport operations supporting the Angolan campaign. A Soviet ambassador arrived in Guyana in 1976, and Guyana apparently applied for membership in COMECON. In March 1979, Prime Minister Eric Gairy in Grenada was overthrown and replaced by Maurice Bishop. Bishop declared himself a Marxist, and an admirer of Cuban revolutionary accomplishments. After U.S. officials issued warnings about Grenada's ties with Cuba, Bishop defiantly visited the Soviet Union, and announced an agreement to sell aluminum on a long-term basis to the USSR.

In Nicaragua, the dictator Anastasio Somoza fled the country after nearly two years of guerrilla warfare against his regime. The Nicaraguan revolution was the most dramatic success for leftist forces, and, it was hoped, might set a precedent. The Soviets undertook a number of assistance projects and trading agreements with these countries, but seemed to be making great efforts not to antagonize the United States. To the extent that the Soviets were active in these countries, it may have been through Cuban agency. By 1980, it was not so much what was going on within these countries with leftist regimes that was bothering the United States, but the prospect that through Cuban aid and assistance, such regimes would seek to change their neighbors forcibly.

GLOBALISM ON THE DEFENSIVE: 1980–1984

Almost without exception, accounts of Soviet foreign policy written since December 1979 have begun with references to the Soviet invasion of Afghanistan, frequently in highly dramatic terms. The invasion is said to represent a "watershed," a "turning point," or a "major departure." So extensively did this event alter perceptions of the Soviet Union that many have used it to identify the rebirth of the cold war. In this atmosphere all Soviet actions have been subject to excitable scrutiny about what they may or may not prove about Soviet aggressiveness (as for example, the suppression of Solidarity in Poland, or the shooting down of a Korean airliner in September 1983).

Soviet-U.S. relations deteriorated sharply. Concern about security in the Gulf added to tensions already generated by a 1979 NATO decision to install advanced medium-range nuclear missiles in Europe. President Jimmy Carter described the Afghan invasion as "the most serious threat to peace since the Second World War" and proclaimed a U.S. commitment to military protection of the Gulf. Secretary of Defense Clark Clifford said a Soviet move to take over this region "would mean war." Steps were taken to set up a military force that could respond quickly to emergencies in the Gulf, and discussions began with Egypt, Somalia, Oman, and Kenya about possible military bases. The United States also announced economic and diplomatic sanctions, which included a grain embargo, restrictions on high technology exports to the Soviet Union, and a boycott of the 1980 summer Olympic Games in Moscow.

The election of Ronald Reagan in the United States confirmed the shift toward anti-Soviet policies and rhetoric. Under Reagan, the United States has undertaken a major arms build-up, sought to stabilize pro-American regimes in Central and Latin America, and advocated overt and covert actions to destabilize leftist ones. Military maneuvers in the Mediterranean, the Gulf of Mexico, Honduras, and Egypt have been accompanied by new commitments to Israel, support to antigovernment guerrillas in Nicaragua, and an outright invasion of Grenada. These developments have tended once more to draw attention to the Third World as an East-West battleground.

The Middle East

The shock of Afghanistan was felt very acutely in the Middle East and for a time prompted a remarkable degree of unity among Arabs eager to protest the assault on fellow Muslims. But this region was torn by two new conflicts: a war between Iran and Iraq, and an Israeli invasion and occupation of Lebanon that divided the states of the region in several ways. The Soviet Union found once again that it had friends on both sides of almost every issue.

Iran and Iraq were at war by the end of 1980. These two Gulf powers had come to blows previously over the Shatt al Arab waterway, which forms a boundary between their countries, a conflict that had been resolved with a treaty in 1975. The change of government in Iran introduced several factors that provoked a reopening of the conflict. For one thing, Khomeini issued a call to Iraq's Shi'ites to overthrow Sadam Hussein's regime. But internal turmoil in Iran may have appeared to offer the prospect of a quick and easy victory, and in September 1980 the Iraqi army invaded Iran. Although the invasion achieved some initial successes, Iran managed to mount an effective resistance, and the war continues in an approximate stalemate.

This new regional conflict sharply divided the surrounding Arab states. Secular, socialist Iraq was supported by traditionalist Saudi Arabia, Jordan, Egypt, and the small Gulf states, which feared Khomeini's messianic appeals. The fundamentalist Shi'ite Islamic Republic of Iran gained backing from only Syria and Libya—both of which are Soviet allies. Although Iraq was a Soviet treaty partner, the Soviets did not endorse Sadam Hussein's military campaign. Instead, they publicly criticized "outside powers" who sought to create instability and an excuse to intervene in the region. The Soviets also urged a negotiated settlement. However, in the first phases of this war, Soviet behavior appeared to favor Iran. The Soviets were careful not to criticize Khomeini's regime and permitted transshipments of arms to Iran from Syria and North Korea. By contrast, arms deliveries to Iraq were slowed. The Iraqis procured weapons from Egypt and Saudi Arabia and from the French, who sold them jet aircraft and Exocet missiles. Hussein publicly complained that Iraq's treaty with the USSR "had not worked."

This Soviet effort to win favor in Teheran was not successful. As long as the hostage crisis continued to dominate U.S.-Iranian relations, Moscow seemed at least a peripheral beneficiary of the political changes in Iran. But with the resolution of this crisis in January 1981, Iranian anti-Americanism turned into anti-Sovietism. The Khomeini regime had at first been rather tolerant of the Tudeh (communist) Party and other opposition groups. But this policy began to change as the Islamic Republic consolidated its new institutions. At the same time, the Gulf war became a national preoccupation. As the Iraqis were rebuffed, the Iranian government rejected cease-fire proposals and pursued its war effort. The Soviets, who continue to recommend a peaceful settlement, resumed arms shipments to Iraq in 1982. For its part, the Iranian government in 1983 arrested several leading communists and expelled many Soviet diplomats.

Security concerns led to several organizational steps in the region. The tension in the Gulf prompted Saudi Arabia to form the Gulf Cooperation Council (GCC) in 1981. Although the Saudis advertised this grouping as one designed to exclude all foreign powers, they increased their own arms purchases from the United States. The Sultanate of

Oman (along with Morocco, Egypt, and Somalia) indicated a willingness to cooperate with U.S. plans for a Rapid Deployment Force and to host its military exercises. In August 1981, three of the USSR's closest and most anti-American friends, Ethiopia, Libya, and South Yemen, joined in a trilateral treaty of friendship and cooperation. In what might be regarded as a kind of mini collective security arrangement, the treaty provides that aggression against one would be considered directed at all. The signatories pledge to "make efforts individually or collectively to strengthen their defensive capabilities." As two of the three signatories (Ethiopia and South Yemen) already had signed friendship and coop-eration treaties with the Soviet Union, this had the appearance of a Soviet defensive network. Algeria and Syria were apparently invited to participate, but chose to decline. (Egypt protested immediately that this pact represented an attempt to spread Soviet influence.) In March 1983, Libya and the USSR announced "agreement in principle" to conclude a friendship and cooperation treaty—but to date no such treaty has been signed.

The Arab-Israeli dispute has not yielded to peacemaking efforts. When comprehensive peace proposals were offered in 1982 by Ronald Reagan and by the moderate Arab states, the Soviets announced one also. The Brezhnev plan, however, has been virtually ignored, despite Soviet efforts to update it. All these plans have foundered over the question of the status of the Palestinians and the terms of negotiations. Moreover, general Arab-Israeli questions have been overtaken by events in Lebanon, which have embroiled two Soviet allies, Syria and the PLO, in a major conflict.

In June 1982, in response to an attack on an Israeli diplomat in London, Israel launched a large-scale invasion of Lebanon. Previous incursions had the character of a retaliatory strike into the border region. This time, Israeli defense forces pushed northward until they reached the outskirts of Beirut, forcing the Palestinians to a humiliating withdrawal from the beaches north of the capital. Despite urgent PLO pleas for help, the USSR did not become directly involved in the fighting. Moreover, the Israelis inflicted major damage on Syrian forces, which had occupied the northeastern parts of Lebanon. Syrian air defenses were heavily damaged, and the bulk of the Soviet-supplied Syrian air force destroyed. This did not do much for the reputation of Soviet military equipment or Soviet reliability in times of crisis. Although more advanced air-defense missiles were subsequently shipped to replace Syria's losses, the Soviets signaled that their treaty did not require them to protect Syrian forces outside Syrian territory. Soviet warnings against U.S. involvement proved ineffectual, as did a Soviet call for an international conference on the situation in Lebanon.

The embattled PLO and the Lebanese eventually accepted U.S. mediation to defuse the crisis. Not only did the United States take responsibility for the safe evacuation of the PLO from Beirut, but U.S. diplomats also helped to secure disengagement agreements between the Lebanese government, the Syrians, and the Israelis. In 1983 U.S. diplomacy resulted in a Lebanese-Israeli treaty in which Israel promised to withdraw from Lebanon if and when the Syrians also pulled back. The treaty implied normal relations between Lebanon and Israel afterwards (and therefore an explicit or tacit recognition of Israel).

Syria denounced the treaty, and increased its support to domestic Lebanese groups that were battling with Amin Gemayel's Christian-dominated government. The Lebanese government was under attack by a number of foes, including Druze and Shi'ite militia, who demanded abrogation of the treaty and a restructuring of the political system. In late summer and fall of 1983, opponents of the Gemayel government attacked U.S. and French troops that were part of the multinational peacekeeping force. These attacks, including a "suicide bombing" of the U.S. Marine barracks, in effect pushed the U.S. troops to fight on behalf of the government. Moreover, at one point in the 1983 fall crisis, it appeared as if a direct confrontation was about to occur between the Soviet-backed Syrians and the United States. In general, Syria's opposition to the treaty and apparent determination to stay in Lebanon has prolonged the crisis. In effect, the Syrian presence has made it impossible to implement an Israeli-Lebanese peace, and has made it next to impossible for the Lebanese government to function.

An additional feature of the Lebanese civil strife further complicated the Soviet position. By 1983, many of the Palestinians driven out by the Israeli advance had returned to Lebanon, only to find themselves once again battling Syrians. This time the Syrians were supporting Palestinian rivals of Yasir Arafat. As these two Soviet allies fought each other, the USSR was unwilling to offer Arafat anything more than verbal support. In December 1983, Arafat and his followers were once again forced to withdraw from Lebanon by sea, this time under protection of a U.S., French, and Italian peacekeeping force. Syria's presence in Lebanon and the disarray in the Lebanese political system have left all outside parties in difficult positions. Reconciliation talks between the warring factions in 1983 and early 1984 seemed to increase Syrian influence over the situation. By March 1984, most of the international peacekeeping force that was helping to maintain some order in Beirut was removed. No internal political settlement has yet been reached, although the Lebanon-Israel treaty was abrogated by the Gemayel government in May 1984. The Soviet Union has supported Syria diplomatically and used its United Nations veto to prevent dispatch of a

UN Peacekeeping Force to Beirut, but faces continued enmity among its closest allies in the region.

Asia

Soviet-Asian relations in this period continued to be dominated by the Afghan situation and by the problem of Vietnamese occupation of Kampuchea. Together these two issues seriously threatened prospects for improving the USSR's standing with Asian governments.

Reactions to the Soviet invasion of Afghanistan were extremely negative. The Soviets quickly vetoed a UN Security Council resolution condemning their invasion, but found themselves overwhelmingly condemned when the General Assembly later voted on a similar denunciation. A few Soviet friends from the Third World voted against the resolution: Afghanistan, Ethiopia, Cuba, Vietnam, Laos, Angola, Mozambique, South Yemen, and Grenada. Some others were absent (Libya) or abstained: India, Algeria, Benin, Burundi, Congo, Equatorial Guinea, Finland, Guinea, Guinea-Bissau, Madagascar, Mali, Nicaragua, São Tomé/Principe, Syria, Uganda, North Yemen, and Zambia. The final vote was 104 to 18, with 18 abstentions. For the first time, the Soviet Union found itself on the receiving end of a Third World majority.

The Soviet invasion of Afghanistan turned into the Soviet occupation of Afghanistan. Despite the somewhat moderate social policies of the new regime, and despite the presence of more than 100,000 Soviet troops, insurgents continue their hit-and-run opposition to the Marxist-Leninist government in Kabul. Although there are Soviet casualties, and although reports have circulated about disaffection among Soviet forces stationed there, so far there are no indications that the USSR intends to leave.

In Southeast Asia, Vietnamese expansionism continues to trouble Soviet efforts to improve its relations with countries of this area. The tenacity of the Kampuchean opposition forces and their support outside Indochina have kept the issue of Vietnam's control of Kampuchea alive. A UN General Assembly resolution in October 1980 called upon the Vietnamese to withdraw from Kampuchea, even as continued insurgent activity necessitated renewed offensives. In 1981 Prince Sihanouk, with Chinese encouragement, began negotiations with the major Khmer opposition groups, and in June 1982 a new coalition government-in-exile was formed. The ASEAN nations swiftly recognized the amalgam of Khmer Rouge, Pol Pot, and Sihanouk, despite a partial Vietnamese withdrawal intended to defuse criticism of its "puppet" Heng Samrin regime. In October 1982 the credentials of the enlarged Kampuchean government delegation were accepted at the United Nations. In the meetings of the 1983 Seventh Nonaligned Summit in New Delhi, Soviet supporters who had recognized Heng Samrin settled for the empty seat formula, which left neither government represented.

The persistence of disputes about the legitimacy of the Kampuchean government has soured Soviet-Vietnamese relations. Soviet aid to Vietnam was reduced substantially during this period, apparently as part of an attempt to coerce the Vietnamese into accepting Soviet guidance in their economic planning. The Vietnamese have made efforts to make up this aid by turning to Western sources but remain dependent on Soviet military supplies. Withdrawals of Vietnamese troops from Kampuchea and efforts to negotiate border security issues with Thailand and China have apparently pleased the USSR. In November 1983, a public declaration reconfirmed the 1978 Soviet-Vietnamese friendship and cooperation treaty.

Other developments in Asia also seemed to reduce Soviet prospects. Burma, which had withdrawn from the Nonaligned Movement in 1979 in protest over its pro-Soviet character, in 1980 accepted its first U.S. aid. In Bangladesh, anti-Soviet military groups effected a coup in 1982. Indira Gandhi was reelected in 1980, just in time to instruct an abstention during the United Nations vote on Afghanistan. She expressed opposition to "outside interference," but indirectly sympathized with Soviet versions of the event by a statement that the Soviet interference in Afghanistan "is not one-sided."[26] Brezhnev visited India in December 1980, with promises of increased military aid. However, the United States was also active, offering to sell military equipment and nuclear material (to which newly devised safeguards were not applied).

The Soviet-Indian relationship continues to receive considerable public attention. At the 1981 Soviet Party Congress, Brezhnev said cooperation with India "holds an important place in the Soviet Union's relations with the liberated countries," and welcomed India's "growing role" in international affairs.[27] Increased U.S. aid to Pakistan has helped to perpetuate the Indian interest in its links with the USSR, despite some efforts to diversify its military purchases. In 1983 the Soviets promised to match U.S. military deliveries to Pakistan with like matériel to India and arranged for an Indian astronaut to participate in a widely publicized space shot in April 1984. However, the October 1984 assassination of Indira Gandhi by Sikh extremists creates new uncertainties in the Soviet-Indian relationship.

Africa

If in the previous period African conflicts permitted the USSR to be an active player in the region, the persistence of inter-African quarrels, liberation struggles, and border wars have most recently proved a hindrance. The polarization of Africa between more or less pro-Soviet radicals and more or less pro-Western conservatives was increasingly visible. It could be seen most clearly in the split within the OAU over recognition of the Sahwari Arab Democratic Republic (SADR) in the Western Sahara. All the radical African states recognize the SADR. They also echo Soviet opposition to the proposed American Rapid Deployment Force for the Gulf (which implies permanent U.S. bases there because of a presumed Soviet threat); base rights for the United States in Africa; and U.S. attempts to challenge the Cuban role in Angola.

By the beginning of 1982, enough African states had recognized the SADR to meet the technical criteria for admission to the OAU. However, when this was announced, Morocco led a walkout that prevented a quorum, and the OAU was unable to meet for about eighteen months (January 1982–June 1983). The Soviet Union itself has never recognized the SADR and because of its close commercial ties with Morocco has avoided taking sides. Although negotiations between the combatants have been attempted, heavy fighting broke out in 1981 and again in 1983. The USSR is on record in favor of a referendum for the territory— a proposal to which Morocco has also agreed. No progress has been made to date on negotiated independence, although the SADR was seated at the OAU in 1984—provoking a Moroccan withdrawal.

The Soviets became implicated in Libyan adventurism—an unfortunate association in the light of post-Afghanistan criticisms of aggressive Soviet behavior. Qaddafi's plans for an "Islamic Saharan confederation" and Libyan interventions in a number of countries provoked ruptures of diplomatic relations with several West African states in 1980. In December, Libyan forces assisted a dissident group in Chad in defeating the incumbent leader, Hissan Habré. Libyan forces withdrew under strong international pressures, and an OAU peacekeeping force moved into the country in 1981. The Libyan client, Goukouni Oueddeï, was soon defeated, but withdrew under Qaddafi's protection. Renewed incursions by Oueddeï and his Libyan patrons alarmed the United States and provoked a French military intervention on behalf of the central government in 1983. Libyans were also charged with subversive intervention in Upper Volta (renamed Bourkina Fasso), Sudan, and Somalia. Numayri of Sudan complained of the "cancer of Soviet encroachment," as he announced that his government would permit the United States to use Sudanese military facilities. In March 1981, Numayri proposed the expulsion of Libya from the Arab League; and in June the Libyan ambassador was ordered out of Sudan. The Libyans have stepped up their military attacks on Sudan, precipitating U.S. air defense assistance in 1984. Somalia, now beset by attacks from Ethiopia as well as internal ethnic oppositionists, has also angrily denounced Libyan interference.

Nineteen eighty-two was to have been the year for Qaddafi to chair the OAU. The dispute over Western Sahara was one obstacle, but at the Tripoli meeting in November, Libyan harassment of the Habré delegation from Chad angered many who had long believed that Qaddafi was unsuited for a leadership role. Siyad Barre of Somalia implied that the OAU's 1982 crisis was at least indirectly related to Libya's association with the USSR. Egypt, Sudan, and Somalia specifically cited Libya's terrorist and subversive activities as reasons for boycotting an OAU summit under Qaddafi's chairmanship. The OAU did meet in 1983 under the chairmanship of an even closer Soviet client, Mengistu Haile Meriam of Ethiopia. But despite some rhetorical unity among radical African states for favored Soviet foreign policy positions, the USSR continues to have image problems in this organization.

Soviet ties to African states suffered as a result of several regime changes and from association with aggressive behavior on the part of some of its clients. The overthrow of Emperor Jean-Bédel Bokassa of the Central African Republic (CAR) in September 1979 ended a short-lived Soviet involvement there. Former President David Dacko, assisted by French troops, announced plans to return the CAR to democratic government. One of his first acts was to break diplomatic relations with both the Soviet Union and Libya in January 1980. In November a coup in Guinea-Bissau shifted that government's orientation to the right. In 1981 Marxist-Leninist groups, allegedly backed by Libyans, attempted a coup in Gambia but were defeated with the aid of Senegalese troops.

The Soviets apparently pressed ahead with requests for strategic access, although they have not been very successful. Cape Verde rejected a request for port facilities in 1980, as did the new government in Guinea-Bissau in 1981. Soviet fishing activities came under suspicion in 1982 in Equatorial Guinea, where the government had moved toward anti-Soviet positions and sought military and security cooperation with Spain.

Even in Southern Africa, the Soviet Union lost ground. Angola had taken steps to improve its relations with Western Europe, although it found the Reagan administration in the United States extremely hostile. The U.S. approach to the Namibian issue rejected a punitive policy toward South Africa and linked Namibian independence to withdrawal of Cuban forces from Angola. This had the effect of encouraging South African military actions against SWAPO and African National Congress (ANC) base camps in neighboring states. Although this has increased the need for Soviet military assistance (Zambia stepped up its military purchases from the Soviet Union in 1981) it is clear the Soviets are reluctant to be drawn into enlarged hostilities. In 1981 President Machel of Mozambique described South African commando raids on his country as "an attack on the socialist camp of which we are a part."[28] Nonetheless, despite the friendship and cooperation treaty, the USSR has shown no signs of willingness to become more directly involved. Mozambique's request to join COMECON was rejected in 1981. Military and party relations have continued to develop since then, but the Mozambican government has expanded its economic links with Portugal and other Western states. Unable to cope with intensified South African military attacks and their disrupting effects, in 1984 Mozambique and Angola both signed agreements with the Pretoria government. These aimed to reduce the level of military conflict and ease overall regional tensions, but leave regional liberation causes with limited hopes for progress.

The African picture remains mixed. The People's Republic of Congo is a Marxist-Leninist state long closely associated with the USSR and a key partner in the Angolan intervention. Although plagued by political instability during this period, the government at Brazzaville adopted a new socialist constitution and formalized its alignment with the USSR by signing a friendship and cooperation treaty in May 1981. Since then, however, the government of the Congo has rejected a Soviet proposal for port construction, brought in French advisors to replace Cubans, and turned to Western countries for economic development assistance. Leftists won elections in Mauritius in 1982 and immediately asserted their interest in pursuing a claim to sovereignty over Diego Garcia (a British-administered island in the Indian Ocean being leased as a U.S. naval base). The Soviets applauded this, but were less pleased when economic difficulties necessitated borrowing from the Western-controlled International Monetary Fund, even though this meant abandonment of domestic socialist schemes.

Latin America

In 1980, Soviet–Latin American ties were stronger than ever before. Moscow benefited from increasing anti-Americanism and radicalism in a number of states. Moreover, the Soviets also continued to expand trade and diplomatic relations in the hemisphere. However, the Soviets have had to contend with a new U.S. aggressiveness about allegedly Soviet-inspired challenges to the existing order. The Reagan administration, which took office in 1981, chose to make Latin America a target of vigorous diplomatic and military anti-Sovietism. The USSR and the Cubans were blamed for "international terrorism" in the region and specifically charged with assistance to leftist rebels in El Salvador. The Soviets have responded to this shift with care.

When the Sandinista Front forced the flight of the Somoza family from Nicaragua in 1979, Soviet observers saw the revolution as a sign of things to come. Diplomatic recognition was quickly extended to the new regime. In its first year, Nicaragua sent delegations to Moscow and established party ties between the Sandinista National Liberation Front (FSLN) and the CPSU. Simultaneously, Cuba provided military, economic, and technical assistance. A significant part of this was intended to lay the groundwork for a Cuban-style health and literacy campaign. In 1981–1982, Soviet assistance included a new arms agreement (including tanks, small arms, and various kinds of military vehicles) and deliveries of wheat. U.S. officials claimed that the USSR had promised Nicaragua MiG-23 aircraft, and in June 1982 announced that the planes had been observed on Cuban airfields awaiting delivery.

The Cubans currently maintain an extensive presence in Nicaragua. Although this certainly reflects Castro's strong sympathy for the Sandinista regime, the Cuban role also serves as a substitute for a more direct Soviet presence. Yet despite their obvious interest in Nicaragua, Soviet public pronouncements have been carefully worded so as to avoid the appearance of a commitment to defend the Sandinistas against U.S. military action. The Soviet leadership was also restrained in its reactions to Reagan's July 1983 statement that Soviet military aid to Nicaragua "cannot be allowed to continue." Shortly thereafter, in July and August, U.S. warships halted Soviet freighters bound for Nicaragua in order to question them about their cargo. Although the USSR protested such actions, it did so very quietly. The Nicaraguans have sought to change the impression that Cuban military advisors are active in their country. Yet Soviet aid shipments persist despite U.S. mining of Nicaraguan ports, increased military surveillance, and warnings about "unacceptable" types of arms assistance.

Until October 1983 the Soviets and Cubans maintained extensive economic and military relations with the tiny island country of Grenada. In 1980 the radical Bishop government (which had come to power in 1979) voted with the USSR and the socialist bloc against the UN Security Council resolution that condemned the invasion of Afghanistan. Other signs of Grenada's desire to establish close relations with the USSR soon followed. Economic assistance agreements were signed with various Eastern European states, and finally, in 1982, a five-year trade deal with the Soviet Union was concluded. Bishop became involved in heated polemics with the United States over its refusal to extradite ex-president Gairy. Meanwhile, Grenada's friendly relations with Cuba brought U.S. charges of cooperation in "terrorism" and in subversion of the government in El Salvador.

The strong U.S. reaction to Bishop's policies probably encouraged the Soviets to keep a low profile in Grenada. As in Nicaragua, it was the Cuban presence that was most visible. In 1982 and 1983, Grenada became increasingly isolated. Other states in the region, encouraged by the United States, criticized the Bishop regime on human rights grounds and sought to condemn it within the OAS. In October 1983, the United States, along with the Eastern Caribbean states, invaded the tiny island during civil disorders that followed Bishop's execution by a revolutionary rival. The U.S. invading force concentrated on an airport construction site, where they expected to find Cuban soldiers. The Cuban construction crew, trained to use anti-aircraft guns, resisted the invasion but were quickly overcome, rounded up, and returned to Cuba. The former British governor general, who was installed to organize a transitional government and supervise an orderly return to democracy, promptly broke relations with the Cubans and ordered Soviet diplomats home. Soviet denunciations of this invasion reflect concern that the United States might have similar plans for Nicaragua—a fear the Nicaraguans express regularly themselves.

Another potential gain for the USSR may well be the continuing unrest in El Salvador. The antigovernment rebels, apparently aided by Cuba and Nicaragua, but not directly by the Soviet Union, have successfully destabilized the regime in San Salvador. The Reagan administration, in response to what it sees as Soviet meddling, has increased military assistance to El Salvador and Honduras and issued a steady stream of denunciations of Soviet aid to Nicaragua. In 1982 NATO forces held joint exercises in the Gulf of Mexico, and the United States has been conducting nearly continuous anti-insurgency exercises in Honduras and Guatemala. In 1983 and 1984, the Reagan administration campaigned energetically but unsuccessfully for congressional support for assistance to antigovernment guerrillas inside Nicaragua.

Elsewhere in Latin America, the USSR has concentrated on trade and formal diplomatic ties. The USSR trades with Uruguay and with Brazil, despite that government's antileftist and anticommunist policies. Leftist Guyana has applied for membership in COMECON. After the United States imposed a grain embargo on the USSR in response to the invasion of Afghanistan, the Soviets increased purchases of wheat and meat products from Argentina. However, the relationship with Argentina became much more political in 1982. In April 1982, Argentineans had taken custody of the Falkland Islands (Malvinas), in defiance of Britain's long-established control. When the British responded by sending an expeditionary force to recapture the islands, the Soviet Union supported Argentina. Indeed, the Soviets could claim that they had supported the Latin American majority against the United States on this issue. After some initial hesitation, the United States had decided to side with Great Britain, and to cooperate with the planning of the naval operation that succeeded in evicting the Argentines in August. This situation permitted the USSR to denounce the United States and its imperialist impulses, although the Soviets kept their distance from the actual fighting.

Aside from Grenada, there were other Soviet setbacks in the region. In 1980, the military government of Peru was replaced by a civilian government under Belaunde Terry. The new government took steps to distance itself from the friendly relations with the Soviet Union practiced by the preceding military government. In Jamaica, Manley was defeated in the 1980 elections. The incoming Seaga government broke relations with Cuba in October 1981, complaining of Cuban support for the "export of revolution." Jamaica's relations with the USSR have cooled considerably since.

NOTES

1. Malenkov's report of the Central Committee is available in *For a Lasting Peace, For a Peoples' Democracy*, October 10, 1952, p. 1.

2. See for example Joseph L. Nogee and Robert H. Donaldson, *Soviet Foreign Policy Since World War II* (New York: Pergamon Press, 1981), p. 131.

3. E. Zhukov, "Porazhenie iaponskogo imperializma i natsional'no-osvoboditel'naia bor'ba narodov vostochnoi Azii," *Bol'shevik*, no. 23–24 (December 1945), p. 85.

4. See V. Vasil'eva, "Sobytia v Indoneizii," *Mezhdunarodnoe Khoziaistvo i Mirovaia Politika*, no. 1-2 (January-February, 1946), pp. 85–93; A. Guber, "Situation in Indonesia," *New Times*, no. 4 (February 15, 1946), pp. 6–10; K. Serezhin, "Events in Egypt," *New Times*, no. 5 (March 1, 1946), pp. 7–10; A. Diakov, "Sovremennaia India," *Bol'shevik*, no. 3 (February 1946), pp. 38–53; and A. Guber, "What's Happening in Indonesia and Indochina?" *New Times*, no. 11 [21] (November 1, 1945), pp. 10–13.

5. E. Zhukov, "Velikaia oktiabrskaia sotsialisticheskaia revoliutsia i kolonial'nyi vostok," *Bol'shevik*, no. 20 (November 1946), pp. 45–46.

6. Andrei Zhdanov, "The International Situation," speech to the founding meeting of the Cominform, September 1947, *For a Lasting Peace, for a Peoples' Democracy*, November 10, 1947, p. 2. Italics supplied. Unfortunately, many translations of this speech published in the West do not reproduce the full text. Deletion of the italicized portions is misleading, for they add considerable flexibility to the supposedly rigid two-camp picture.

7. E. Zhukov, "Obostrenie krizisa kolonial'noi sistemy," *Bol'shevik*, no. 23 (December 1947), pp. 51–64.

8. Iu. Frantsev, "Natsionalizm, oruzhie imperialisticheskoi reaktsii," *Bol'shevik*, no. 15 (July 1948), p. 54.

9. "Narody v bor'be protiv kolonial'nogo gneta," *Pravda*, February 21, 1952.

10. G. Akopian, "O natsional'no-osvoboditel'noi dvizhenii na blizhnem i srednem Vostoke," *Voprosy Ekonomiki*, no. 1 (January 31, 1953), p. 59. The citation is from Stalin's "Ob osnovakh Leninizma" (1924) in *Sochineniia*, vol. 6 (Moscow: Gospolitizat, 1947).

11. It is surprising that so many Western works on Soviet foreign policy ignore this important episode in Middle Eastern policy. Several recent studies are available that have explored the Soviet-Israeli alliance from 1947–1951. See for example Alden Voth, *Moscow Abandons Israel for the Arabs: Ten Crucial Years in the Middle East* (Washington, D.C.: University Press of America, 1980).

12. See Sylvia Woodby Fain, "Evolution of Soviet Attitudes Toward Colonial Nationalism, 1946–1953: South and Southeast Asia," (Ph.D. diss., Columbia University, 1971).

13. Adam Ulam, *Expansion and Coexistence: Soviet Foreign Policy, 1917–1973*, 2nd ed. (New York: Praeger Publishers, 1974), p. 628.

14. At first, the Soviets suggested a four-power summit plus India, then a Security Council meeting. After an emphatic protest from China, this was changed to a proposal that heads of state attend a session of the UN General Asembly, where the situation could be discussed.

15. Robert Alexander, "Impact of the Sino-Soviet Split on Latin American Communism," in Donald Herman, ed., *The Communist Tide in Latin America* (Austin: University of Texas Press, 1973), p. 93.

16. Alexander George, "The Basic Principles Agreement of 1972: Origins and Expectations," in Alexander George, ed., *Managing U.S.-Soviet Rivalry: Problems of Crisis Prevention* (Boulder, Colo.: Westview Press, 1983), pp. 107–118. Adam Ulam has argued that fear of China was exceptionally important in Soviet willingness to conclude agreements with the West. See his *Expansion and Coexistence: Soviet Foreign Policy, 1917–1973* (New York: Praeger Publishers, 1973) p. 728; and *Dangerous Relations: The Soviet Union in World Politics, 1970–1982* (New York: Oxford University Press, 1983), pp. 39–82.

17. At the 24th CPSU Congress, Brezhnev had referred to the importance of links between revolutionary democratic parties and communist parties— specifically including links with the communist parties in their own countries. The more "progressive" revolutionary democratic parties in the Third World had of course been encouraged to establish formal relationships with the Soviet communist party for some time. It may be recalled that Khrushchev had apparently sanctioned the notion that communist parties should in some cases dissolve themselves and join ruling front parties. Obviously the Brezhnev group was more prepared to try to defend the cause of local parties and help secure a place in a formal political coalition with the ruling pro-Soviet group where this was possible and appropriate. See Robert O. Freedman, *Soviet Policy Toward the Middle East Since 1970*, rev. ed. (New York: Praeger Publishers, 1978).

18. Marvin and Bernard Kalb, *Kissinger* (Boston: Little, Brown, 1974), p. 490; Alvin Z. Rubinstein, *Red Star on the Nile: The Soviet-Egyptian Influence Relationship Since the June War* (Princeton: Princeton University Press, 1977), pp. 275–277.

19. See Seymour Hersh's account in *The Price of Power: Kissinger in the Nixon White House* (New York: Spectrum Books, 1983), for example, Chapter 27, pp. 363–377. Nixon and Kissinger apparently believed that China and the USSR had been maneuvered by what they called "triangular diplomacy" into helping produce results the United States desired at several points.

20. For details, see David K. Hall, "Soviet Naval Diplomacy in West African Waters," in Stephen S. Kaplan, ed., *Diplomacy of Power: Soviet Armed Forces as a Political Instrument* (Washington, D.C.: Brookings Institution, 1981), pp. 519–569. Vocal criticism of Soviet activities in Africa in the wake of the demise of Keita and Nkrumah was often expressed by President Houphouet-Boigny of Ivory Coast, firmly pro-Western. In 1969, he ordered Soviet diplomats out of his country because of alleged involvement in student riots against his regime. Later he was to support a dialogue with South Africa, thus further distancing himself from more radical anticolonial opinion.

21. See documents and commentary in Stephen Clissold, ed., *Soviet Relations with Latin America, 1918–1968: A Documentary Survey* (London: Oxford University Press, 1970), pp. 57–58; 304–306.

22. Carmela Mesa-Lago, *Cuba in the Seventies: Pragmatism and Institutionalization* (Albuquerque: University of New Mexico Press, 1974), p. 9.

23. See Shirin Tahir-Kheli, "The Soviet Union in Afghanistan: Benefits and Costs," in Robert H. Donaldson, ed., *The Soviet Union in the Third World: Successes and Failures* (Boulder, Colo.: Westview Press, 1981), pp. 217–231; Stephen Hosmer and Thomas Wolfe, *Soviet Policy and Practice Toward Third World Conflicts* (Lexington, Mass.: Lexington Books, 1983), Chapter 9, pp. 109–123.

24. Brezhnev's report to the 25th PCSU Congress, in *Current Digest of the Soviet Press* [hereafter CDSP], vol. 28, no. 8 (1976), p. 8.

25. See David Morison, "Soviet and Chinese Policies in Africa," in *Africa Contemporary Record*, vol. 10 (1977–1978), pp. A94–A101, and vol. 11 (1978–1979), pp. A73–A78. U.S. officials were among those who charged that the Shaba rebel forces had been trained and equipped by the Soviet Union and Cuba. For an account that accepts Soviet responsibility, see Morris Rothenberg, *The USSR and Africa: New Dimensions of Soviet Global Power* (Miami: University of Miami Press, 1980), pp. 51–66.

26. *New York Times*, January 4, 1980.

27. Brezhnev's report to the 26th CPSU Congress, CDSP, vol. 33, no. 8 (March 25, 1981), p. 8.

28. As cited in *Keesing's Contemporary Archives*, February 12, 1982, p. 31328.

Third World Openings and Soviet Opportunities

From the perspective of the early eighties, we take for granted that the Soviet Union is a major force in the Third World. But it was not until the mid-fifties that Stalin's successors began to seek out and cultivate ties wtih the less-developed countries. Since then, as the preceding chapter indicates, there has been a marked proliferation of Soviet ties with the Third World and a tremendous expansion in the range of Soviet relations with them to include diplomatic ties, trade, and military agreements. Additionally, the Soviets pursued these involvements with a complex variety of goals in mind. It would be far from accurate, however, to suggest that Soviet policy in the LDCs is the product alone of the Kremlin's aims or perceptions. Changing Third World realities clearly affect Soviet attitudes and actions and thus the outcome of Soviet policies. Indeed, the Third World terrain may actually influence which goals the Kremlin attempts to pursue.

Since the end of World War II, more than one hundred states have gained independence, and the headlines of the last thirty years should remind us of the diversity and fragility of these nascent political systems. The very process of decolonization and the attenuation of ties, if not outright antipathy, between the metropole and former colony created many opportunities for friendly Soviet approaches to the new states. Identifying itself with LDC aspirations for complete independence, the Soviet Union sought to mobilize anti-Western sentiments within the United Nations and the Nonaligned Movement. Moreover, successive Soviet leaders have attempted to turn decolonization and anger about European subjugation into anti-imperialism and, wherever possible, pro-Soviet orientations.

Political conflict and domestic instability seem endemic to the Third World. In some cases of domestic upheaval, outside support is requested either by the threatened regime or by rival cliques. Either invited or on their own initiative, the Soviets may lend aid and support to one or more factions competing for power. In still other cases, a leadership change may bring to power a pro-Soviet regime. Similarly, interstate conflicts present opportunities to Moscow insofar as the Kremlin may offer friendship and aid to one state or another or to two or more simultaneously.

This chapter will analyze those aspects of Third World politics that have facilitated Soviet policy objectives. These openings may be divided into four analytical categories: local conflicts, political instability, de-colonization, and alignment shifts. The record of Soviet involvement shows that, in Moscow's search for opportunities, the Kremlin took advantage of some openings and not others and did so with varying degrees of success. If the Kremlin leadership has been aggressively opportunistic, it is also true that it would have been foolish to let the opportunities slip away.

LOCAL CONFLICTS

Interstate conflict has been a frequent feature of Third World politics. In some cases the boundaries between states were artificial creations from the outset, and in others ideologically opposite regimes came to power in contiguous areas. In still other situations, ambitious Third World regimes came to power seeking territorial aggrandizement at the expense of neighbors. Each instance represents a source of potential local conflict. That conflict may take the form of verbal sparring and propaganda disputes or may in fact involve covert or overt military activity.

Border wars and other forms of local conflict provide avenues for Soviet involvement when Moscow provides support for one side over the other. A willingness to offer military aid in such situations may permit the Soviet Union to initiate long-term relationships. Through offers of arms assistance and friendship, including diplomatic support, the Soviets can demonstrate their reliability, thereby gaining prestige and gratitude. Such aid is frequently intended as an inducement to the leadership of the Third World state in question to seek the favor of the Kremlin.

The Arab-Israeli dispute is an obvious example of a regionalized conflict that has repeatedly permitted Soviet intrusion into the Middle East. While the initial Soviet contact with Egypt may have been more a function of Nasir looking for alternative arms supplies than a product of the Arab-Israel dispute, by the time of the 1956 Suez Canal crisis the Soviet Union was clearly in the Arabs' corner. The Soviets claimed the credit for forcing the withdrawal of the joint Israeli-French-British invasion force. While never denying the existence of the State of Israel, Moscow has consistently been on the Arab side of the dispute ever since 1956.

By the time the conflict erupted again in 1967, the volatility of the region, combined with prior Soviet support for the region's progressive states, created a situation in which the Soviets wound up arming an increasingly aggressive Arab camp. Although there is ample evidence to indicate that the Kremlin would have preferred to avoid the 1967 Six Day War, the consequence was a set of Arab clients dependent on the Soviet Union for crucial large-scale resupply. The war and the Arab defeat were thus an opening for the Soviet Union to garner ever more influence in the region. During the 1970 War of Attrition along the Suez Canal, the Soviet Union increased its commitment to Egypt and its presence in the region by providing pilots to fly interceptors across the canal. Again in 1973 the Soviets supported the Arab cause by threatening to become directly involved if the United States were unable to restrain Israel. In addition, Moscow actively replaced military equipment lost by the Arabs during the course of the war.

Active U.S. intervention in the Middle East following the 1973 war at first appeared to reduce Soviet opportunities and altered the political terrain in terms of the Soviet presence. Yet, despite the signing of the Egyptian-Israeli peace treaty in 1979, the very existence of the Arab-Israel dispute and the persisting enmity toward Israel on the part of the other confrontation states continue to facilitate a Soviet involvement. Moscow applauded the creation of the so-called Steadfastness and Rejectionist Front and proffered aid to its members, including Algeria, Libya, and Iraq. Ties with Syria, strained as a consequence of the Syrian intervention in Lebanon in 1976, improved following the Israeli invasion of Lebanon in June 1982. The growing hostilities between Israel and Syria prompted the Soviets to supply Damascus with diplomatic and military support, including additional Soviet military personnel and sophisticated antiaircraft missiles. The level of Soviet support represents a significant development in the Soviet-Syrian relationship: This is the first time that such advanced Soviet military equipment has been deployed outside of the Soviet Union and Eastern Europe.

The perennial conflict on the Indian subcontinent between India and Pakistan over Kashmir also provided the Soviet Union with the opportunity to cultivate a major regional power. Friendly Soviet-Indian relations date back to 1955. In February of that year a major aid agreement was signed and in June Prime Minister Nehru received a warm welcome in Moscow. At that time, the Soviet leadership declared itself in favor of Indian sovereignty over the disputed territory of Kashmir. Pakistan, it should be noted, was considered in the late fifties a firm U.S. client. Except for a brief period following the 1965 Indo-Pakistani War, when Moscow attempted to curry favor with both sides, the Kremlin has maintained a consistently pro-Indian position.

Soviet opportunities in the Indian subcontinent were complicated, however, by Sino-Indian hostilities. Twice in the ten years between the initiation of Soviet-Indian ties and the 1965 Indo-Pakistani War, war broke out between India and China. The far more serious hostilities occurred in 1962 when India was soundly defeated by Chinese forces. The Soviets chose to back India in this conflict, which further embittered Sino-Soviet relations. The Soviet choice, however, reinforced the friendship with India.

When Pakistan and India went to war over Kashmir in 1965, the Soviets at first called for an end to hostilities. Moscow appeared reluctant to become involved but warned China to stay out of the conflict. As the fighting continued, the Soviet Union offered to mediate the dispute; representatives of the two sides, meeting at Tashkent under Soviet auspices, discussed the conflict and agreed to end this round of fighting. They did not resolve the Kashmir issue. The Soviets may have offered mediation so as to minimize their risks in the area, but whatever their reasons, Moscow's evenhanded approach garnered widespread praise in the Third World. In this instance, a regional conflict facilitated a major Soviet victory in terms of international and regional prestige.

In the early seventies, civil war in East Pakistan and the resulting strain in India caused by refugees from the conflict again brought the subcontinent to war. As the situation in East Pakistan disintegrated, the Soviets clearly reinforced their choice of India as preferred partner. Against this background of impending conflict, India renewed the negotiations for a Moscow–New Delhi treaty that had been curtailed a few years earlier. The August 1971 treaty, which praised Soviet-Indian friendship and increased cooperation, called for "mutual consultations" in the event of attack or threat of attack from a third party.[1]

The treaty formalized the Soviet-Indian relationship and, perhaps more importantly from the Soviet perspective, firmly stated that the Kremlin expected to be consulted before the Indians initiated any military action with Soviet weapons. In addition to the treaty, the Soviets pursued a policy of simultaneously urging peaceful resolution to the burgeoning conflict while speeding supplies of arms to India. Some scholars argue that the flurry of Soviet diplomatic activity was designed to forestall another Asian war in which China would aid Pakistan and potentially gain in the region.[2] The war proved inevitable, but the Indian victory demonstrated Soviet support of a Third World ally and dealt the Chinese a serious blow. Thus, through Soviet intervention in the regional dynamic, the Kremlin accomplished two regional goals: to solidify its ties with India and to counterbalance the perceived Chinese encroachment. In addition the Soviets could boast of ties with the newly created state of Bangladesh.

On occasion, depending on the parameters of the specific conflict, the Soviet Union may try to "play" both sides. By proclaiming neutrality and proffering limited support to both parties to the dispute, Moscow has tried to win or sustain two or more clients simultaneously. In the Gulf and on the Horn of Africa internal political changes, combined with eruptions of local hostilities, presented the Soviet Union with multiple problems and opportunities.

The Soviets signed friendship treaties with Iraq in 1972 and with Somalia in 1974 that reflected each state's obvious geopolitical advantages. Soviet relations with Somalia netted extensive port and related support facilities for the Soviet fleet; ties to Iraq resulted in Soviet permission to call at Umm Qasr and an arms dependency that began to pay off in hard currency. Yet each came into conflict with a neighbor whom the Soviets also courted. Soviet interest in Ethiopia and Iran was spurred by internal revolutions that changed the global orientations of both governments. The USSR provided arms to both despite the probability that the weapons would be used against a Soviet friend. Moscow armed Ethiopia slowly so as not to alarm the Somalis and provided indirect and, according to some, direct aid to Iran in an attempt to buy Khomeini's favor.[3] When hostilities broke out on the Horn of Africa, the Soviets sped up arms shipments to Ethiopia but did not cut off all supplies to Somalia at first. In the Gulf, initially, the Soviet Union appeared to side with Iran, yet permitted the Eastern-bloc allies to maintain supplies to Iraq. As will be discussed in Chapter 4, this type of opening in both the Gulf and on the African Horn proved to be short-lived.

The one instance where thus far the Kremlin has managed to keep both sides on the line, with only periodic fighting, is the long-term dispute between the Yemen Arab Republic (YAR) and the People's Democratic Republic of Yemen (PDRY). Soviet bilateral relations with the YAR date back to the 1962 antimonarchical coup. In subsequent years, republican forces, backed by Egyptian support and troops and supplied with Soviet military equipment, fought Saudi-supported royalists. Following the Egyptian defeat in the June 1967 Six Day War, Nasir withdrew from the conflict, and the Soviets became directly involved. The Soviet equipment and logistical support proved decisive in the eventual royalist defeat in 1969.[4]

Almost simultaneously, Marxists assumed control of the government of Aden (PDRY). In the 1970s the YAR acted to reduce its dependence on the Soviet Union (while still maintaining relations), and the increasingly radical PDRY drew closer to the communist bloc. By the late seventies it was clear that South Yemen was by far the favored client. Nineteen seventy-eight saw domestic political strife in both countries, and in early 1979, the PDRY, now headed by a pro-Soviet leader, attacked the North. The military crisis was successfully resolved by Arab League mediation and by the early eighties there were even discussions regarding possible unification. The Soviets have given verbal support to the unification scheme, but ideological differences would seem to preclude a merger. Moscow's support for the negotiations seems to echo a tactic used in the conflict on the Horn: There Cuba proposed a federation of pro-Soviet states in order to avert hostilities between the two Soviet clients.

Soviet arms flow to both YAR and the PDRY. Aden, of course, receives more, while North Yemen supplements Soviet supplies with purchases from the West. The PDRY has hosted many high-ranking Soviet military officials in the recent past, some of whom have promised "unlimited" Soviet support.[5] Thus far the Soviets have not been forced to make a choice, but it can be argued that their toehold obtained in the YAR through arms transfers could indeed prove valuable should their fortunes change in the PDRY.

As noted at the outset, conflicts that provide Moscow with opportunities to cultivate Third World leaderships need not be full-scale, or long-term armed confrontations. Examples abound of perceived security threats and common foreign policy stands that have prompted the LDC elites to request Soviet military aid. In North Africa, Algeria received increasing amounts of Soviet military assistance during and after the short-lived border war with Morocco in the fall of 1963. Moreover, there are reports that Cuban troops were present in Algeria at that time. More recently, Libya stepped up its arms purchases from the Soviet Union following Muammar Qaddafi's final break with Anwar Sadat in 1974. In sub-Saharan Africa, security problems continue to facilitate Soviet involvement. For example, Sékou Touré renewed his ties to Moscow when, during the final stages of the Portuguese colonial wars, a Portuguese contingent attacked bases of PAIGC located in Guinea. In return (until 1977), port facilities at Conakry were available for Soviet ships.

In Southern Africa, until early 1984, continuing low-level military conflicts between the Republic of South Africa and its neighbors plus African hostility to the white supremacist government in Pretoria provided openings for the Kremlin. Angola, faced with South African occupation of its territory and with continuing opposition supported by South Africa, remains dependent on Cuban and Soviet security assistance. While the Cubans have mostly remained in their barracks during South African raids on the camps of the South West African People's Organization (SWAPO), they are simultaneously guarding Gulf Oil installations from attacks by Cabinda separatists, thus performing a major political and economic service. Mozambique, a radical pro-Soviet state, also faced a threat from South Africa in the form of the Pretoria-backed National Resistance Movement. The Soviets have expressed concern over the situation and in 1982 there were several exchanges of military delegations, although the USSR is clearly not willing to serve as guarantor of Mozambique's security. In South Africa itself the Soviets support the African National Congress, which it considers the sole legitimate national liberation movement there. While the Soviets are careful not to provoke Pretoria, they do hope to use black dissatisfaction with the white supremacist government.

Demands for the liberation of Namibia and for the containment of South Africa may present still other opportunities for the Soviet Union throughout Southern Africa. On the one hand, the Soviets proffer aid to SWAPO, a national liberation movement fighting a hated power and international pariah, and on the other, the very existence of U.S.–South African ties allows the Soviet Union to use anti-American feelings to cultivate the so-called frontline states. Indeed, the OAU has condemned the recent South African agreements with its neighbors.

In sum, major and minor border wars provide the Soviet Union with openings through which to enter regional politics in assorted geographic areas. Continuing support for the Arabs against Israel or for Angola against South Africa allows the Soviet Union to demonstrate its reliability as an external power and friend. In return, Moscow gains a presence in sensitive regions from which it can further utilize regional tensions for its own purposes.

POLITICAL INSTABILITY

Political instability within individual Third World states has also often proven to be a catalyst of Soviet intervention of one type or another. In many cases, the disparate groups that comprised the independence movements proved unable to maintain their unity of action once the metropolitan power departed. The resulting contenders for power frequently offered varying visions of the future of their country. The groups included the intelligentsia, independence leaders, the church, and the military and covered the ideological spectrum. The Soviets found that they could offer military and/or economic support to one or more of the groupings competing for power.

In many young societies, tribal and ethnic divisions comprise the basis for ongoing political turmoil. The Soviets approached these situations pragmatically and cautiously. Moscow has made propagandistic approaches to the central governments by holding the USSR up as *the* model multiethnic society. The Soviet Academy of Sciences periodically invites Third World scholars and notables to scientific conferences dealing with the solution to the nationality question in the Soviet Union and its applicability to the Third World. On the policy level, Soviet decision makers in many cases found it expedient and productive to support central governmental authorities faced with secessionist demands.

In the sixties, the Soviets chose the central government side in Nigeria where the secession of the Ibo-dominated eastern region precipitated a major civil war. Until the Biafran secession, Lagos, while maintaining diplomatic relations with the Soviet Union, received its military supplies from Britain and West Germany. When the war broke out in 1967, Britain and the Soviet Union both supported the central government. Yet London refused to supply certain offensive weapons that Moscow was happy to provide. The arms supply, including MiGs and a few Ilyushin bombers, began almost immediately. Moscow also provided Nigeria with military advisors. The Soviets profited from the indirect intervention, which helped initiate a friendly relationship with the Lagos government. The effects of Soviet military aid enhanced Moscow's relations with Black Africa following the overthrow of the pro-Soviet governments in Ghana and Mali. Clearly, good relations with Nigeria, the most populous Black African state and a major economic and political force on the continent, is to the benefit of the Soviet Union. Nigeria has become the largest Soviet trading partner in sub-Saharan African, and Soviet development assistance is held up as an example of "disinterested" Soviet aid. The continuing cultivation of Nigeria should be understood against the background of the regional dynamics of Southern Africa and the need to legitimize the Soviet presence in Angola.[6]

Even in cases where the secessionist demands were not wholly tribally based, the Soviets judged it advantageous to support central governmental authorities. During the Khrushchev era, Moscow, in its effort to cultivate the Sukarno regime in Indonesia, assisted Djakarta in suppressing a rebellion based on the island of Sumatra. The Soviet courtship of Sukarno began in 1952–1954 with the signing of several trade agreements between Djakarta and Eastern Europe and picked up when the first Soviet economic aid was offered in 1956. In May 1957 General Voroshilov visited Indonesia, thus initiating a military connection as well. The rebellion began on February 15, 1958, when regional military commanders and national leaders opposed to Sukarno announced creation of a revolutionary countergovernment. The Kremlin came out in favor of the central government in the context of Western displeasure with Sukarno that included U.S. clandestine aid for the rebels. Additionally, Sukarno and the central government were supported by the large

Indonesian Communist Party (PKI). During the course of the short-lived rebellion, Soviet military assistance arrived in Indonesia at a stepped-up pace. The Sukarno government would in all probability have defeated the rebels without Soviet military aid, but Moscow demonstrated reliability with its assistance, countered the United States, and initiated a relationship that was to survive until 1965.

At the same time, the Kremlin has found it convenient to keep certain states stirred up, that is, to support the tribal or national dissidents in their demands against the central government. The Soviets have also been known to pursue two opposing policies simultaneously. Pragmatism and opportunism combine to induce the Soviet Union to deal, in many cases quite cordially, with the central governments while aiding irredentist and ethnic separatist groups. In the early sixties, Moscow supported Kurdish separatists in Iraq at the same time that it was establishing warm relations with the radical Qasim regime. Armed with Soviet weapons, the Kurds periodically challenged several Iraqi leaders. The Soviets seem to have varied their assistance to the Kurds to show displeasure with the state of Moscow-Baghdad relations. But in the early seventies when the central government agreed to legalize the local communist party, Soviet support went to Baghdad against the separatists; and by 1974, the solidification of Soviet–central government relations appeared a necessity to Moscow.[7] Support for irredentist movements is next to impossible in Africa where there is a fundamental consensus regarding the sanctity of borders. Yet, the Soviets did provide covert assistance to Eritrean rebels prior to the Marxist revolution in Ethiopia.

In many instances of political instability, one or more of the operative political forces may be a self-proclaimed socialist, national liberation, or even a communist group. In general, Moscow maintains ties with nonruling communist parties, socialist-oriented or vanguard parties, revolutionary democratic parties, and national liberation movements. All, according to Soviet theory, merit support because, taken as an undifferentiated whole, they comprise a major force in the world-wide revolutionary movement. According to a recent survey of the nonruling groups, there are at least nine progressive parties and eight national liberation movements with ties to the Soviet Union and international communist front organizations. The survey, an annual listing published by the journal, *Problems of Communism*, construes the Soviet connection from participation in conferences sponsored by the *World Marxist Review* and from attendance at CPSU meetings. The progressive parties represent groups from disparate geographic areas such as Peru, Egypt, and Bangladesh. And the national liberation movements range from Southern Africa to Oman and from the Middle East (namely, the Palestine Liberation Organization) to El Salvador and Guatemala.[8] While all the progressive groups could conceivably be instrumentalities of Soviet policy and in certain circumstances represent openings to the Kremlin, it is the national liberation movements that seem to provide the most advantageous opportunities to Moscow.

National liberation movements, the most broadly based of the groupings, are organizations that according to Soviet theorists are fighting against foreign domination and what the Soviets call local reaction, i.e., those individuals, groups, or regimes supporting pro-Western tendencies. From Moscow's perspective, the situation becomes a microcosm of the world revolutionary process. Justice, according to this logic, is on the side of the anticapitalist/anti-imperialist forces. Over the years, the Soviet Union proffered moral and some clandestine military support to the Algerian FLN in its eight-year struggle against France. Elsewhere in Africa, Moscow aided one of the liberation movements in Rhodesia (now Zimbabwe) and supports the South West African People's Organization (SWAPO) in the struggle to free Namibia from South Africa. In addition, as noted above, Moscow also supports and arms the African National Congress fighting in South Africa. The Vietnamese fight in Indochina, the Dhofar rebellion in Oman, the Palestine Liberation Organization's activities, and the rebel forces in El Salvador are examples of the opportunities presented by national liberation movements and the limits of Soviet involvement.

In one of the earliest instances of Soviet involvement with a national liberation movement, Moscow cautiously became a supporter of the Vietminh. Although it would seem logical to expect Soviet assistance to Ho Chi Minh when he fought the French, it was not until 1950 that the USSR recognized the Vietminh. China had previously done so. At the 1954 Geneva Conference, convened after the decisive French defeat at Dienbienphu, the Soviets supported a negotiated settlement for the region. The accords resulted in the de facto division of Vietnam into North and South; in 1960, Ho Chi Minh set out to "liberate" South Vietnam. Although the Soviets supported the struggle, the Chinese were for a long time the major military supplier. Even though the United States increased its commitment to South Vietnam, it was not until 1965 that the Soviets stepped up their shipments of military equipment to the war zone. Following the first U.S. bombings of the North, the USSR issued veiled threats to send "volunteers" into combat.

Soviet-Vietnamese relations in this period complicated and were complicated by relations between Moscow and Washington. The United States wanted Moscow to restrain its North Vietnamese allies, but the USSR lacked the leverage Washington wanted it to exercise. As for the Vietnamese, it would seem fair to suggest that Hanoi could not have been pleased when the Soviet leadership went ahead with the scheduled summit meeting with the United States while U.S. attacks on North Vietnam were broadening. The Soviets received the proverbial best of all worlds—they did not lose North Vietnam and Washington signed the Strategic Arms Limitation Treaty despite the continuation of the war.

The Popular Front for the Liberation of Oman (PFLO) is significant for the levels of Soviet aid and the longevity of the relationship with Moscow. Consisting of rebels from the Dhofar region of Oman, the PFLO was created in 1964. At first, it received only a trickle of support from Mideast powers, but in the late sixties, the movement was taken over by Marxists. Expanding its goals, the movement was renamed the Popular Front for the Liberation of Oman and the Arabian Gulf (PFLOAG) and received Soviet aid via the PDRY. At the peak of hostilities in 1972, Moscow provided arms and military training to the rebels. Moreover, they received additional military training in PDRY, Iraq, and PLO camps. The fortunes of war proved detrimental to the organization and in 1976 the PFLOAG reverted to the PFLO. It continues to exist and receive Soviet support in its struggle "against the military presence of the USA and its allies in Oman."[9]

When the PLO was created in 1964, the Soviet Union issued no official statement; however, the Soviets seemed to have altered their position around the time of the June 1967 Six Day War. In her book on the Soviet-PLO relationship, Galia Golan claimed that Kremlin support for Syrian-backed raids on Israel were tantamount to support for Fatah, the major Palestinian guerrilla organization. Moreover, by late 1968, while continuing to criticize "extremist" Palestinians, the Kremlin permitted some arms transshipments to the Palestinian guerrillas.[10] The extent of Moscow's support, both diplomatic and military, changed as the volatile Middle East situation warranted. First, in the aftermath of the 1967 war, other Arab countries began to see the Palestinian question as central to the Middle East situation. Second, according to Golan and others, subsequent to the 1972 expulsion of Soviet advisors from Egypt the PLO acquired additional significance as a Soviet-supported force in the region.[11]

Despite signs of increasing Soviet backing for the PLO, full-scale relations were slow in coming. In 1969, the Soviets referred to the PLO as a national liberation movement, yet it was not until 1974 that Yasir Arafat received the first governmental invitation to Moscow. Previously, PLO representatives attended meetings only of the Afro-Asian Solidarity Committee. It was still two more years before the official PLO office was opened in Moscow. Full diplomatic recognition was extended to the PLO in 1981.

The forces impelling Moscow to back the PLO are as numerous as those that constrain a full alliance. As noted above, Moscow consistently upholds Israel's right to exist, even going so far as to offer Soviet guarantees for Israeli security.[12] This support complicates any discussion between the Palestinians and the Kremlin leadership regarding a future Palestinian state: Who the Palestinians are and where the state should be located all revolve around the border question. The organization and Moscow have also disagreed about the use of terror. While the Soviets seemed to accept the legitimacy of armed struggle on the West Bank, they condemned as counterproductive other activities such as the massacre of Israeli athletes at the 1972 Munich Olympics.

The contradictory pressures for and against Soviet backing of the PLO are nowhere more obvious than in Moscow's reaction to the Israeli invasion of Lebanon in June 1982 and its aftermath. Clearly, Soviet policy was dictated not by concern over the PLO but by the desire to avoid escalation of the Syrian-Israeli confrontation that might directly involve the superpowers. Indeed, the Soviets made it clear that although they offered verbal and diplomatic support to the besieged Palestinians, no direct military aid was to be forthcoming. By the same token, the Soviets cannot afford to ignore and to dissociate themselves totally from the Palestinian cause. Moscow claimed (as the Israeli occupation continued through 1983) that the United States was trying to remove the PLO as a force in the Middle East. Moreover, Moscow asserted that Arabs rejected the 1982 Reagan peace initiative because it did not recognize Palestinian rights. Reports also surfaced that Moscow was displeased with what amounted to Syrian destruction of Arafat's independent PLO.

In contrast, the Kremlin's involvement with or aid to Latin American liberation movements is exceptionally low-key. This is not to say that the existence of leftist antigovernmental forces in various countries is not an opening for Moscow. Rather, the Soviets are circumspect in their ties because of Central (and Latin) America's distance from the Soviet Union and proximity to Washington. Despite Reagan administration claims to the contrary, direct Soviet ties to leftist forces are difficult to document. El Salvador is a case in point.

Between 1932 and 1979, El Salvador enjoyed only nine months of civilian rule. During that period the so-called Fourteen Families, supported by rightist military leaders in government, consolidated their hold on economic power. In the sixties, attempts at land reform and democratization under the Alliance for Progress failed miserably. Within this context, opposition groups proliferated and by the late seventies armed guerrilla groups formed to wage a military campaign against the government. Simultaneously, rightist groups' use of terror with quasi-official sanction further polarized the political scene. On October 15,

1979, a group of young military officers, claiming to support Salvadoran social reform, staged a coup d'état. However, substantive divisions within the military as to the extent and pace of reforms hindered the establishment of a civilian-military coalition and after a short period brought reforms virtually to a halt. At the same time the leftist groups stepped up their pressure on the new government. It has been argued that the left failed to comprehend the significance of the splits within the military and, therefore, played into the hands of the military hard-liners.[13] The ongoing civil war testifies to the tenacity of both the oligarchy and the opposition forces.

The Soviet role in all of this is difficult to determine. While Moscow has verbally backed the opposition forces, evidence of direct military support is scant. Castro has openly and directly given his support and has sent arms clandestinely to the leftists. The Soviet Union in all likelihood backs the covert transshipment of arms; however, the United States has been hard put to prove that Cubans or Soviets have been actively assisting revolutionary forces in El Salvador.

Although at times the ties between Moscow and liberation movements and other progressive forces in the Third World are tenuous, the Soviet Union has utilized the openings these groups represent. As we have seen, the Kremlin took advantage of opportunities either by supporting the groups in question or in cases of separatist movements by supplying the threatened central government with verbal and military support. Either way, the goal clearly was and continues to be the cultivation of additional friends in the Third World.

DECOLONIZATION

As noted at the outset of this chapter, decolonization as a process presented multiple openings to the Soviet Union. Moscow was able to take advantage of the newly won independence insofar as it meant attenuation of ties with the European powers. Not only did Moscow see each declaration of independence as the death knell of imperialism, but also certain Third World leaders invited Soviet entrée into their regions when, as affirmation of their independence from the former metropolitan power, they sought alternative sources of economic and military assistance. In North Africa, for example, the Algerian FLN received Soviet support to counterbalance economic relations with France.

In other instances, the openings were created not only because the Third World leadership desired neutrality but also because of what was seen as Western arrogance and miscalculation. For example, when

Egyptian army officers overthrew the corrupt and dissolute monarchy, the Soviets at first accused the plotters of working in concert with the British and U.S. imperialists. Despite some evidence of earlier softening, it was the 1955 delivery of Soviet arms to Egypt that signaled both the reorientation of Egyptian policy and the change in Soviet attitudes. By 1956, when the United States equivocated on an earlier aid proposal, Moscow agreed to finance the construction of the first stage of the Aswan Dam, thereby not only continuing the cultivation of Egypt but also reaping tremendous propaganda advantage.

Guinea provides an even more striking example than Egypt because Sékou Touré was the one Black African leader in former French West Africa to sever all his ties to France. When no Western leader would assist Guinea for fear of offending French President Charles de Gaulle, Sékou Touré turned to Moscow for aid. (This relationship, however, proved to be exceptionally stormy.) Also in Africa, the Ugandan regime of Idi Amin Dada, having been refused economic assistance by the Western powers, turned to the Soviet Union. Moscow appeared only too happy to respond, since Kampala's neighbors were anti-Soviet and in Tanzania's case pro-Chinese. In Ethiopia prior to the Somalian invasion, the Soviets began providing military assistance to the nascent Marxist regime after the United States cut off military aid because of human rights violations.

A particular kind of opening seems to be presented by sudden decolonization in the last vestiges of vast European empires. This phenomenon was created not by the long anticolonial struggles, but by the short periods of time between the announced departure of the Europeans and the actual declarations of independence. The Soviets aided a separatist government in the former Belgian Congo and radical national liberation movements in the Gulf and Southern Africa.

When the Belgian government announced its intention to grant independence to the Congo, rival Congolese leaders maneuvered for power. Almost immediately the barely stable government faced the secession of mineral-rich Katanga. Dissatisfied by UN assistance, Prime Minister Patrice Lumumba requested and received Soviet military aid. However, within two months Lumumba was ousted by the rival Mobutu-Kasavubu faction and UN troops closed Congo's airports to Soviet planes. Thus, while this first intrusion of Soviet power ended in failure, the Soviets showed that they would take advantage of the openings created by precipitous decolonization.

In the late sixties and early seventies, precipitous European withdrawal seemed to increase Soviet opportunities. In 1968 Great Britain, the paramount power in the region for 150 years, announced its intention to withdraw from all territories "East of Suez" by 1971. At the time of the announcement, the British had already pulled out of the Protectorate of Aden. In the course of the decolonization process, Arab radicals seized power in Aden, transforming the Protectorate into the People's Democratic Republic of Yemen. Yet the PDRY received little from the Soviets until the British actually withdrew in 1971. Moscow's hesitation has been attributed to two factors: early Chinese involvement and the intense factional fighting within the Yemeni leadership that forced Moscow to adopt a wait-and-see attitude.

The British left the Gulf area rife with territorial disputes and political complexities, including several indigenous radical groups. In addition, the Soviet-PDRY relationship, which has been consolidated since 1971, may well help the Soviets to manipulate future instabilities. The PDRY proved to be a staging area for Dhofari rebels, and there are indications that the Kremlin is watching other regional powers for signs of instability. Moreover, the port of Aden has acquired increased importance since the loss of facilities at Berbera, Somalia.

The major opportunities that rapid decolonization, as it occurred in the Third World in the seventies, provided the Soviets are also demonstrated by the Portuguese withdrawal from its African territories: Angola, Mozambique, and Guinea-Bissau. In 1973 it was unthinkable that within two years the Portuguese would abandon their African possessions, leaving behind three radicalized former territories.

The Portuguese withdrawal, initiated by the military government that seized power in Lisbon in April 1974, altered the South African terrain. Angola, Mozambique, and Guinea-Bissau all became Soviet friends in a relatively short period of time. In both Mozambique and Guinea-Bissau, the Portuguese transferred power to the single national liberation movement in the territory. FRELIMO, the Mozambican liberation movement, was formed in 1962 out of disparate anticolonial groups. Over the years of the struggle against Lisbon, the ideological center of the movement shifted to the left as radicals acquired a firm hold on power. Prior to independence, FRELIMO received assistance from both the PRC and Moscow; in fact, according to most observers, the movement was far more a Chinese than a Soviet client. After the final Portuguese withdrawal, FRELIMO moved closer to the Soviet Union. By 1977, the government at Maputo had signed a treaty of friendship and cooperation with Moscow, and in 1981 Soviet warships appeared in Mozambican harbors. Prior to independence the Guinea-Bissau liberation movement, PAIGC, was based in Guinea, where it received extensive Eastern-bloc training assistance and arms. In fact, following a Portuguese attack, Moscow sent ships to Conakry to rescue PAIGC leaders. Upon independence, Guinea-Bissau established close ties to Moscow and permitted the Soviets and Cubans to use its territory as a transshipment point en route to neighboring Angola. Despite a coup in 1980, Guinea-Bissau continues to maintain its ties to Moscow.

The Angolan situation, in contrast, was far more complex. Three national liberation groups, each in part tribally based and each receiving support from different outside patrons, competed for power. The Soviets and the Cubans both maintained relations with the most Marxist of the three groups, the Popular Movement for the Liberation of Angola (MPLA), while the Chinese and the CIA aided the Front for the National Liberation of Angola (FNLA). The third group, the National Union for the Total Independence of Angola (UNITA), benefited from U.S., Chinese, and South African aid.

The ultimate if shaky victory of the Soviet-backed MPLA was not the result of military superiority alone. External political factors seemed to play a major role in keeping the MPLA in power. First, the United States, preoccupied with the collapse of Saigon, did not offer timely verbal support to the agreement for a coalition transitional government, thus depriving the already fragile accords of authority.[14] Second, Pretoria, responding to requests for assistance from FNLA-UNITA forces, supplied military advisors and then in October 1975 sent between 1,500 and 2,000 troops into Angola. Third, according to Colin Legum and others, in mid-1974 the Soviets stepped up aid to the MPLA as a reaction to increasing Chinese aid to the FNLA.[15] Although all these factors combined to affect the outcome of the struggle for power, the major intervention came in the form of Cuban troops that began to arrive shortly after the South African incursion into Angola. In many respects, the South African intervention legitimized the Soviet-Cuban rule, since the OAU recognized the MPLA. Currently, Cuban troops remain on the scene to shore up the MPLA position.

The inducements for Soviet intervention were many, but it was the rapid decolonization of Angola that turned pre-existing Soviet ties with the MPLA into a tangible asset. The Soviets, as a result, have a forward position from which to support SWAPO and in which they sit poised to take advantage of the explosive situation in South Africa. Moreover, their support for the MPLA helps to bolster their position as self-proclaimed champion of the world-wide national liberation movement while they simultaneously condemn South African–U.S. ties.

ALIGNMENT SHIFTS

In instances of rapid and frequently revolutionary changes, the alignment changes may be quite dramatic. Prime examples would be Ethiopia,

Somalia, Iran, Cuba, Nicaragua, Grenada, and Peru. In each, a pro-Western government lost out to radical elements.

Until 1970 the Soviet Union and Latin America were, as one Western scholar put it, "worlds apart."[16] Prior to that time, the sole Soviet prospect in the hemisphere was Cuba. The overthrow of the Batista government in Cuba brought to power Fidel Castro, who, although anti-American, was not at first either a communist or pro-Soviet. When the United States sought to isolate Cuba and to crush by economic and then military means the new government in Havana, Castro turned to the Soviet Union for assistance. Despite the many disagreements between Cuba and the USSR (see Chapter 4), the pro-Soviet orientation of the Cuban elite has remained intact. In the seventies, as Moscow expanded its ties beyond Havana, Soviet trade relations with Latin America have substantially increased and new leftist governments have sought out Soviet assistance. In both Grenada and Peru, governments favoring close relations with the Soviet Union came to power. In the case of Grenada, Maurice Bishop and his New Jewel Movement acceded to power, claiming to be socialist and pro-Soviet. They set out actively to court the Soviet Union, including voting "no" on the UN resolution condemning the Soviet invasion of Afghanistan. Both Cubans and Soviets assisted Bishop by offering credits and technical assistance. Until the 1983 coup and U.S. military intervention there, Cuban technicians were at work building a major airport on the tiny island.

In Peru, although the military junta headed by General Velasco was not communist, it introduced agrarian reforms and nationalization of key industries. Moreover, Velasco evicted U.S. military advisors from Peru. In 1969, Soviet and Peruvian representatives negotiated their first trade agreeement, and in 1971 an agreement on economic and technical cooperation was signed. Significantly, Peru is unique in Latin America as a major recipient of Soviet military equipment. The Peruvians pay for the equipment, but supposedly on relatively easy terms.[17] The Lima government purchased tanks, fighter bombers, SA-3s and SA-7s and artillery. According to U.S. estimates, the value of Soviet arms transfers to Peru between 1975 and 1979 was US$650 million.[18] Despite the burgeoning ties, Soviet-Peruvian relations cooled considerably in 1980.

Nicaragua is unique because the current pro-Cuban and pro-Soviet government came to power not through a coup but through armed revolution. Moreover, the former government had been established with the help of U.S. forces in the thirties and had remained staunchly pro-Washington. The Soviets or, indeed, Cubans had little to do with the wave of unrest that culminated in the Sandinista revolution. In fact, the communists were but one of many groups of oppositionists. Prior to the final Sandinista victory, the Soviet press reported the imminent end of the Somoza dictatorship under "powerful blows" from "popular forces."[19]

Nonetheless, the Soviets moved immediately to recognize the new government and to court it assiduously, but carefully. Cuba, which had contributed barely at all during the civil war, quickly lent military, technical, and economic assistance to help consolidate the regime. The Soviets, during the Sandinistas' first year in power, hosted several Nicaraguan delegations and established party-to-party relations with the Sandinista National Liberation Front (FSLN). In 1981–1982 the pace of Soviet assistance quickened with the signing of new military agreements and the provision of 20,000 metric tons of wheat. There is a large Cuban presence in Nicaragua and, by comparison, a much smaller, lower-key Soviet presence. By all indications the Soviets, while rhetorically supportive of the Sandinista government, have exercised extreme caution in cultivating Managua. Still, by 1984, Soviet assistance was increasingly direct and visible.

On the Horn of Africa, the Soviets benefited from a regime change in Somalia. Following his rise to power in 1969, Siyad Barre intensified his country's pro-Soviet orientation. He proclaimed his socialist intentions, which the Soviets quickly welcomed: Aid was forthcoming, and in 1972, the USSR began work on the port of Berbera. In 1974, the two signed a friendship and cooperation treaty.

One Middle Eastern example stands out as an anomaly. Libya, a monarchy until 1969, did not become a radical state until several years later. Qaddafi, although vehemently anti-American, become pro-Soviet only in 1974. Even then, the Soviets have approached him cautiously. Despite his self-proclaimed socialist ideology, his support for Arab and radical causes, and the massive Soviet arms sales to Libya, the Soviets have refrained from a full embrace. In March 1983, Moscow and Tripoli publicized an agreement in principle to sign a friendship and cooperation treaty. To date, no treaty has been signed and official analyses of Soviet-Libyan relations no longer mention the agreement.[20]

Given Moscow's goals, the Third World clearly presented multiple openings to the Soviet Union. As we have seen, indigenous radical groups of varying colorations permitted Moscow a foothold in several locations. In many cases, the existence of these groups allowed the Soviet leadership to hedge its bets, that is, to support a potential contender for power and the individual in power simultaneously. The Soviets found opportunities in instances of tribal or politically motivated rebellions as well. Depending on the specifics, they supported either the central governmental authorities or the would-be new Third World state. Moreover, regional conflicts not only gave the Soviet Union access to particular regions, but sometimes developments permitted the Soviets to cultivate two regional actors simultaneously.

Openings seemingly abound. However, their successful long-term utilization is problematic. Many openings to Soviet power and influence projections turned out to be disappointments, if not traps. The dynamics of regional and domestic politics, while inducements to Soviet activity, have in many cases proved to be obstacles to Soviet involvement and Soviet goals. These constraints on and obstacles to Soviet penetration are the subject of the next chapter.

NOTES

1. See the text of the treaty in *Pravda*, August 10, 1971, p. 1.

2. Joseph L. Nogee and Robert H. Donaldson, *Soviet Foreign Policy Since World War II* (New York: Pergamon Press, 1981), p. 167.

3. Shahram Chubin, "The Soviet Union and Iran," *Foreign Affairs*, vol. 61, no. 4 (Spring 1983), pp. 921–949.

4. Bruce Porter argues that Soviet pilots flew combat missions during the war. See his "Soviet Military Intervention: Russian Arms and Diplomacy in Third World Conflicts" (Ph.D. diss., Harvard University, 1979).

5. Carol R. Saivetz, "Soviet Policy Toward Iran and the Persian Gulf: Legacies of the Brezhnev Era" (Paper presented at the Midwest Slavics Conference, Chicago, Ill., May 1983).

6. Seth Singleton, "Soviet Opportunities and Vulnerabilities in Africa" (Paper presented at the American Association for the Advancement of Slavic Studies, Kansas City, Mo., October 1983).

7. Robert O. Freedman, "Soviet Policy Toward Ba'athist Iraq, 1968–1979," in Robert H. Donaldson, ed., *The Soviet Union in the Third World: Successes and Failures* (Boulder, Colo.: Westview Press, 1981).

8. Wallace Spaulding, "Checklist of 'National Liberation Movements,'" *Problems of Communism*, vol. 31 (March-April 1982), pp. 77–82.

9. TASS, June 18, 1982, *Foreign Broadcast Information Service* [hereafter FBIS-SOV] 82-119 (June 21, 1982), p. H5.

10. Galia Golan, *The Soviet Union and the Palestine Liberation Organization* (New York: Praeger Publishers, 1980), pp. 7–8.

11. Ibid., pp. 47–48.

12. See for example *Pravda*, April 24, 1975, or *Pravda*, September 25, 1975.

13. Cynthia Arnson, *El Salvador, A Revolution That Confronts the United States* (Washington, D.C.: Institute for Policy Studies, 1982) p. 44.

14. Larry C. Napper, "The African Terrain and U.S.-Soviet Conflict in Angola and Rhodesia: Some Implications for Crisis Prevention," in Alexander L. George, ed., *Managing U.S.-Soviet Rivalry: Problems of Crisis Prevention* (Boulder, Colo.: Westview Press, 1983) p. 159.

15. Colin Legum, "The Soviet Union, China and the West in Southern Africa," *Foreign Affairs*, vol. 54, no. 4 (July 1976), pp. 745–763.

16. Cole Blasier, *The Giant's Rival, The USSR and Latin America* (Pittsburgh: University of Pittsburgh Press, 1983), pp. 3–16.

17. Ibid., p. 43.

18. U.S. Arms Control and Disarmament Agency, *World Military Expenditures and Arms Transfers, 1970–1979*, ACDA Publication 112 (released March 1982).

19. *Izvestiia*, June 13, 1979, p. 4, in FBIS-SOV 79-121 (June 21, 1979), p. K1.

20. A. V. Frolov, "Vashington i Arabskie Strany Afriki," *SShA*, no. 10 (October 1983), pp. 31–42.

Chapter Four

Third World Obstacles and Soviet Vulnerabilities

Given the multitude of Third World openings that provided the Soviet Union avenues of penetration and that continue to facilitate Soviet access, we in the West tend to emphasize the proliferation of Moscow's ties with the Third World and the spread of Soviet influence there. However, a more balanced picture, one that includes Soviet problems and setbacks, is required for a complete assessment.

The terrain in the Third World, despite the openings it presents, has proven to be treacherous. First, the variety of nationalist ideologies so characteristic of the Third World seems to make local leaders suspicious of Soviet motives. Although Moscow was and still is attractive as an alternative supplier and patron, the elites of the Third World states are reluctant to increase their dependence on the large powers. Second, political volatility and highly personalized domestic politics sometimes result in the fall from power of pro-Soviet leaders or in sudden shifts of alignment. In addition, some of the local conflicts that provided Soviet entrée outlive their usefulness and tend to complicate Soviet relations with regional powers. Third, the Soviets find themselves handicapped by the history of their own involvement in the Third World. They have been tainted by past actions, and in some instances the label "ugly Russian" is most fitting. Finally, economic development problems pose an additional and perhaps insurmountable obstacle to the consolidation of Soviet relations even with its most favored "friends" in the Third World.

IDEOLOGIES AND NATIONAL INTERESTS

Underlying the Soviet quest for influence in the nonindustrial world is the need to convince Third World leaders that their interests coincide with those of the Soviet Union. Indeed, Soviet rhetoric and official statements as well as routine exchanges of delegations are all designed to encourage the LDCs to identify with the Soviet Union. Yet, it seems that questions of national identities and interests as expressed in Third

World nationalist ideologies are exceedingly sensitive issues to the LDCs. Most postindependence elites have sought to create new national identifications to redress what many see as the embarrassment of colonial domination. The use of non-European languages and the emphasis on traditional values underscore national distinctiveness. Even in those countries in which the colonial experience was relatively benevolent, ideologies were devised to differentiate the new state from the former metropolitan powers. Third World leaders use their national ideologies as the basis for a unifying, mobilizing, and legitimizing political culture. The ideologies have helped leaders to rally diverse forces around central governments and to create support for their tenure in power. Many of these ideologies combine statements of national distinctiveness with religious traditions and socialisms of the Marxist and non-Marxist varieties. Soviet leaders have not always been tolerant of what they obviously perceive as "unscientific" ideas, and over the past several years, they have wound up engaging in bitter polemics with Third World elites over various aspects of their nationalist ideologies. For many of the new states, ethnic groupings such as the Islamic Conference and regional organizations, for example, the Organization of African Unity (OAU), proved to be equally important components of their identities and interests. From the Soviet perspective, this labyrinth of crosscutting identities has on many occasions proven to be a complicating factor in the continuing cultivation of Third World powers.

Ironically, these nationalisms are the product of the same process of national liberation that Moscow supports. However, the very idea of nationalism has always been problematic both for the Soviet leadership and for theoreticians charged with elaborating political processes in the Third World. When assessing international politics, Soviet analysts both appreciate the implications of Third World nationalisms and are wary of their impact on Soviet foreign policy. The Soviets, of course, claim to understand and to sympathize with the aspirations of the Third World for independence. Soviet conceptions acknowledge that nationalism can be extremely valuable in international politics in that anticolonialism makes an important contribution to the defeat of capitalism. On a doctrinal level, the Soviets constructed a tentative formula linking nationalism with "progressiveness" up to the point at which it contradicts proletarian internationalism, i.e., Soviet interests. Implicitly, Third World nationalisms are progressive insofar as they are anti-Western.

However, there is a fine line between anti-Westernism and generalized suspiciousness of all outside powers. These nationalisms may render the LDCs less amenable to Soviet influence and this is equally true of moderate and the more radical LDCs. National self-assertiveness may clash with obvious Soviet military and/or political presence in a given locale. For example, Burma, one of the earliest recipients of Soviet aid, has turned down offers of military assistance from Moscow. Even though Soviet commentators labeled Burma a state on the noncapitalist path of development, Rangoon has maintained cool relations with Moscow over the years. And while India maintains close relations with the USSR, it has hosted fewer Soviet military personnel than many smaller states.[1] Among the Middle Eastern states, Algeria, despite its close ties with the Soviet Union, has never permitted Soviet bases on its territory. And Iraq, a firm client in the mid-seventies, allowed Soviet calling rights at Umm Qasr, but never a permanent base. In fact, no Third World state, however close its relations with the USSR, currently grants Moscow a permanent military base.

From the Soviet perspective, nationalism as a domestic political force implies a total disregard for class issues, which are so important in Marxism. Marxism-Leninism postulates the inevitability of the class struggle as the driving force in history, and nationalism would mute class antagonisms. Thus, Soviet theorists view nationalism as a barrier to efforts made by the Soviet Union and the local communist parties toward the promotion and cultivation of proletarian interests. Soviet observers and propagandists warn the Third World repeatedly of the dangerous domestic implications of nationalism. They appear to feel that pro-Soviet orientations will thrive best where class and other common issues dominate the political rhetoric.

Consequently, the Soviets have tried to chip away at those aspects of nationalist ideologies that seemed to conflict with their interests. Where religious elements have been incorporated into nationalist rhetoric, the Soviets initially railed against those components. But the strident atheism usually associated with Marxism-Leninism created a deep mistrust on the part of potential allies. African leaders frequently combine Christian humanist traditions with their socialist rhetoric, and Middle Eastern elites have incorporated Islam into their socialisms. Many thus insist they are not atheists, but something more in keeping with their own traditions. For example, Robert Mugabe, the prime minister of Zimbabwe, issued the following statement in response to questions regarding Zimbabwe's brand of socialism: "Shona traditions of land ownership, and Christian principles, too, of love and charity. And at the end of the day we have what we believe to be our own brand of socialism. Not a system which is the blueprint of the Soviet Union."[2]

In the Middle East, Islamic issues resurface periodically to trouble even the best Soviet-Arab relations. As the Soviet leadership assiduously courted Nasir in the early sixties, the Islamic content of Egypt's ideology evoked Soviet criticism. More recently in the Middle East, the Kremlin has confronted Islamic insurgents in Afghanistan and the Islamic fundamentalism of the Khomeini regime in Iran. At first, Moscow simply tried to downplay the revolution's religious content. However, as Khomeini became increasingly anti-Soviet, the Kremlin responded by issuing numerous denunciations of the Shi'ite clergy in Iran.[3] But in general, the Soviets have sought to understand Third World phenomena such as these and to soften their hostility to them.

Many states also adopted socialism as part of their self-definitions. It was attractive because of its appeal to equality and its emphasis on imperialism. Although the Soviets tried to use the popularity of socialism to stress their philosophical affinities, the many varieties of socialism proved to be a complicating factor in Soviet approaches to the Third World. For example, while Khrushchev could claim that he had more in common with the Arab worker than he had with other Soviets of differing class origins, just a few years earlier Muhammed Hassanein Heikal, the well-known journalist and Nasir confidant, wrote in *Al Ahram* that communism as an ideology did not suit the Arab East.[4]

To the extent that the value clash produces arguments or hostility, claims of class affinity proved an ephemeral solution. The issue of class origin opened the Pandora's box of just how authentically socialist these radicals and their ideologies truly can be. Soviet academic studies have recognized that most Third World socialisms fall short of orthodox Soviet-style socialism—a phenomenon that they blame on the class origins of their sponsors. Nevertheless, while they have argued that such ideologies are worthy of Soviet support, they apparently expected to have conflicts over them with Third World elites.

In the seventies, the issues in the debate changed. Many Third World socialists became explicitly Marxist-Leninist in their approaches. These socialists claimed to recognize the inevitability of the class struggle and adopted other jargon from the Soviet political vocabulary. Yet some of the "new wave" depart significantly from Soviet positions. They remain part of the world capitalist system and, in contrast to their ideological pronouncements, encourage and willingly accept investment from the West. Moreover, on a political level, they support Third World demands for a New International Economic Order (NIEO), which is not wholly acceptable to the Kremlin. As for the Soviets, even in the mid- to late seventies, African socialisms were suspect. In the words of one Soviet observer, "Anticommunism takes different forms. . . . [In] tropical Africa it frequently appears under the flag of 'African socialism.' "[5]

In spite of their self-proclaimed socialist ideologies, a majority of Third World states do not practice Leninism. Their political systems lack the trappings of Soviet-style socialism, particularly communist parties. It is clear that the Soviets gave up hopes very early that Third World communist parties would be significant agents of desirable political change. Instead, the Soviets have worked with existing cliques, in the hopes that these groups might be taken over or converted into reliable allies. Chapter 1 pointed out the role Soviet ideology ascribes to political parties; in practice, the Soviet leadership has exerted considerable pressure on its most sympathetic friends to create vanguard political organizations that would replicate the Soviet party in structure-and-control functions. Some self-declared Marxist-Leninist states, including Congo, Angola, and the PDRY, have followed this advice. Yet most Soviet allies have been unable or unwilling to create this kind of institution. In the early years of Soviet involvement in the Third World, the Kremlin urged Algeria and Egypt, without effect, to tighten party discipline and control.[6] Even Ethiopian leader Mengistu, despite his proclaimed faith in Marxism-Leninism, long resisted Soviet urging to create a vanguard political organization. He eventually convened the Commission for Organizing the Party of the Working People of Ethiopia (COPWE), designed to investigate and lay the groundwork for a vanguard political party. In 1984 Mengistu announced the creation of a bona fide Marxist-Leninist party in Ethiopia, called the Ethiopian Workers' Party. It would seem fair to speculate that many Third World leaders view Soviet-style parties as threats to their positions. A vanguard party might serve as a Soviet policy instrument or a base of power for a future political rival.

A corollary to each state's nationalism and national identity is its regional identification. Most Third World states belong to one or more regional organizations. It is important for example to Africans to be part of the Organization of African Unity (OAU) and for Arabs to be members of the Islamic Conference and the Arab League. The Kremlin has adopted careful approaches to these organizations; its attitudes toward the major regional groups vary with the region and the issue. The groups are each in slightly varying ways obstacles to Soviet penetration insofar as they are exclusive clubs to which Moscow cannot belong.

In Africa, the OAU has effected some policies that constricted Soviet maneuverability and others that were compatible with Soviet positions. For example, in 1971 the organization condemned any dialogue with South Africa, thus facilitating the Soviet preference for confrontational tactics. But just a few years later the OAU established a liberation committee through which all aid to Southern African liberation movements was to be funneled. Moreover, the OAU has endorsed peaceful negotiations, accepted Western mediation and resisted efforts to polarize liberation movements along East-West lines. Soviet ability to affect the liberation struggle in both Zimbabwe and Namibia was constrained by the parameters of the crisis as defined by the OAU. Particularly since the mid-seventies, the Soviets have praised the OAU and tried to show

how Soviet foreign policy positions are consonant with African positions. They have also done what they can to express concern over the crisis in Chad and the question of seating the POLISARIO Front as a member of the OAU, two questions that threatened the very existence of the regional organization.

In the Middle East, the Islamic Conference and the Arab League have given the Soviet Union pause. In light of Soviet attitudes toward Islam, it is hardly surprising that Moscow's attitude is one of ambivalence. Since the Kremlin's Arab friends are members, the Soviets try to emphasize similarities in positions, especially in regard to the Palestinian question and anti-Israel statements. However, the Conference loudly condemned the Soviet invasion of Afghanistan and according to Soviet observers engineered a "campaign of slander" against the Soviet Union. Moreover, in 1980 the conference suspended Afghanistan.

The Soviets have been equally circumspect in their attitudes toward the Arab League. Because it is composed of radical, moderate, and conservative Arab states, the Soviets are concerned about the balance among the members at any given time. In general, to the extent that its positions are anti-Western, Moscow has praised its decisions. The Soviets could not but be pleased when the League expelled Egypt in 1979. At the same time, many of its actions seemed to work against Soviet regional objectives. For example, when Somalia joined the Arab League, Mogadishu was able to solicit funds from conservative Arab states and, thereby, lessen potential dependence on Moscow. It should be noted that Soviet attempts to curry favor with these organizations are due in large measure to the fact that many Soviet friends are members.

Other regional intergovernmental organizations reflect efforts to exclude all foreign influences and, therefore, have fared less well in Soviet assessments. Moscow's criticisms of the Association of South East Asian Nations (ASEAN) and the Gulf Cooperation Council (GCC) clearly indicate that the Soviet leadership supports regionalism only insofar as the organizations are a barrier to Western influence. Moscow was hostile to ASEAN at its inception. While rhetorically applauding some of its aims, the Soviets view ASEAN as a "tool of imperialism." This seemed confirmed when the organization refused to admit communist Vietnam, Laos, and Kampuchea into its ranks. Recently, the Soviets implicitly criticized ASEAN members for their ties to the United States, which it charged was attempting to convert ASEAN into a military bloc.[7] The GCC is even more suspect. Founded by Saudi Arabia and other conservative Gulf states, some of which do not even maintain diplomatic relations with Moscow, the organization is clearly anti-Soviet. Although the principles of the GCC include hostility to foreign bases and support for the Palestinian cause, Moscow seems to fear not only that the GCC is a barrier to Soviet interests but also that the United States will utilize the conservative nature of the organization to further anti-Soviet objectives in the region. Steps taken in 1984 to create a military arm of the GCC have increased Soviet concerns.

Third World states have also created several international organizations such as the Nonaligned Movement and the Group of 77 to express their common interests. To a certain extent, these organizations represent obstacles to Soviet–Third World involvement. The Nonaligned Movement has rejected outside interference and on occasion has explicitly criticized the Soviet Union for its activities. Moscow, in attempting to overcome this potential obstacle, has consistently sought to identify nonalignment with "anti-imperialism." As Brezhnev said at the Twenty-Sixth CPSU Congress in 1981: "Its strength lies in its orientation against imperialism and colonialism. . . . We are convinced that the key to a further heightening of the Nonaligned Movement's role in world politics—and we would welcome this—is its fidelity to these underlying principles."[8]

The NIEO, championed by the Group of 77, amounts to a demand for the redistribution of the world's wealth and a dramatic restructuring of international economic relations in favor of the "South." It includes plans for the mechanics to stabilize Third World export prices, more development assistance from the West, and reform of the International Monetary Fund and the World Bank. At the outset, the Soviet Union applauded these demands, but gradually Soviet verbal support gave way to reservations and some open disagreements. First, whereas the program blamed both the West and the East equally for the ills of the Third World, the Kremlin has taken great pains to dissociate itself from the "North" and to advertise its "disinterested" aid. Second, since the Soviets hoped to increase trade ties with the West and South, they objected fundamentally to any dramatic restructuring of international economic relations.[9] Moscow has apparently reached the conclusion that its interests in becoming a greater part of the world economic system would be damaged by progress toward the NIEO. No longer is the USSR an unqualified supporter of all Third World economic demands upon the North. As with other issues and as with the question of regional organizations, Soviet backing can be expected only insofar as there is a clear anti-Western (not anti-Soviet) impact on international relations.

It is one thing when ideological incompatibilities arise and quite another when there are major disagreements over specific policy issues. From Moscow's point of view, religion, patriotism, and home-grown socialism can combine to form a national interest that may not be congruent with Soviet foreign policy goals. Conversely, Moscow's policy line and expectations of an ally or potential client may conflict with the national goals of that state. The effect of a given conflict of interest would appear to depend on the salience of the disputed issue for both parties and the costs of alternative policies to either. Such conflicts need not cause problems in long-term relations where the perception of mutual benefits allows tolerance for disagreements.

One of the Soviets' earliest experiences with the phenomenon of diverging national goals occurred in the sixties during the first phase of their relationship with Cuba's Fidel Castro. Castro's drive to be revolutionary leader of Latin America, his attempts to export the Cuban revolutionary model, and his advocacy of violent revolution conflicted with Moscow's interest in expanded trade relations with moderate Latin American states. Castro's rhetoric and aid to local radical groups frightened Latin American leaders and in effect prompted many Latin American states to strengthen their ties to the United States.[10] The issue proved salient to both sides. The Soviets coerced Castro by withholding oil shipments from Cuba and by threatening to withhold economic assistance. In addition to Soviet pressure, the failure of some Cuban-backed guerrilla operations and the murder of Ernesto "Che" Guevara in Bolivia in 1967 ultimately forced a resolution. Castro abandoned his revolutionary zeal, and in 1968 he offered a lukewarm endorsement of the Soviet invasion of Czechoslovakia. Cuba accepted Soviet suggestions on restructuring the economy and in 1972 was admitted to the CMEA. In the long run, the interests of both parties have been served in that Cuba vitally needs Soviet aid and in that Moscow clearly benefited from the use of Cuban naval facilities and the availability of Cuban troops for combat in Africa.

Although the Soviet Union supported Vietnam during the long Indochina War and benefited directly from the unification of Vietnam under communist control, relations between the two communist allies have been less than ideal. Vietnam's relations with neighboring Kampuchea have seriously hampered Soviet policy in the rest of the region. In January 1979, Vietnam invaded Kampuchea and deposed its leader, Pol Pot, who was Chinese backed. In retaliation, China invaded Vietnam. Although the Vietnamese invasion of Kampuchea could not have occurred without some assent from Moscow, Hanoi's continuing occupation of Kampuchea is not necessarily in the USSR's best interests. First, the military situation itself and the outside intervention in Kampuchean politics have embarrassed the Soviet Union and complicated Moscow's diplomacy toward the ASEAN countries. In June 1980, for example, the Vietnamese were so intent on quelling all Khmer Rouge opposition to the Heng Samrin government that they pursued rebels into Thailand. Apparently, the Vietnamese never informed Moscow of its intention to enter Thailand although the Soviets had previously given their assurances to ASEAN that no such incursions would take place. Second, within Kampuchea itself a rivalry for influence seems to exist between the Soviet Union and Vietnam. Hanoi seems intent on establishing itself as the leader of a quasi federation of Vietnam, Laos, and Kampuchea while Moscow appears to prefer bilateral relations on an equal basis with each of the three.[11]

Thus far divergent regional goals have not caused a major attenuation of relations between Moscow and Hanoi. The Vietnamese are economically dependent on Soviet assistance for rice, other foodstuffs, and oil, while the USSR finds Vietnam a logical counter to China in Southeast Asia. (There are, nonetheless, strains in the relationship with regard to the amounts of Soviet assistance and its management within Vietnam.) Politically, Hanoi enjoys Soviet sponsorship, although not complete endorsement of its policies, and the Soviets have use of the major naval facilities left by the United States at Cam Rahn Bay.

Despite the generally close ties between Moscow and Cairo in the years of Nasir's reign, following his death in September 1970, Soviet-Egyptian relations floundered frequently because of divergent interests. From the outset, Sadat's relations with the Kremlin were cooler than his predecessor's. When the Egyptian president's "year of decision" (1971) passed without military action against Israel and without progress toward the recovery of the Sinai, Sadat's prestige and Arab nationalism were on the line. But at this time the Soviets were actively pursuing détente with the United States and, therefore, were not willing to condone a fourth Middle East war. By 1972 these disagreements became public. The issue's salience to Egypt was so great that, unlike Castro, Sadat did not acquiesce in Soviet wishes; instead, he expelled some 20,000 Soviet advisors. In a little more than a year, the Soviets agreed to President Sadat's war aims. Yet despite Soviet support to Egypt during the 1973 Yom Kippur War, relations between Moscow and Cairo were never again so cordial and in 1976 Sadat abrogated the friendship and cooperation treaty.

Policy disagreements have also troubled the Soviet-Indian relationship. Despite the overall coincidence of interests, the limits to Soviet influence, which reflect diverging goal assessment, may be seen in several instances. In 1968, when the USSR offered military aid to Pakistan, the furor in India was so great that the Soviets were forced to reaffirm their choice of New Delhi as the preferred regional ally. In the seventies, India refused to endorse Soviet proposals for an Asian collective security arrangement and also sought to ameliorate relations with China. Moreover, New Delhi clearly hesitated in recognizing the new regime in Kampuchea and offered only a tepid endorsement of the Soviet invasion of Afghanistan.

Soviet-Algerian relations parallel the Indian case. Although Algeria is usually considered a Soviet friend in North Africa, divergent foreign policy concerns appeared for a short time in 1975–1976 when war broke out in the Western Sahara between Algerian-backed POLISARIO (Popular Front for the Liberation of Saquia-el-Hamra and Rio de Oro) guerrillas and the Moroccan army. Initially Moscow refused to support the Sahrawi guerrillas because to do so might have threatened the developing economic relationship with Morocco, and because the fighting increased the feuding among a number of Arab states with which the Soviet wanted good relations. The Kremlin not only urged the late President Boumedienne to calm the crisis but, according to some reports, even warned against POLISARIO use of Soviet equipment. By the end of 1976, Moscow acceded to Algerian interests: Following a flurry of high-level meetings, Soviet advisors and equipment began flowing into guerrilla camps in Algeria.

The Soviets continue to confront similar situations in their relations with the LDCs. Currently, Soviet-Syrian ties are being tested. Although Syria is a client of long standing, fundamental differences have been manifested over the years. Moscow disapproved of initial Syrian intervention in the Lebanese Civil War in 1976 and President Assad retaliated by briefly denying calling privileges to Soviet ships. Moscow, however, could not afford to endanger what became after 1979 its last major confrontationist toehold in the region. Arms shipments were eventually resumed, and the Soviets became reluctant patrons of the Syrian occupation of Lebanon. Despite the signing of a treaty of friendship and cooperation in 1980, substantial disagreements over the course of relations in this tangled and volatile region remain. President Assad's intervention in Lebanon, his attacks on Yasir Arafat and his followers within the PLO, and his "Greater Syria" expansionism contravene Soviet interests in the region. These activities are also clearly dividing the Arab world. President Assad's prestige is linked to Greater Syria, but the issue seems far less important to the Soviets. Although they have rearmed the Syrians, the Soviets must clearly be concerned about being dragged into a Middle East war not of their choosing.

POLITICAL VOLATILITY

The uncharted terrain in the Third World displays a volatility not characteristic of the first or second worlds. The USSR (and for that matter the United States) has been surprised on occasion by events detrimental to their interests, such as power changes within individual countries and eruptions of local wars. Domestic political upheavals are significant because in many cases the state's pro-Soviet orientation revolved around a certain leader or elite group.

The Soviets first learned that the dynamics of the Third World could work against them in the sixties when they discovered that a palace coup could as easily displace a leader considered progressive as it could bring radicals to power. Within a short period of time, Ben Bella of Algeria and Nkrumah of Ghana were both ousted by less radical regimes. In each of these cases military officers pledging to purge their respective countries of corruption and of foreign influences came to power. Personal ambitions clearly played a part, but the net effects were setbacks for the Soviet Union. No sooner had the first wave of coups subsided when President Keita of Mali, another progressive leader, fell from power in 1968.

An unanticipated regime change may jeopardize the total structure of Soviet ties. We have seen that the accession to power of Anwar Sadat ultimately altered the tenor and longevity of Soviet-Egyptian relations. Sadat went as far as to purge pro-Soviet elements from leadership circles. Soviet leaders are known to have met with experts on Egypt to discuss ways of removing Sadat from power. Two other cases, the fall from power of the Emperor Bokassa in the Central African Empire (now Republic) and of President Macias Nguema in Equatorial Guinea, meant a subsequent loss of influence for Moscow.

Events in Iran proved to the Soviets the dangers inherent in the unpredictable Third World environment. In the course of the seventies, Teheran and Moscow had worked out mutually beneficial economic ties despite periodic arguments over the price of oil and natural gas. By all indications, the events surrounding the fall of the Shah Reza Pahlevi surprised Moscow as much as Washington. Initial Soviet responses were ambivalent: While in some ways the fall of the shah was regretted, the new regime's anti-Americanism seemed to hold great promise for Soviet policy makers. Nonetheless, it is significant to note that the internal dynamic and logic of the Iranian revolution proved detrimental to long-term Soviet interests. Despite efforts to capitalize on the Ayatollah Khomeini's anti-Americanism, he turned out to be as anti-Soviet as he was anti-American. In February 1983, Khomeini arrested key members of the communist Tudeh Party and in May expelled Soviet diplomatic personnel.

Instability in Afghanistan turned out to be no less costly. In 1973 a coup overthrew the Afghan monarchy and in 1977 the government began to seek closer ties with the West. The peculiar volatility of Afghan politics, particularly the rivalry between the two branches of the communist party and between the party and the Islamic rebels, further complicated the picture. The advent of a Marxist government through a coup in April 1978 enmeshed the Soviet Union in a long-term conflict situation. The Soviets moved immediately to recognize and to aid the new regime. Within a year and a half, however, internal dynamics took their toll on Afghanistan. The regime headed by Nur Muhammed Taraki, clearly the Soviet choice, was overthrown by Hafizullah Amin. The policies of the new Afghan ruler further jeopardized the Marxist-Leninist regime. By December 1979 it was apparent that the political infighting and the burgeoning tribal rebellion would lead to the collapse of the regime. The Soviets chose military intervention to put a pliable leader in power and simultaneously to prop up the dying Marxist regime.

In Latin and Central America, the volatility of domestic politics resulted in the overthrow of progressive regimes in Chile and Grenada; elections replaced a pro-Soviet leader in Jamaica and adversely affected Soviet fortunes in Peru. In Chile, Salvador Allende, a Marxist, was elected president with the support of the pro-Soviet Chilean Communist Party and other leftist groups. Divisions among the coalition partners and right-wing protests about activities of the militant left and the growing economic crisis weakened the government and precipitated a major crisis in Chilean politics. In the end, a rightist military coup overthrew and killed Allende, thus terminating the short-lived progressive turn in revolutionary fortunes in Latin America.

The Peruvian case clearly illustrates the problems of basing relations on personalized rule. As noted above, between 1970 and 1980, Peru was unique in Latin America because of its close ties with the Soviet Union and its purchases of Soviet military equipment. However, when Belaunde Terry was elected in March 1980 he altered his country's orientation and basically undid the fabric of Soviet-Peruvian relations.

Another more recent case would clearly be Grenada. In September 1983, the pro-Soviet Maurice Bishop was removed and later killed by the left wing of his own Marxist government. The new leadership claimed to be even more radical than its predecessors. But the coup and the uncertainty that followed provided the incentive for an U.S. invasion of the Caribbean island, under cover of an Eastern Caribbean command. Thus, as a result of an internal power struggle, the Soviets and the Cubans suffered a major setback and Grenada was forcibly returned to the pro-Western fold. Each of these cases shows that volatility may endanger Third World foreign policy alignments. The endemic instability of the Third World affects not only the politics of individual LDCs but also the relations among them.

Complex interstate relations have also rendered Moscow vulnerable to setbacks. The same local conflicts that initially permit Soviet penetration can pose long-run dangers. Regional rivalries and persistent local disputes can acquire a momentum all their own. Long after the disputes have outlived their utility for Soviet purposes, these conflicts may continue to complicate Soviet relations with regional powers and the parties to the conflict. Such disputes can create agonizing dilemmas in which the Soviets are pressured to choose sides or to become involved in risky or expensive operations of little direct benefit to themselves. In either case, the USSR may face losses of influence, restrictions on options, or damage to other objectives elsewhere.

The best illustrations of this phenomenon occur in and around the Middle East, an area that has long been an object of Soviet interest and involvement. The Soviets have been brought into three subregional conflicts that the Kremlin has so far been unable to control. In each of these the Soviets tried at the outset to maintain a balance between the protagonists.

They proved least successful in the war between Somalia and Ethiopia. The Soviets already had a close relationship with Somalia but ran into problems when they began to offer military aid to the new Marxist government of Ethiopia, an age-old Somali rival. Mogadishu clearly saw the Soviet build-up in Ethiopia not only as a threat but also as a betrayal by its benefactor. The Soviets tried without success to manage a juggling act, and Fidel Castro even traveled to the region to attempt to persuade Somalia and Ethiopia to join with the PDRY in a Marxist federation. President Siyad Barre refused and instead decided to invade the Ogaden region. The Marxist-Leninist orientation of Ethiopia, combined with Somalian appeals to the West for aid, determined which state the Soviet Union would back in the long run. Until the Somalian invasion, the actual Soviet and Cuban commitment to Ethiopia's Marxist regime was relatively small. But after the second Somalian offensive, it became clear that Mengistu's regime needed a massive infusion of support. In the end, Siyad Barre abrogated the treaty of friendship and cooperation and expelled Soviet and Cuban advisors, while Cuban troops and Soviet military advisors helped Ethiopia to repulse the Somalian invasion.

In the Gulf, the Iraqi attack on Iran in September 1980 brought to a head their long-smoldering territorial and ideological disputes, which had been exacerbated by the Iranian revolution. Iraq, of course, had signed a friendship treaty with the Soviet Union in 1972 and, despite an on-again–off-again relationship with Moscow, never abrogated the treaty. Soviet relations with Teheran were described above. At first, official Soviet policy was one of careful neutrality that seemed to tilt toward Iran. At the beginning of the war, Moscow held up arms shipments to Iraq and delayed delivery of spare parts but permitted Eastern European shipments to fill the void. By 1982 the prolongation of the war created major complications in Soviet policy. Not only was Khomeini becoming increasingly anti-Soviet, but the Kremlin policy of studied neutrality further alienated the Iraqis, who began to hint of a willingness to deal with the United States. Moreover, the war exacerbated divisions in the Arab world so that no one came to the aid of the PLO in Lebanon when Israel invaded in June 1982.[12] The internal dynamic of the Iranian revolution forced a final decision: While continuing to push for an end to the conflict and continuing to proclaim no interest in it, The Soviets have quietly tilted back toward Iraq.

The third conflict, the fighting in the Western Sahara, provides another example of a difficult choice for the Soviets to make, since the Kremlin prizes relations with both Algeria and Morocco. The war that broke out in 1975 pitted Algerian-sponsored POLISARIO guerrillas against Morocco, with which the Soviet Union hoped to negotiate a multibillion-dollar deal for phosphates. As the war progressed, Moscow simultaneously provided arms to Algeria (transshipped to the POLISARIO) and managed to conclude the phosphate agreement with Morocco. The Soviet investment in Morocco—with a price tag of US$9 billion—represents the largest Soviet project in the Third World. Thus far, eight years since the war began, the Soviets have managed to retain their unique relationship with both Algeria and Morocco. However, as the war drags on, the Moroccans have turned increasingly to the United States for military aid. Reportedly, U.S.-Moroccan agreements include not only arms, but also use of Moroccan bases by the American Rapid Deployment Force if needed. Thus, from the Soviet perspective, the prolongation of the Western Saharan War may lead to an internationalization of the conflict that could further push Morocco into the Reagan administration's arms. This both raises overall Soviet risks and could conceivably threaten the much-needed phosphate source.[13] The apparent rapprochement between Morocco and Libya in 1984 has not yet resolved these dilemmas.

The central Mideast conflict is without question the Arab-Israeli dispute. Detailed studies of regional politics abound as do analyses of Soviet policy there. What seems clear is that, although the dispute and the periodic wars have facilitated Soviet intervention, the dynamics of this conflict often frustrate Soviet objectives. Despite its role as armorer to the Arab states and of treaty partner with Egypt and later Syria, the USSR has not been able to control the choices of either war or peace. Instead, although Arab military successes in the 1973 war were achieved with Soviet weapons and training, both the 1967 war and particularly the 1973 war had the effect of increasing the U.S. role in the Middle East. The series of disengagement agreements, the Camp David Accords, and the Egyptian-Israeli peace treaty all were products of U.S. diplomacy. Egypt's final withdrawal as a confrontationist state was a double blow to the Soviet Union. Not only was the Soviet Union eliminated from a major role in the movement for peace in the Middle East, but Egypt changed from a Soviet to a U.S. client in the region. Moreover, the intractability of the Arab-Israel dispute presents continuing problems for the Kremlin. Presently, Syria remains the sole confrontationist state that is a firm Soviet client. Yet, as noted above, that relationship contains inherent dangers. The intransigent complexities of the region create a situation in which the local clients are dragging the patron behind them. And the reluctant patron finds that it risks losing Syria unless President Assad's claims to a Greater Syria are supported.

SOVIET HANDICAPS

When the Soviet Union entered the ranks of the outside powers seeking to play a role in the politics of the Third World, few if any of the nonindustrial states had had any prior contact with Moscow. In effect, unlike the Western countries that were former colonial powers, Moscow had an untarnished reputation. Simultaneously, of course, the USSR was locked in an uncompromising rivalry with the United States and its Western allies, which made the role of alternate patron and supplier ultimately attractive. Moscow was more than willing to step in as arms supplier or benefactor for development projects when the West had already refused. Soviet rhetoric enhanced the Kremlin's image: The repeated emphasis on national liberation and the struggle for true independence struck a responsive chord in the Third World.

By the early sixties, Moscow no longer possessed an unblemished record, nor was it free to choose friends without regard to prior commitments. Guinea, the site of the Soviet breakthrough into Black Africa, also proved to be one of Moscow's first problems. In 1962 Sékou Touré charged the Soviets with interference in Guinean domestic affairs and expelled the Soviet ambassador. As if the Guinean setback were not enough, Khrushchev's withdrawal of offensive weapons from Cuba, reportedly without consultating or informing Castro, could hardly enhance Moscow's image as partner.

Ten years later, Egyptian President Sadat charged that the Soviets were interfering in the internal politics of the Arab Socialist Union (ASU). History seems to repeat itself for the Kremlin. In the summer of 1983 reports circulated of Soviet attempts to infiltrate Syrian Air Force units under the direct control of Hafez al-Assad. Despite the Syrian dependence on Soviet military help, Assad sent certain Soviet officers home.[14] And in early 1984 the Soviets ran into trouble again.

Ethiopian President Mengistu expelled two Soviet diplomats on espionage charges, thus sending a clear signal to Moscow that however close Soviet-Ethiopian relations were, interference was not to be tolerated.[15]

Moscow has also been charged with arrogance and racism—two allegations that can only further complicate relations between the Soviet Union and individual Third World countries. The number of Soviet economic and military advisors abroad has grown substantially, as has the number of Third World students and military trainees in the Soviet Union. Although this reciprocity is frequently beneficial to both sides, it is not without its problems. Over the years, the Soviets have earned a reputation for high-handedness and arrogance. Technicians, when sent abroad, frequently do not possess requisite language skills and often fail to learn even the polite rudiments of the host country's language. Additionally, stories circulate of Soviets looking down their noses at their Third World students. Charges of racism seem to arise most when Third World students study in the Soviet Union. Civilian students, especially those from Black Africa, more often than not wind up at Patrice Lumumba University in Moscow, which caters to foreign students. There they are kept segregated from Soviet students, who attend Moscow State University, and the foreign students have allegedly been subjected to insults and racial slurs on the streets of Moscow. At the military academies, Third World students also attend classes separate from their Soviet counterparts.

As Moscow became more deeply involved in the Third World, the Soviet leadership found that it could not remain unscathed. The Soviets have been blamed as well for the activities of local communist parties. Whether the communist parties are or can be effective instrumentalities of Soviet policy and whether or not such suspicions are well founded is open to question. The impact on local politics of local communist party activity and of ties between Moscow and the local organizations is at issue only in certain parts of the Third World. In the Middle East and Asia there are several active communist parties, but, in contrast, in Black Africa communists are few and far between, mainly remnants of the communist parties of the former colonial power. In several Latin American countries, the communist parties are legal; however, in most they have not been in the forefront of revolutionary activity.

Generally, Third World elites fear these parties because they are independent power bases offering competing programs and policies. A heritage of mistrust is created not only because of international ties to other communists and to the Soviet Union, but also because of past histories. In Algeria, for example, the communist party was never trusted because, as part of the French Communist Party, it initially opposed independence. At the Twenty-Third CPSU Congress, the FLN delegate walked out to protest the presence of an Algerian communist at the meeting. In other instances, communist activity or alleged involvement in antigovernmental affairs obviously creates suspicion. Many Third World countries ban all communist organizations even if other opposition parties are permitted to function. Even where they are legalized, the existence of communist parties continues to be problematic. The Iraqi and Syrian parties have regularly been harassed by their pro-Soviet governments. Indian regimes under Nehru and Gandhi have been intolerant of hostile domestic communist factions. The pro-Soviet CPI has learned that it criticizes the government at its own peril. The uneasy if not proscribed relationship between rulers and local communist organizations would, therefore, seem to be a complicating factor in Soviet cultivation of Third World regimes.

The Soviet leadership is keenly aware of this problem. In practice, Moscow has been more than willing to sacrifice local communists for better relations with progressive leaders. Depending on local circumstances, the Kremlin has urged the local organizations to dissolve and to form "united fronts" with the ruling groups. But this policy has not always worked. In the Sudan, when Gafar Numayri came to power in 1969, he proclaimed himself anti-imperialist and pro-Palestinian and included representatives of the large Sudanese Communist Party in his cabinet. The Soviet leadership took special interest in Numayri: He traveled to Moscow and signed several cooperative agreements, and Soviet ships visited Port Sudan. However, the Sudanese Communist Party opposed the merger of Libya, the UAR, and Sudan, which was proposed in 1971. The open communist opposition to his policies prompted Numayri to crack down on the party. In July 1971 a group of army officers backed by the communist party staged a coup while Numayri was out of the country. However, with the help of Egypt and Libya, he was reinstated three days later. Numayri angrily charged Moscow with trying to unseat him, and he executed the leader of the party. He is reported to have said: "we will teach them [USSR] a lesson and show them Sudanese originality. We will not accept colonization from the Soviet Union or anyone else."[16]

Other Soviet activities in the nonindustrial world and policy decisions also contribute to a wariness on the part of potential allies. When the Soviet Union switched sides on the Horn of Africa a number of countries were distressed. Not only did the change of sides illustrate Soviet opportunism, but Somalia, as a Muslim country, was supported by a large percentage of the Arab states. Many of them also had long supported the largely Muslim liberation movement in Eritrea—a movement the new Soviet-backed Ethiopian government has been trying to crush. The Soviets have also allied themselves with several harsh dictators around the world. They endorsed Nguema in Equatorial Guinea and Idi Amin Dada in Uganda. Although the Soviets could claim adherence to international law when they helped the Ethiopians repulse the Somalian attack, their support of the Vietnamese invasion of Kampuchea and of course their own invasion of Afghanistan raised a number of questions about their international behavior. Just how opportunistic are they? Would they switch sides again in a regional conflict? Would they endorse territorial aggression against more clients in the future? While it is difficult to answer any of these questions, their implications for Soviet–Third World relations are troubling. The USSR has shown itself to be a superpower that could abandon allies, resort to force, and contravene internationally accepted norms.

All of these problems are clearly detrimental to the consolidation of Soviet–Third World relations. But none is more serious than the inability of the Soviet Union to provide economic development assistance on the scale expected by its Third World clients. Since 1974 when the Group of 77 first issued the call for an NIEO, it has become fashionable to discuss and analyze the North-South dialogue. As discussed above, while supportive of Third World demands for a greater share of the world's wealth and a restructuring of the international economic system, the Soviets have assiduously tried to dissociate themselves from the North. As with many other issues, Moscow cheers the demands for the NIEO insofar as they are demands upon the West.

Central to the Third World proposals is what amounts to a shopping list of economic needs: food, development assistance, convertible currency to purchase manufactures, energy (mainly oil), and consumer goods. It seems obvious that failure to meet these basic needs is as serious a problem as political volatility or divergent national interests. Indeed, persistent food shortages, balance of payments deficits, huge foreign debt, and generalized slow if not negative growth rates all contribute to the seemingly inherent instability of the nonindustrial world. For Soviet and Third World policy makers, the crucial question is who will supply those needs.

In the past, Moscow, while never equaling the amounts proffered by the United States, had offered credits and some outright grants to favored Third World states; however, the Soviets learned that development assistance is an endless operation. Current economic problems within the Soviet Union prevent the Kremlin from dispensing so much as previously. Economic assistance as an instrumentality of Soviet foreign policy will be discussed in Chapter 5, but in the context of obstacles and constraints to Soviet foreign policy objectives the inability of the Soviet Union to provide large amounts of development assistance must rank along with their other handicaps.

The Soviet economic system suffers from problems of low labor productivity, declining work force, decreasing funds available for capital investment, major agricultural declines both weather- and system-related, and the need to import sophisticated Western technology. In the early eighties, the gross national product increased by around 2 percent, although 1983 stands out with a 4 percent increase. The combined toll of these factors has forced and will continue to force the Soviet leadership to confront some difficult choices. The Kremlin will have to establish economic priorities, among them economic aid to Third World states.[17]

Academic studies by Soviet economists corroborate these Western analyses. For example, a Soviet scholar in an amazingly frank article in *Voprosy Filosofii* acknowledged the problems created by the "definite lowering of the tempo of socio-economic development of the socialist countries."[18] In another recent article, the deputy chairman of the State Committee for Foreign Economic Relations hinted that Soviet defense spending limited resources available to Third World friends. He wrote: "the dynamics of cooperation [with the Asian countries] is influenced by a number of internal and external factors of an *economic* and political nature. We have to bear considerable expenses to maintain the country's defense capability in the conditions of the arms race forced upon [us] by . . . international conditions and imperialists."[19]

The most current aid statistics reveal that new Soviet aid/credit commitments fell to a four-year low in 1981. Although this might not indicate by itself less interest in economic credits and aid as a foreign policy tool, the terms of recent agreements reflect a concern also for the costs to the Soviet economic system. Newer agreements are clearly designed to promote Soviet equipment sales and to be much less concessional than in the past.[20]

During the Brezhnev era, Soviet specialists on the Third World reluctantly concluded that the LDCs would remain enmeshed in the world capitalist system for the foreseeable future. Moreover, they admitted that the Soviet Union could not replace the West as aid supplier. Instead, they argued in the words of one economist: "[the] friendly help and support of the socialist countries is a most important factor which has created the favorable external situation for the choice of the noncapitalist perspective of development."[21]

One aspect of Brezhnev's "rationalization" of Soviet programs was a shift to joint ventures and trade-linked investment in nonprogressive states. The most significant example is the multibillion-dollar phosphate deal signed with Morocco in 1978. The Soviets are to supply untied currency loans to develop a major phosphate complex, and in return Morocco will guarantee shipments of phosphate fertilizers under terms of a barter agreement extending over thirty years. Clearly, the sorry state of Soviet agriculture made the deal immeasurably attractive to the Kremlin.

Additional evidence of economic constraints on Soviet foreign policy toward the Third World may be found in the shift to arms transfers (and away from economic aid) as an instrumentality of foreign policy. Currently, nearly two-thirds of Soviet commitments involve military equipment and training. And among these a significant percentage go to countries able to pay with hard currency. This has meant that oil-rich Arab countries that can finance their purchases directly, for example, Libya, Algeria, Iraq (prior to the Iran-Iraq war), or that receive development assistance from Saudi Arabia, such as Syria, have overwhelmingly dominated the recipients' field.

In the fifties and sixties, the Soviets reaped tremendous political advantage from their assistance to nonaligned states. By the seventies, many progressive LDCs, counted by most to be in the Soviet camp, seemed to expect large amounts of Soviet (and CMEA) assistance. The stringencies on Soviet economic largesse have elicited bitter complaints from the USSR's Third World clients. One need only look at Mozambique, a self-proclaimed Marxist state, which encourages economic trade with and investment from the West. FRELIMO security chief Sergio Vieira is quoted as saying that Mozambique "would not like to be a model of poor socialism."[22] In fact, Mozambique has concluded several major agreements with Portugal, its former colonial ruler.

The increasingly difficult straits the LDCs find themselves in mean that their requirements for economic aid and their demands from the North can only increase. The Soviet Union, faced with major economic difficulties, is clearly not in a position to answer their requests. This situation could presage a parting of the ways between the socialist bloc (especially the Soviet Union) and its clients. How can the Soviet leadership explain investment in Morocco and not a poorer socialist-oriented state? Neither Andropov nor Chernenko has altered this approach.

Soviet involvement in the Third World has not been without its setbacks. Differing ideological outlooks and divergent goals scuttled even the best relationships. The terrain in the Third World has clearly contained its "traps" for the Soviet Union: Political volatility and local conflicts turned out to be disadvantages as well as means of entrée. Lastly, the USSR itself is handicapped in many respects. As we have seen, the Kremlin is a captive of the legacy of its own earlier involvement in the Third World. Policy decisions and choices of clients clearly hold implications for regional friends and in some cases for all the Soviet Union's allies. In terms of handicaps, probably no factor is more significant than Moscow's inability to distribute huge amounts of development assistance. That this is a major concern to the Soviet leadership seems clear. In fact, at least one Soviet specialist has urged a reappraisal of the criteria by which the Kremlin dispenses assistance. He advocated greater selectivity in the client list and argued that the Soviets can enhance their prestige by avoiding "compromising ties with repressive antipopular (*antinarodnye*) regimes" that in some cases "discredit the idea of socialism."[23]

NOTES

1. M. Rajan Menon, "The Military and Security Dimensions of Soviet-Indian Relations," in Robert Donaldson, ed., *The Soviet Union in the Third World: Successes and Failures* (Boulder, Colo.: Westview Press, 1981), p. 246.

2. *The Financial Gazette* (Salisbury), September 19, 1980, p. 11.

3. For example, Pavel Demchenko, *Pravda*'s Mideast correspondent, wrote: "it seems that it is these groups [the right-wing clergy] who want to put up obstacles to the expansion of Soviet-Iranian relations." (Author's translation). "USSR-Iran in the Interests of Good Neighborliness," *Pravda*, March 9, 1982, p. 4. *Pravda* also charged "reactionary conservative circles" with attacking "patriotic" forces and disrupting Soviet-Iranian ties. "Against the National Interests of Iran," February 19, 1983, p. 4.

4. Quoted in V. Mayevskii, "Hassanein Haykal's Sortie," *Pravda*, February 19, 1959, p. 4, in *Current Digest of the Soviet Press* [hereafter CDSP], vol. 11, nos. 6–7 (March 18, 1959), p. 27.

5. P. I. Manchka, "Communists, Revolutionary Democrats and the Noncapitalist Path," *Voprosy Historii KPSS*, no. 10 (October 1975), pp. 57–69, in CDSP, vol. 27, no. 51 (January 21, 1976), p. 4.

6. Soviet observers paid careful attention to party developments in both Egypt and Algeria, two early progressive states. They urged the leadership, in each case, to tighten party organization and to strengthen indoctrination. It is also interesting to note that in the postmortems on Sadat's turning away from the Soviet Union, scholars and officials alike argued that Nasir realized he needed to build up the ASU, but his untimely death cut short party development. Hence, according to the Soviets, Sadat was able to reverse course.

7. Moscow World News Service, January 22, 1984, *Foreign Broadcast Information Service* 84-016 (January 24, 1984), p. E4–6.

8. *Pravda* and *Izvestiia*, Feburary 24, 1981, pp. 2–9, in CDSP, vol. 33, no. 8 (March 25, 1981), p. 8.

9. For a detailed discussion, see Elizabeth K. Valkenier, *The Soviet Union and the Third World, An Economic Bind* (New York: Praeger Publishers, 1983), pp. 109–146.

10. For the ins and outs of Soviet-Cuban debates in the period, see W. Raymond Duncan, "Moscow and Cuban Radical Nationalism," in his *Soviet*

Policy in the Developing Countries (Waltham, Mass.: Ginn-Blaisdell, 1970), pp. 107–132.

11. Leif Rosenberger details the political infighting in Phnom Penh over Kampuchea's ties to the Soviet Union and Vietnam in his "The Soviet-Vietnamese Alliance and Kampuchea," *Survey*, no. 118/119 (Autumn/Winter, 1983), pp. 207–231.

12. See Carol R. Saivetz, "Soviet Policy Toward Iran and the Persian Gulf: Legacies of the Brezhnev Era" (Paper presented at the Midwest Slavics Conference, Chicago, Ill., May 1983), and Galia Golan, "The Soviet Union and Israeli Action in Lebanon," *International Affairs*, vol. 59, no. 1 (Winter 1982/1983), pp. 7–17.

13. Carol R. Saivetz, "Periphery and Center: The Western Sahara Dispute and Soviet Policy Toward the Middle East" (Paper presented at the American Association for the Advancement of Slavic Studies, Kansas City, Mo., October 1983).

14. *Ha'aretz*, August 7, 1983, p. 2.

15. *New York Times*, March 8, 1984, p. A7.

16. Agence France Presse, August 6, 1971, cited in Robert O. Freedman, *Soviet Policy Toward the Middle East* (New York: Praeger Publishers, 1975), p. 54.

17. Despite all the publicity accorded Soviet economic difficulties, most Western scholars conclude that the USSR is *not* on the verge of collapse.

18. Iu. S. Novopashin, "Vozdeistvie real'nogo sotsializma na mirovoi revoliutsionnyi vopros: metologicheskie aspekty," *Voprosy Filosofii*, no. 8 (August 1982), p. 9.

19. Iliodor Kulykov, "Economic and Technical Cooperation of the USSR with Asian Countries," *Asia and Africa Today* (Moscow), no. 6 (November/December 1982), p. 23. Italics supplied.

20. U.S. Department of State, *Soviet and East European Aid to the Third World, 1981* (1983), p. 5.

21. N. A. Ushakova, *Arabskaia Respublika Egipta: Sotrudnichestvo so stranami sotsializma i ekonomicheskoe razvitie* (Moscow: iz. Nauka, 1974), p. 3.

22. Sergio Vieira, "Viability of Scientific Socialism," *World Marxist Review*, March 1979, p. 60.

23. Novopashin, "Vozdeistvie real'nogo sotsializma," pp. 14, 15.

Chapter Five

Tools
of Soviet
Involvement

W e have thus far analyzed the record of Soviet involvement in the Third World, noting the expansion of relations and examining those aspects of politics in the Third World that presented both openings for and obstacles to Soviet penetration. In our discussions we referred to, but did not analyze, the several foreign policy tools used by Moscow to achieve its goals in the Third World. These instrumentalities include Soviet economic assistance, economic credits, trade, military transfers, diplomatic ties, and party-to-party relations. None is uniformly a discrete category and in most cases relations of one type coexist with other types of ties.

Data for the categories are not necessarily readily available. The Soviets themselves publish trade statistics and some development assistance statistics but barely mention arms transfers. In this regard, Soviet statements on occasion refer to all-round assistance rendered or to military assistance lent to embattled progressive forces. Collecting data on arms transfers is hampered additionally by a CIA decision to cease publishing exact data on a recipient country-by-country basis. Even diplomatic data are harder to come by than might be expected. The Soviets frequently exaggerate the level of ties with assorted LDCs; in some cases representatives of the USSR have been expelled or embassies in Moscow (or in specific nonindustrial states) remain unassigned.

Since the USSR first offered small economic credits to Afghanistan in 1954, and since the Egyptian-Czechoslovak arms deal of a year later, the scope of Soviet economic and military relations with the states of the nonindustrial world has expanded dramatically. According to recent data, the Soviets have extended US$22.35 billion in economic aid to the LDCs, with an added US$665 million from Eastern Europe. On the military side, Moscow's military agreements total some US$70 billion.[1] It is important to realize, however, that much of this assistance has gone to a few chosen recipients. The geographic and numerical range of Soviet diplomatic relations also has expanded: The Soviets claim and indeed seem to desire formal relations with as many states as possible regardless of their political leanings and ideological orientations. The patterns of these ties and their interrelationship will be discussed below.

ECONOMIC ASSISTANCE AND FOREIGN TRADE

When the Soviet Union first sought to break out of its postwar isolation and to change its image in the emerging Third World, the Kremlin's chosen tool was economic assistance. As previously noted, the Soviets' initial gesture was in the form of small-scale economic credits to neighboring Afghanistan. This 1954 experiment was followed in rapid succession by the 1955 agreement with India to construct the Bhilai steel complex, and later to assist in building the Bokaro steel mill, and the 1956 offer to finance construction of the first stage of the Aswan Dam in Egypt. The Indian and Egyptian aid offers proved typical of Khrushchev era economic assistance programs. Both were large-scale showy projects in the public sector, and both Bokaro and Aswan came on the heels of political and economic disputes with Western countries. The New Delhi government chose Soviet plans for Bokaro after an earlier U.S. offer was rejected. The Soviets offered a scaled-down version, which included the use of tools from a Czech-financed local company. In this way, the Soviets could claim that two native industries would be built simultaneously and moreover that India would not be dependent on imported equipment (which the U.S. plan called for). Aswan, as noted in Chapter 4, also permitted the Soviets a significant propaganda advantage, further enhancing Soviet prestige as a Third World patron. It is ironic that despite the rupture in Soviet-Egyptian relations and despite the fact that the dam has turned out to be an ecological disaster, Moscow continues to point to it as one of the Soviet Union's major Third World successes. Some Soviet aid wound up in showy yet unproductive projects. One of Moscow's largest investments in Indonesia was in a huge stadium—which can hardly be considered infrastructure development.

That Khrushchev saw economic assistance as a major foreign policy tool is clear. Under his leadership the Soviet Union dispensed some US$3.8 billion of economic aid to the Third World, primarily to assist public sector development.[2] It is widely speculated that one factor in Khrushchev's unceremonious ouster in 1964 was an additional US$277 million credit promised to Egypt on the spur of the moment, without consulting his colleagues in the Politburo.

With the end of the Khrushchev era, Soviet economic aid policies changed: The leadership became more cautious and conservative in dispensing credits. The Soviets appeared more concerned about the ability of recipients to absorb development assistance and in general more care was given to feasibility studies. Along with the push for economic rationality, Moscow began to look for domestic benefits, which the Kremlin called mutually advantageous relations, from aid. This post-Khrushchev period also saw the establishment of joint venture programs in recipient countries. While the Middle East, North Africa, and India remained favored recipients, the Soviets worked out agreements with monarchical Iran and made tentative offers to Hassan's Morocco. Overall, the Kremlin signed agreements totaling US$6.3 billion between 1965 and 1974.[3]

By 1974, changes in the world economy induced by the rise in oil prices and consequent recession forced yet another shift in Soviet development-assistance programs. Moscow seemed to become more concerned with securing raw materials necessary for Soviet economic growth and began to urge its recipients to sign broad cooperation agreements effective for several years. This arrangement was intended to provide the client with a firm base for long-term planning and insure Moscow stable supply patterns.[4] Examples are the fifteen-year US$3 billion agreement for development projects signed with Iran and the 1978 phosphate agreement with Morocco. As Alexei Kosygin said at a state dinner honoring the visiting Moroccan prime minister: In return for assisting Moroccan economic development, the Soviet Union was interested in "obtain[ing] more fertilizers which we intend to use in developing our agriculture."[5] The new agreements for the 1975–1979 period total US$8.1 billion.[6] The most recent economic assistance data are contained in Table 5.1.

What data such as these do not show is the composition of the various Soviet aid programs. Whereas at first the Soviets contributed to large-scale industrial and infrastructure projects, they are starting to endorse projects geared to agricultural improvement, geologic exploration, and light industry development. This is particularly true in sub-Saharan Africa. In Latin America the Soviets have lent assistance in the fields of hydroelectric power and mineral prospecting. And in the Middle East–North African region the Soviets have helped construct large-scale enterprises and petroleum-related industries. A breakdown of Soviet development assistance is contained in Figure 5.1.

Another increasingly significant aspect of Soviet development assistance is the stationing of economic technicians in recipient countries and the training of Third World students in the USSR. At the end of 1981, approximately 96,000 Soviet and Eastern European technicians were assisting seventy-five countries; moreover, there were an additional 23,000 Cuban advisors abroad. The Soviets claim that their personnel abroad in the LDCs provide vital training services so that the host country can be self-sufficient in the long run. By the same token, approximately two-thirds of these are at work in Arab countries where

Table 5.1 USSR and Eastern Europe: Economic Aid Extended
to Non-Communist LDCs, by Country (Million US$)

	1954-1981		1980		1981	
	USSR	Eastern Europe	USSR	Eastern Europe	USSR	Eastern Europe
Total	22,355	11,885	2,070	1,330	445	665
North Africa	3,250	980	315			
Algeria	1,045	525	315			
Mauritania	10	10				
Morocco	2,100	215				
Tunisia	95	230				
Sub-Saharan Africa	2,870	1,990	310	280	125	115
Angola	30	100				
Benin	10	NA			5	
Burundi		NEGL				
Cameroon	10					
Cape Verde	5	5				NA
Central African Republic	5					
Chad	5					
Congo	45	60				
Equatorial Guinea	NEGL					
Ethiopia	400	355			10	5
Gabon		NEGL				
The Gambia	NEGL					
Ghana	95	145				
Guinea	215	110	5			
Guinea-Bissau	10	5				
Ivory Coast		NA				
Kenya	50					
Liberia	NEGL					
Madagascar	70	35	50	35		
Mali	100	25			5	
Mauritius	5					
Mozambique	175	100			NA	
Niger	NEGL					
Nigeria	5	220				20
Rwanda	NEGL					
São Tomé and Principe	NA	NA				
Senegal	10	35				
Sierra Leone	30					
Somalia	165	10				
Sudan	65	270		30		
Tanzania	40	75				
Uganda	25	25				
Upper Volta (Bourkina Fasso)	5					
Zambia	20	165		30		
Other	1,275	250	255	185	100	90
East Asia	260	665		40		
Burma	15	215		40		
Indonesia	215	365				
Kampuchea	25	15				
Laos	5	5				
Philippines		65				

Table 5.1 (continued)

	1954-1981		1980		1981	
	USSR	Eastern Europe	USSR	Eastern Europe	USSR	Eastern Europe
Latin America	1,420	2,135	250	195	170	50
Argentina	225	300				
Bolivia	100	75		15		
Brazil	145	780		150	55	10
Chile	240	145				
Colombia	215	80				
Costa Rica	15	10				
Ecuador	NEGL	20				
Grenada	NEGL	NA		NA		
Guyana	NA	35				
Jamaica	30	285				
Mexico	NA	45				
Nicaragua	80	70	NA	30	80	40
Panama		5				
Peru	275	215	250			
Uruguay	60	30				
Venezuela	NA	10				
Other	35	25			35	

Source: U.S. Department of State, <u>Soviet and East European Aid to the Third World, 1981</u> (February 1983).

Figure 5.1 USSR: Sectoral Distribution of Aid to Non-Communist LDCs, 1954-1979

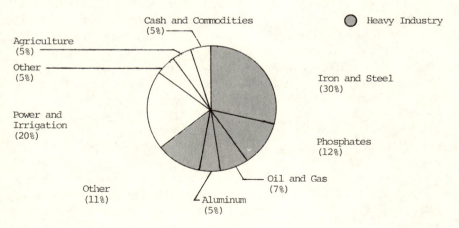

Source: C.I.A. Foreign Assessment Center, <u>Communist Aid Activities in Non-Communist Less Developed Countries, 1979 and 1954-1979</u>, (October 1980).

they are paid with hard currency.[7] The Soviets and Eastern Europeans also offer academic training to students from the Third World. Statistics from 1981 reveal that 72,000 students have studied at Soviet and Eastern European academic institutions, many on full scholarship. The pattern of scholarships seems to favor the African countries. Among these, Angola, Congo, Ethiopia, Ghana, and the Sudan send the most students to the USSR. The Soviet leadership seems to see this program as a long-term investment both by showing how helpful the USSR can be and in terms of influencing the political orientation of future leaders in a given country.

Any assessment of Soviet economic assistance to the LDCs should include discussions of foreign trade because increasingly the two are becoming intertwined. As the Kremlin sought to make assistance less costly, aid assumed the form of credits for the purchase of Soviet equipment and manufactures. Indeed, a significant part of Soviet exports to the developing countries consists of machinery and related equipment for the Third World development projects. From the early years through the sixties, trade with the LDCs was conducted by means of governmental agreements that specified exchanges of goods at preestablished prices. In many cases, the exchanges were made with nonconvertible currencies. Lately there has been a marked shift to covering trade in convertible or hard currencies. Much of the Soviet trade with the Third World consists of commodities needed by the USSR, including crude oil, natural gas, food imports, and metallic ores.

In the seventies, trade as a foreign policy tool permitted Moscow increasing penetration of Latin America, a continent where hitherto there was little Soviet contact. The majority of Latin American countries proved reluctant to accept Soviet economic assistance; thus, with the exceptions of Chile under Allende and Peruvian military purchases, most Soviet–Latin American contacts consist of trade relations. According to the Central Intelligence Agency, most credits extended to Latin and Central America have been trade related, the first going to Argentina in 1958.[8] Unfortunately from the Soviet perspective, only a small percentage of the credits have been drawn, creating a huge Soviet trade deficit of approximately 4.5 billion rubles.[9] Over the years, the Soviet Union has tried to promote trade in this part of the world, but Western products remain more attractive. The trade imbalances with Latin America were exacerbated by large-scale Soviet purchases of Argentine wheat and corn in 1980, following the U.S. grain embargo. Moscow has also imported sorghum, soybeans, and fresh-frozen meat from Argentina.

In other areas, except the Middle East, the USSR also runs a deficit, although at a much lower rate. In the Middle East, trade surpluses are created by purchases of arms with hard currency. The latest trade data available are contained in Table 5.2.

Overall, it seems fair to conclude that it was with a keen eye for political opportunities that Moscow became involved in the assistance business. Indeed, the Soviets derived propaganda victories from the timing of certain assistance offers and political pluses as they endeavored to show how "disinterested" their aid programs were. But the Soviets discovered that development aid can be an endless and sometimes thankless task, with the poorer countries clamoring for more aid and others reneging on promises to repay loans. Moreover, several recipients have criticized the Soviets for building the wrong factory in the wrong place, for equipment that performed poorly, and for the arrogant behavior of Soviet technicians who did not speak native languages.

Changes in the world economy coupled with the slowdown in Soviet economic growth (see Chapter 4) altered Soviet perspectives on development assistance. As we saw, more credits are tied to trade and the terms of the agreements are far less concessionary than in the past. Currently, Moscow policy makers urge their allies to be more self-sufficient. All these problems and changes notwithstanding, development assistance continues to be a major Soviet foreign policy tool.

MILITARY ASSISTANCE

Over the last several years, the Soviet Union has increasingly turned to military assistance as a foreign policy tool. From the initial 1955 Egyptian-Czechoslovak arms deal to big business, the Soviet Union's arms trade through 1981 was estimated to have totaled over US$68 billion. Today the Soviet Union ranks second only to the United States as a supplier of arms to the Third World.

In the early years (1955–1970) the Kremlin seemed willing to make arms available on favorable terms. Most deals included Soviet credits for the purchase of arms at 2 to 2.5 percent interest with a 10- to 12-year recoupment period. Moreover, many of the early arms agreements allowed for repayment in local currencies. A dramatic escalation in Soviet arms sales occurred in the seventies. This reflected Soviet willingness to sell weapons that were more sophisticated than previously and the massive Soviet resupply of its Arab clients during and after the 1973 Yom Kippur War. The traditional Soviet interest in the Middle East and the dramatic increase in Arab oil revenues combined to spur Soviet arms trade to a record US$34 billion between 1974 and 1979.[10] Despite the apparent shift to stiffer terms and to sales to oil-producing

Table 5.2 Soviet Trade with Third World Countries

		Millions of Rubles[a]	
		1981	1982
ASIA			
Afghanistan	Turnover	655,8	691,0
	Export	339,2	412,5
	Import	316,6	278,5
Bangladesh	Turnover	53,4	54,9
	Export	28,7	27,6
	Import	24,7	27,3
Burma	Turnover	31,4	9,9
	Export	9,3	8,8
	Import	22,1	1,1
Vietnam	Turnover	891,8	1 010,7
	Export	724,6	804,2
	Import	167,2	206,5
India	Turnover	2 397,9	2 514,0
	Export	1 064,1	1 040,2
	Import	1 333,8	1 473,8
Indonesia	Turnover	93,1	53,8
	Export	34,1	34,4
	Import	59,0	19,4
Jordan	Turnover	20,9	90,7
	Export	20,4	90,5
	Import	0,5	0,2
Iraq	Turnover	909,4	994,1
	Export	905,5	975,9
	Import	3,9	18,2
Iran	Turnover	878,5	766,0
	Export	409,0	577,3
	Import	469,5	188,7
Yemen Arab Republic	Turnover	22,9	34,4
	Export	22,5	34,1
	Import	0,4	0,3
Kampuchea	Turnover	61,6	55,7
	Export	59,7	53,4
	Import	1,9	2,3
Cyprus	Turnover	42,5	49,1
	Export	25,8	29,5
	Import	16,7	19,6
China	Turnover	176,8	223,5
	Export	82,6	120,1
	Import	94,2	103,4
N. Korea	Turnover	529,2	681,0
	Export	278,9	318,5
	Import	250,3	362,5

(continued)

[a]In this table a comma is the equivalent of a decimal point.

Table 5.2 (continued)

| | | Millions of Rubles | |
		1981	1982
Kuwait	Turnover	18,2	6,1
	Export	12,7	6,1
	Import	5,5	0
Laos	Turnover	37,1	66,2
	Export	36,2	64,2
	Import	0,9	2,0
Lebanon	Turnover	22,9	23,9
	Export	14,8	17,5
	Import	8,1	6,4
Malaysia	Turnover	190,0	250,6
	Export	15,0	15,9
	Import	175,0	234,7
Mongolia	Turnover	1 035,9	1 232,7
	Export	787,3	918,9
	Import	248,6	313,8
PDRY	Turnover	98,9	73,0
	Export	92,8	67,1
	Import	6,1	5,9
Nepal	Turnover	22,0	23,8
	Export	20,0	22,1
	Import	2,0	1,7
Pakistan	Turnover	124,6	142,0
	Export	76,3	71,4
	Import	48,3	70,6
Saudi Arabia	Turnover	25,5	14,3
	Export	25,5	14,3
	Import	–	–
Singapore	Turnover	117,2	71,4
	Export	49,0	30,6
	Import	68,2	40,8
Syria	Turnover	530,0	511,6
	Export	278,5	210,8
	Import	251,5	300,8
Thailand	Turnover	320,4	141,8
	Export	8,0	8,9
	Import	312,4	132,9
Turkey	Turnover	448,4	248,2
	Export	318,4	152,8
	Import	130,0	95,4
Philippines	Turnover	157,5	93,6
	Export	0,5	13,1
	Import	157,0	80,5
Sri Lanka	Turnover	24,0	21,1
	Export	2,8	3,1
	Import	21,2	18,0

(continued)

Table 5.2 (continued)

		Millions of Rubles	
		1981	1982
Japan	Turnover	3 029,5	3 682,4
	Export	816,8	756,6
	Import	2 212,7	2 925,8
AFRICA			
Algeria	Turnover	197,5	178,5
	Export	113,3	132,4
	Import	84,2	46,1
Angola	Turnover	115,1	64,4
	Export	107,0	61,0
	Import	8,1	3,4
Ivory Coast	Turnover	103,0	70,9
	Export	1,0	1,0
	Import	102,0	69,9
Ghana	Turnover	39,0	37,4
	Export	0,3	0,4
	Import	38,7	37,0
Guinea	Turnover	84,0	43,9
	Export	20,9	15,4
	Import	63,1	28,5
Egypt	Turnover	511,3	520,7
	Export	244,0	218,6
	Import	267,3	302,1
Cameroon	Turnover	22,1	14,0
	Export	3,0	3,3
	Import	19,1	10,7
Congo	Turnover	12,4	12,4
	Export	6,9	8,4
	Import	5,5	4,0
Liberia	Turnover	14,4	15,0
	Export	11,5	14,4
	Import	2,9	0,6
Libya	Turnover	551,1	1 346,9
	Export	189,9	221,1
	Import	361,2	1 125,8
Madagascar	Turnover	10,2	6,1
	Export	2,5	3,8
	Import	7,7	2,3
Morocco	Turnover	261,1	194,7
	Export	126,9	136,1
	Import	134,2	58,6
Mozambique	Turnover	37,0	50,9
	Export	35,7	44,2
	Import	1,3	6,7

(continued)

Table 5.2 (continued)

| | | Millions of Rubles | |
		1981	1982
Nigeria	Turnover	176,4	279,0
	Export	156,9	265,1
	Import	19,5	13,9
Sudan	Turnover	39,5	9,2
	Export	1,4	0,4
	Import	38,1	8,8
Sierre Leone	Turnover	10,3	9,8
	Export	6,8	1,8
	Import	3,5	8,0
Tanzania	Turnover	12,3	10,8
	Export	2,1	3,9
	Import	10,2	6,9
Tunisia	Turnover	15,1	11,2
	Export	12,7	6,1
	Import	2,4	5,1
Ethiopia	Turnover	156,3	195,5
	Export	136,2	182,3
	Import	20,1	13,2
LATIN AMERICA			
Argentina	Turnover	2 402,9	1 292,9
	Export	30,6	27,5
	Import	2 372,3	1 265,4
Bolivia	Turnover	21,5	21,9
	Export	9,8	2,8
	Import	11,7	19,1
Brazil	Turnover	550,2	595,4
	Export	16,3	179,9
	Import	533,9	415,5
Colombia	Turnover	15,4	20,2
	Export	3,3	6,8
	Import	12,1	13,4
Cuba	Turnover	4 807,0	5 840,5
	Export	2 754,5	3 131,4
	Import	2 052,5	2 709,1
Mexico	Turnover	22,7	28,8
	Export	4,0	7,8
	Import	18,7	21,0
Nicaragua	Turnover	10,4	42,5
	Export	4,7	36,6
	Import	5,7	5,9
Panama	Turnover	21,6	8,2
	Export	21,6	8,2
	Import	–	–

(continued)

Table 5.2 (continued)

		Millions of Rubles	
		1981	1982
Peru	Turnover	35,2	25,2
	Export	13,0	14,5
	Import	22,2	10,7
Uraguay	Turnover	51,7	53,2
	Export	1,8	1,0
	Import	49,9	52,2
Equador	Turnover	6,1	7,8
	Export	2,7	1,7
	Import	3,4	6,1

Source: Ministry of Foreign Trade, Foreign Trade of the USSR, Moscow, 1983.

(hence hard currency) customers, the political component remains. Moscow has been willing on occasion to reschedule debt payments, for example, to Peru and Syria.

Based on Arms Control and Disarmament Agency data, the major recipients of Soviet arms (through 1980) in descending order were Libya, Syria, Iraq, India, Ethiopia, Algeria, Peru, PDRY, North Yemen, and Angola. According to the same data, six countries were wholly supplied by the Soviet Union and an additional nine received more than 50 percent of their arms from Moscow. Table 5.3 contains the data on Soviet transfers and recipients. Libya, Syria, Iraq, Algeria, and Angola are known to pay with petrodollars while India, in the aftermath of the invasion of Afghanistan, reportedly received exceptionally concessionary terms for its purchases. Furthermore, the four Middle East countries accounted for 70 percent of all Soviet arms trade in the 1974–1979 period. Thus, from the Soviet perspective, arms sales have become a lucrative hard currency operation.

The USSR's climb to the number two spot in the arms business was facilitated by several features of the arms manufacturing industry in the Soviet Union. First, the USSR built up a huge industrial capacity to handle the Soviet military's conventional force modernization program. Second, because of the standardization of Eastern European and Soviet equipment the Kremlin has at its disposal an even larger base than might be expected. Taken together, this means that the USSR can deliver significant quantities of arms very quickly. Third, the Soviets wisely did not cease producing certain older equipment, making it available for export where less than top-of-the-line equipment would be adequate.[11]

The Soviet Union is a willing and capable supplier, but there are Third World factors that enabled Moscow to become a major purveyor

of arms. On a very general level, many of the newly independent states were armed only with "hand me down" colonial arsenals. The Third World leaders consequently sought to modernize their military establishments by seeking arms from all suppliers. A great deal of effort has often been spent on the military in these Third World states, partly because the army is the sole multiethnic institution and therefore a symbol of national sovereignty and partly because the military is in a position of political power. Moreover, these states were not always able to get weapons from the West or on so favorable terms as the Soviet Union was willing to provide. To complete the picture, one needs also to consider the nature of the openings presented the Soviet Union. As we noted in Chapter 3, many of the Soviet opportunities occurred in the form of armed rivalries in which Moscow provided weapons to one or the other combatant. By offering weapons at reduced cost in time of crisis, the Soviets acquired a list of customers.

For the Third World states, the choice of arms supplier has, in many respects, become a political statement. When Nasir turned to the Soviet Union for military assistance, he was in effect thumbing his nose at the West, which had refused his requests. And the same is true of other countries. Most recently, King Hussein of Jordan publicly announced his willingness to purchase arms from Moscow if the United States were not willing to provide him with the types of weapons he wanted. A look at the list of key Soviet recipients reconfirms this trend. Most of the states are considered radical if not quasi-Marxist. The exceptions are India, a Soviet client although not radical, Tanzania, and Zambia. And both of those are part of the frontline states opposing South African (and by extension U.S.) positions in Southern Africa.

For the Kremlin leadership, arms transfers were a way of accomplishing several goals. The Soviets clearly hoped that the arms could buy them influence or, at the least, a voice in certain foreign policy debates of the recipient states. However, the degree to which that in fact has occurred is open to question. As noted previously, the Soviet expulsion from Egypt, despite the significant levels of Soviet military assistance extended over the years, was a stunning defeat. The investment in the Indonesian military "disappeared" after Sukarno's fall and the Somali expulsion of the Soviets negated the long-term Kremlin effort in arming them and building up their port facilities. However, certain Soviet recipients seem to toe the mark. For example, in the PDRY and Somalia (until 1977) not only did the general outlines of their respective foreign policies coincide, but the Soviets also enjoyed the use of port facilities at Berbera and Aden. In between there is a range of Soviet ability to buy influence or a voice with arms provisions. What is at issue are questions of created dependency: Do the recipients become dependent on the supplier and to what extent? Or conversely, do suppliers become hostages of the recipients?

There is no doubt that to some extent the pipeline of arms from the Soviet Union to the Third World does contribute to a sense of dependence. While there is no direct quid pro quo, for example, for bases, the Soviets seem to exercise a modicum of "leverage"[12] over their recipients. For example, the Soviet Union's Arab clients are dependent on Moscow's willingness to provide arms and, therefore, must maintain good relations with the Kremlin leadership. This potentially dependent relationship may appear in the form of a need for spare parts, or for technicians and advisors to help train the local military in the uses of the equipment. These advisors do not have to be Soviet; in many cases, Cubans and East Germans provide the training.

Arms shipments also create risks for the Soviet Union. The build-up of arms may in fact create a preponderant regional power. Such a power could conceivably pursue expansionist goals based on its military strength. In that eventuality, the Soviets could be dragged behind the recipient into an unwanted regional conflict that could be detrimental to Soviet foreign policy goals. A case in point is the Soviet sales of weapons to Libya. The mercurial Qaddafi is distrusted, and his Islamic unification schemes are perceived by other potential Soviet allies as threatening and Soviet supported.

Consequently, the Soviet Union has faced on more than one occasion requests from recipients for larger shipments of sophisticated weapons that it may not want to fill. Nondelivery of weapons bought or refusal to honor requests for additional matériel at the least creates strains in relations. According to Ismail Fahmy's recent memoirs, Soviet reluctance to honor agreements with Egypt not only contributed to Sadat's decision to expel Soviet advisors in 1972, but also led to his decision to abrogate the friendship and cooperation treaty in 1976, claiming that the Soviets had not abided by the provisions of the treaty (that is, to deliver arms).[13] And in Syria, Soviet-Syrian relations reached a low when the Soviets refused President Assad's request for new and more sophisticated weapons in 1978.

Failure to supply the sought-after weapons may well prompt the disappointed recipient to seek arms elsewhere. This threat clearly represents a diminution of Soviet influence. But that potential for influence is also lessened by the ability of the superrich recipients to pay for their weapons. Algeria, Iraq, and Libya are all able to buy from Western and Soviet sources and have done so on several occasions. Precisely because they do not need concessionary terms from the USSR, they retain their freedom from Soviet leverage. Just as the initial choice of supplier may

Table 5.4   Arms Diversification Trends: Major Identified Arms Agreements

Country	1980-1981		1981-1982		1982-1983	
	East	West	East	West	East	West
Algeria	X		X	X		X
Angola		X				X
Cape Verde						
Congo						X
Ethiopia						
Guinea-Bissau						
Guinea						
Libya	X	X	X	X	X	X
Madagascar						
Mali						
Mozambique						
Nigeria		X		X		X
Somalia		X		X		X
Tanzania		X				
Uganda						
Zambia		X				
Kampuchea						
Laos						
Vietnam						
Cuba						
Peru		X		X		X
Iraq	X	X		X	China	
Syria	X		X		X	
Yemen (Aden)						
Yemen (Sanaa)						
Afghanistan	X					
India	X	X	X	X	X	X
Jordan		X	X			X
Botswana			X			

Source: Information from: International Institute for Strategic Studies, "The Military Balance" (London) 1981-1982, 1982-1983, 1983-1984.

be considered a political statement, so too may be the decision to diversify. (See Table 5.4.)

   While the focus of our discussions is Soviet policy instruments, we would be remiss not to include other communist bloc aid to the Third World, particularly in the military sphere. According to all available data, the Eastern Europeans contribute in a modest but significant way to the Soviet effort in the Third World. In the early years, Czechoslovakia played the role of Soviet front. This was true in all three of the first Soviet arms shipments to the Third World—to Israel, Guatemala, and Egypt. In the current period, East Germany has replaced Prague as the major Eastern European actor in the Third World.

   The East Germans, in the early years of their activity in the Third World, were concerned primarily with establishing their own political recognition through formal diplomatic ties. They assertively sought out relations with a variety of Third World states and by 1970 established contacts with Congo-Brazzaville, Somalia, Algeria, Central African Republic, and ties with the Southern African liberation movements, PAICG, FRELIMO, and the MPLA. The most significant German role appears to be in the form of security training for Third World regimes. Not only are Germans engaged in training local security forces, but they are also known to be the palace guard for Mengistu, Machel, and Ismail in the PDRY. Keeping those leaders in power is clearly in the Soviet interest.

The other major non-Soviet communist actor in the Third World is clearly Cuba. Much has been written about Cuba's role in Africa, with scholars disagreeing on the nature of the Soviet-Cuban relationship. Whether surrogate, proxy, or "international paladin,"[14] there can be no doubt that the Cubans have performed and continue to provide a vital service for the Soviet Union. As noted in Chapter 4, Cuban desires to be Third World revolutionary leader brought Havana into conflict with Moscow in the early sixties. Cubans made their appearance in Africa at about the same time. In 1963, Cuban troops assisted the Ben Bella regime in Algeria in a short-lived border war with Morocco, and in 1964–1965 Ernesto "Che" Guevara toured Africa. PAIGC guerrillas were apparently trained by Cubans in camps in Guinea in the sixties, and in the seventies Cubans stationed in the PDRY assisted Dhofari rebels. During the 1973 Middle East war, Cuban troops fought with the Syrians on the Golan Heights, and after 1975 they trained Zimbabwe fighters in Mozambique. By the mid-seventies, Castro's "Third Worldism" aided the Kremlin in several ways. As a leading spokesman for the Nonaligned Movement, Castro was able to persuade the organization to adopt many pro-Soviet stands (until the invasion of Afghanistan). Cuban ties with African national liberation movements, especially the Angolan MPLA, facilitated Moscow's successes in Angola. Although many Latin Americanists argue that Cuba maintains an independent foreign policy, a careful analysis of Cuban involvement in Angola and Ethiopia clearly shows that the USSR and Cuba have worked in tandem. Cuba could not have responded to Agostinho Neto's request for aid during the civil war of 1975–1976 without Soviet logistical and transport support. The evidence of cooperation between Moscow and Havana is even more striking in Ethiopia. There, Cuban troops operated under direct Soviet control.

Sending Cuban rather than Eastern European or Soviet troops deflected some of the international criticism directed at Moscow in the aftermath of the USSR's African adventures. Furthermore, the use of Cuban troops in Angola was a stroke of genius. Largely comprised of blacks and mulattoes, the Cuban troops possessed a linguistic affinity and as another Third World state could not be labeled imperialist. As of early 1984, Cuban troops are continuing their withdrawal from Ethiopia, but are still in Angola. As the situation there remains precarious, high-level consultations among Soviet, Cuban, and Angola officials are taking place in Moscow, thus indicating continuing coordination of policies between Cuba and the USSR.

In sum, arms transfers are an attractive foreign policy tool that the Soviets seem willing and able to use. The distribution of Soviet equipment and the increasing numbers of Soviet military advisors add to the sense of Moscow's presence in the Third World. But presence, as the Soviets have learned, does not necessarily translate into influence. Conflicts may create the need for arms, but there is a limit as to how much any one recipient nation can absorb. Will the arms be used? Will they rust in the field? Will the military establishments employ the arms, not against external enemies or even domestic dissidents, but to seize power? The Soviets are beginning to recognize the limitations on arms transfers, particularly with regard to the last question posed above. They are increasingly concerned over the possibility of reactionary military coups staged with Soviet weapons against so-called progressive regimes and are urging local elites to purge the ranks of the military and to put in place extensive educational and mobilizing institutions—on the line of those in the Soviet military. It would seem, nonetheless, that as long as there are persistent and endemic conflicts between Third World states, arms are a necessity.

DIPLOMACY

Proffering economic aid and agreeing to sell arms, whether at concessionary rates or for hard currency, are but part of the network of relations the USSR has constructed with the Third World. They complement the active diplomacy of the Soviet Union. The Kremlin leadership seems to conduct its diplomacy with a peculiarly Soviet style and that diplomacy, itself, is multifaceted. It includes state-to-state relations, CPSU ties with ruling progressive and socialist-oriented parties, activities in international arenas, and the signing of friendship and cooperation treaties.

The style of Soviet diplomacy is significantly different from that of other nations. On a general level, Soviet diplomacy has been variously described as shrewd, deliberate, and masterly. Of course, it has not always been gracious. The image of Khrushchev banging his shoe at the UN remains. And many Third World dignitaries report that Brezhnev would explode with rage and lecture them about international issues and bilateral relations.

At a minimum, the Soviets use diplomacy to demonstrate at least some commonality of views in all their relations. Through communiqués, joint statements, and formal agreements, an impression is created of shared values and goals. The impression of common outlook and common commitment to peaceful coexistence and to the avoidance of nuclear war represents an achievement, at least of a negative sort. That is, such statements erode ideas that the Soviet Union is a disruptive or hostile force and help to create a climate in which friendly relations and close ties may be appropriate.

The joint communiqués are also useful for us as students of Soviet international behavior. Frequently what is absent is more significant than what is contained in the statements. The listing of common views implies priorities. And the by now routinized press descriptions of high-level meetings give us further clues to the state of relations. "Frank" discussions usually imply major disagreements while "friendly atmosphere" connotes good relations.

As an adjunct of direct diplomacy, Moscow seeks to popularize Soviet positions and common views by providing cheap propagandistic literature as well as more scholarly works to many Third World countries. According to recent statistics, the Soviets publish material in sixty-eight languages. Some are written specifically for export, and others are translations of Russian materials. These include obviously propagandistic pamphlets and translations of journals such as *New Times*—a major Soviet news weekly. An example of the importance Moscow attaches to these publications as tools of foreign policy may be seen in the availability of the journal *Latinskaia Amerika,* published by the Academy of Sciences. The Spanish language version appears regularly and (as with the Soviet version) contains at least one article in each issue written by a representative of one of the twenty-three Latin American communist parties.[15] Table 5.5 provides the latest available data on Soviet publications in non-Soviet languages.

The Soviet leadership conducts its diplomacy both in international forums and bilaterally. We have already discussed Soviet policy toward regional international governmental organizations and toward the Non-aligned Movement, but mention must be made of Soviet activities at the United Nations. It seems clear that the Soviets accord much more importance to the United Nations than do the United States or other Western countries. The UN has provided the arena for much of the assiduous cultivation of Third World states. In their efforts to promote common interests, the Soviets could point with pride to their support of all the UN declarations on decolonization and on economic rights.

160

Table 5.5   Soviet Books and Brochures in Foreign Languages, 1982

LANGUAGE	BOOKS	COPIES (Thousands)
Albanian	2	3.2
English	1,191	24,308.7
Arabic	121	893.2
Afghan	34	285.6
Amharic	11	93.3
Bulgarian	29	833.8
Hungarian	74	1,304.4
Vietnamese	34	843.3
Dutch	14	73.7
Greek	7	196.3
Danish	18	92.1
In languages of the people of India	272	2,262.3
Indonesian	2	6.9
Spanish	391	11,636.3
Italian	55	400.0
Chinese	13	46.5
Korean	10	42.6
Khmer	11	193.6
Laotian	15	114.4
Latin	22	326.1
Macedonian	3	15.0
Malgash	3	13.6
Mongolian	20	201.4
German	445	10,956.6
Nepalese	10	30.5
Norwegian	15	86.2
Persian	34	294.1
Polish	86	2,744.1
Portuguese	109	1,250.8
Romanian	23	619.5
Serbo-Croatian	25	272.1
Singhalese	14	245.1
Slovak	25	353.5
Slovenian	1	5.0
Swahili	15	80.8
Turkish	3	190.8
Finnish	66	403.3
French	463	6,645.2
Czech	30	748.2
Swedish	20	191.8
Japanese	13	59.2
Esperanto	1	3.0
Other	29	373.7

Source: Pechat' v SSSR (Moscow: iz. Financy i Statistiki, 1983).

Over the years, the Soviets have voted increasingly with the majority of Third World states, while the United States has found itself on the receiving end of many of those resolutions. Despite this use of the United Nations to promote Soviet and Third World interests, the Soviets devote even more attention to their bilateral relations with each of the Third World states.

The USSR prides itself on the number of states with which it has diplomatic relations. These relations, in the Soviet view, symbolize its acceptance as a superpower. Formal relations, no matter how cool, are touted; the Soviets claim that they seek no advantage—only to maintain disinterested ties world-wide. Currently, the USSR maintains diplomatic relations with ninety-two Third World countries. Of course, these vary from close relations with the socialist-oriented states to less than cordial relations with others. For a number of years, there was no Soviet ambassador in Egypt. The current number represents a marked increase due to additional states having gained independence since the sixties and to an extensive and intensive diplomatic offensive. For example, Soviet representation in Latin America has grown from four countries in the late fifties to nineteen as of 1983. Six were added only since 1970. There are in Latin America several countries that do not maintain diplomatic ties to Moscow: These include El Salvador, Honduras, Chile (since 1973), Haiti, and Paraguay.

Moscow has been successful in Africa. The two countries with which the Soviet Union does not enjoy diplomatic relations are the Ivory Coast and South Africa. The Asian picture is almost as complete. Bhutan does not maintain relations with the USSR, but the major (and logical) exception is South Korea. The Middle East presents a very different picture. Even though the region has been the arena for so much Soviet involvement, the list of Middle Eastern states with state-to-state relations with Moscow displays significant gaps. First, the USSR broke diplomatic relations with Israel in the aftermath of the 1967 Six Day War and has never restored ties. The lack of formal contact has become a liability since then, because without ties to Israel, the USSR can never assume the Middle East peacemaking role it seems so ardently to desire. Second, in the Gulf area, a number of countries do not maintain relations with the Soviet Union. Saudi Arabia is clearly the most significant and important regional power among these, and the Soviets have long sought to rectify this situation. Among the others are Oman and the United Arab Emirates.

This marked proliferation of normal state-to-state relations is complemented by the interconnected relations between the CPSU and ruling progressive parties. In the Soviet view, party relations exist on a higher plane than state/governmental ties. They represent not only recognition, but also ideological affinity. Relations on the party level facilitate numerous exchanges of delegations, such as of youth organizations (affiliated with the parties), party workers, and the like. Party ties permit the Soviet Union an additional channel in which to stress relations. For example, the delegates of certain ruling parties have been invited to address the congresses of the CPSU. This is a way for Moscow to emphasize its close ties to these states and to continue the cultivation process.

State/governmental international relations do not preclude Soviet ties with local communist parties. The problems attendant upon Moscow's connections to local communist organizations were discussed in the preceding chapter. In the context of our analysis of tools we must note that in many countries the USSR pursues a double-, if not triple-, track approach. In addition to frequently close governmental ties and even party relations, the CPSU deals with local communist organs. According to a recent survey there are 60 nonruling communist parties in Third World countries. These vary in size and role. Some have a membership of only 100 or fewer while others claim membership of more than 20,000. Among the largest Third World communist parties are Argentina's (estimated 65,000), Mexico's (with around 200,000) and India's two organizations (one pro-Moscow and one pro-Beijing: together some 700,000).[16] Although these communist parties have been buffeted by the Sino-Soviet rift, splintered, and repressed, they do continue to exist. Some are legal participants in the respective governmental and electoral processes and others are proscribed, if not outlawed. And despite the handicaps they may offer, they do present to Moscow a potential policy instrument. Of course, not all parties are docile tools. Pro-Beijing factions are hardly likely to cooperate with Moscow, and their very existence may complicate Soviet relations with the ruling government and parties. The two- or three-track policy means that Moscow can hedge its bets. It can deal closely and profitably with regimes in power, even with ruling progressive parties, as well as with opposition forces.

In addition to seeking party ties with a number of progressive Third World states, Moscow has also sought to formalize relations with a chosen group of states through friendship and cooperation treaties. This type of treaty, as distinct from specific cooperative agreements, seems designed to regularize contacts between Moscow and the contracting party and to promote long-term close cooperation. The first such treaty was signed with Egypt in June 1971 and was followed in August of that year by one with India. Since then, Moscow signed similar treaties with Iraq (1972), Somalia (1974), Angola (1976), Mozambique (1977), Vietnam, Ethiopia, and Afghanistan (1978), the PDRY (1979), Syria (1980), and the Congo (1981).

These friendship and cooperation treaties were signed with diverse states in a variety of circumstances. Egypt, at the time of the signing, represented a major Soviet bridgehead into the Middle East. Indeed, precisely because the Kremlin was less sure of Sadat than of his predecessor, the treaty should have been seen as a means to consolidate relations and, perhaps from Moscow's perspective, to prevent their deterioration. The agreement with India was apparently sought by the New Delhi government; it was signed as the situation in East Pakistan deteriorated and may have been viewed as a guarantee of Soviet support during the impending war. For their part, the Soviet leadership hoped to ensure that the USSR would be consulted before Soviet matériel was used in that war. The treaties with Iraq and Somalia served to secure footholds at opposite ends of the vital Middle East area. The Iraqi treaty was signed amidst serious disagreements, but was designed to secure the strategic relationship despite the policy disputes. The agreement with Somalia not only reinforced the political relationship, but also consolidated the Soviet military commitment (especially in light of the construction at Berbera). The treaties with Angola and Mozambique formalized the preexisting Soviet commitment to the MPLA and were an expression of the new Soviet presence in Southern Africa. The Ethiopian accords were intended to regularize the patron-client relationship especially in light of the extensive Soviet-Cuban commitment. It also signified the Soviet switch on the Horn from Somalia to Ethiopia.

Moscow's treaty ties to Vietnam seem to be of a different order. With their large military and economic commitment to Vietnam, the Soviets sought to formalize fraternal relations and to ensure Vietnam's anti-Chinese orientation. The agreement with Afghanistan is similar to that with Vietnam in that it was signed with fellow Marxist-Leninists. Afghanistan's location on the Soviet border, Moscow hoped, would ensure the loyalty of the new radical state. The treaties with the PDRY and Syria, although both Middle Eastern countries, were signed under circumstances very different from each other. The Kremlin signed the treaty with the PDRY following a coup in which a pro-Soviet leader was brought to power (perhaps with Moscow's help). Having risked the attenuation of ties with the PDRY, the Soviets obviously hoped to retain their relations with this Gulf state. Syria was a reluctant treaty partner. Although Moscow had been pushing for a treaty for several years, closer ties were increasingly important following the loss of Egypt. Ironically, it was Assad who, for a variety of domestic and regional reasons, at the time needed the treaty with Moscow. Finally, the Congo is somewhat of an anomaly. Although it has signficant economic ties with the West, Brazzaville permitted the stationing of a Cuban garrison as an early-staging area for the Angolan operation. The language of the treaty implies that Moscow wanted to ensure similar Congolese cooperation in the future.

A comparison of the texts of the treaties reveals both some interesting similarities and some striking differences. Each document contains a preamble outlining the signatories' common views on certain international issues, for example, anti-imperialism, reductions in international tension, and peaceful coexistence. There are of course some specific variations in that the treaties with Arab countries refer to anti-Zionism and those with sub-Saharan African countries, apartheid and racism. The agreements with Vietnam and India are implicitly concerned with the Chinese threat. The treaties all contain promises to expand "friendly cooperation" in the fields of economic, technical, and cultural affairs and to institute consultations on all international issues of significance to the parties. These routinized phrases clearly represent an attempt to coordinate positions on international and regional issues. For a nonroutine occurrence, the treaties state: "In the event of any situation arising that may create a danger to peace or disturb peace, the High Contracting Parties shall immediately establish contact with each other in order to coordinate their positions in the interests of removing the danger or restoring peace." The means by which the threat would be eliminated are not specified, but some sort of Soviet commitment seems implicit.

Most of the treaties also include articles dealing with military cooperation between the USSR and the Third World ally. The standard article reads: "In the interest of strengthening the defense capabilities of the High Contracting Parties, they will continue to develop cooperation in the military field on the basis of agreements concluded between them." However, there are exceptions to this: Military measures are treated distinctively in the agreements with Egypt, India, Vietnam, and the Congo. The treaty with Egypt went beyond the general clause on military cooperation to identify two specific areas of military assistance: personnel training and strengthening offensive and defensive capabilities. The Indian treaty lacks the general clause. Instead, several references imply a Soviet pledge not to aid Pakistan against India, as well as an Indian pledge not to side with China against the USSR. A mutual nonaggression clause adds a commitment for consultations in the event either is attacked.

The USSR-Vietnam treaty uses completely different language. In this case the pledge is for "fraternal assistance" and socialist unity. The agreement contains a commitment to mutual consultations in case either party is attacked—an obvious reference to China's hostile posture toward Vietnam. The accord with the People's Republic of the Congo lacks the general reference to defensive capabilities. However, it does say that both will cooperate in support of independence struggles.

Although intended as a tool of institutionalization of relations, in many instances these mutual commitments have proved largely rhetorical. Both Egypt and Somalia abrogated their treaties (in 1976 and 1977, respectively) when the interests of each and Moscow proved incongruent. Mozambique, despite its treaty, has endured attacks from South African–backed rebels and South Africa itself and recently concluded a non-aggression pact with Pretoria. Iraq specifically complained bitterly that the USSR had not lived up to its treaty obligations when Moscow withheld spare parts in the fall of 1980. The Soviets also seem wary of any additional commitments. No new treaties have been signed since 1981, and talk of one with Libya was allowed to die quietly.

In a search for the "right approach" to Third World states, the Soviets have utilized economic aid, trade, military aid, diplomacy, and friendship and cooperation treaties. Each of these tools has worked well on occasion but has failed in other instances. As a result, the Soviets have attempted to apply a variety of policy blends. As Soviet bilateral relations with the Third World states continue to evolve, we may expect to see continued adaptation and perhaps even some experimentation with these tools.

NOTES

1. U.S. Department of State, *Soviet and East European Aid to the Third World, 1981,* (February 1983), p. 4.

2. C.I.A. Foreign Assessment Center, *Communist Aid Activities in Non-Communist Less Developed Countries, 1979, and 1954–1979,* ER80-10318U (October 1980), p. 7.

3. Ibid.

4. Ibid., p. 8.

5. Moscow in Arabic, March 9, 1978, *Foreign Broadcast Information Service,* 78-48 (March 10, 1978), p. F4.

6. C.I.A., *Communist Aid Activities,* p. 7.

7. U.S. Department of State, *Soviet and East European Aid,* p. 6.

8. C.I.A., *Communist Aid Activities,* p. 41.

9. Cole Blasier, *The Giant's Rival, The USSR and Latin America* (Pittsburgh: University of Pittsburgh Press, 1983), p. 51.

10. C.I.A., *Communist Aid Activities,* p. 5.

11. U.S. Department of State, *Conventional Arms Transfers in the Third World, 1972–1981,* Special Report 102 (August 1982), p. 8.

12. Bruce E. Arlinghaus defines leverage as the creation of influence for later use. See his "Linkage and Leverage in African Arms Transfers," in his *Arms for Africa* (Lexington, Mass.: Lexington Books, 1983), pp. 3–17.

13. See the details of Sadat's relations with Brezhnev in Ismail Fahmy, *Negotiating for Peace in the Middle East* (Baltimore: Johns Hopkins University Press, 1983) especially Chapters 7 and 8, pp. 123–152.

14. Edward Gonzalez uses the term "paladin" because he argues that Cuba pursues its own objectives within the parameters of Soviet interests. See, for example, his "Cuba, The Soviet Union and Africa," in David Albright, ed., *Communism in Africa* (Bloomington: Indiana University Press, 1980), pp. 145–167.

15. Morris Rothenberg, "Latin America in Soviet Eyes," *Problems of Communism*, vol. 32 (September-October 1983), p. 15.

16. Robert Wesson, "Checklist of Communist Parties, 1982," *Problems of Communism*, vol. 32 (March-April 1983), pp. 94–102.

Chapter Six

Accounting for Soviet Behavior

Accounting for Soviet–Third World relations is a task that raises many questions about the nature of the Soviet state and the process by which its foreign policy is made. But it is also a task that in a general way resembles all efforts to explain state behavior. One must decide what is meant by foreign policy and what factors or forces are most likely to affect it. Different assumptions about the answers to these questions frequently lead to quite different explanations for a state's behavior.

One of the most difficult problems in evaluating explanations of Soviet foreign policy is the possibility that many of them reflect and confirm prior assumptions about the nature of the Soviet state. For those who assume that the Soviet Union is by nature expansionist and combative, all Soviet behavior can be interpreted as confirming these characteristics. Assertiveness is taken as aggressiveness, and caution can be explained as tactical accommodation. In contrast, for those who assume the Soviet Union operates from a position of weakness, the same behavior can have an opposite explanation: Caution is accepted as the norm, and assertiveness is defensive and responsive to perceived threats. Evidence abounds on both sides of almost every argument of this kind. For those to whom the Soviets are clever diplomats, every move can be seen as part of a plot; for those who see the Soviets as clumsy, a long list of gaffes can establish their ineptitude. This chapter, in its review of the factors that may account for Soviet behavior, will attempt to avoid some of these more obvious pitfalls. We will suggest both general and specific explanations incorporating a broad spectrum of possibilities.

The term "foreign policy" itself suggests choice. Indeed, one of the most familiar approaches assumes that foreign policy reflects conscious design or strategy—that is, the purposeful pursuit of objectives. If one believes that there is purpose behind action, then one can, by reasoning backwards, establish motive. This approach is especially attractive in the case of the USSR, a state that explicitly describes itself as dedicated to the triumph of the socialist cause and regularly assesses its progress toward this end. The combative rhetoric of Marxism-Leninism and the image it projects of an international political system engaged in a life-or-death struggle with the forces of reaction provide a framework within which every Soviet action is alleged to make "scientific" sense. In practice, it is up to the observer to sort through actions and statements to decide which particular goals, values, or preferences make sense out of a state's behavior. This can be exceedingly difficult, since the USSR is a major international power, interacting simultaneously with many other actors on many levels. Moreover, it is impossible to prove conclusively that any particular objective actually inspired or accounts for any Soviet action.

Nevertheless, one need not assume that all Soviet foreign policy is necessarily coherent or carefully planned. Assumptions of purposiveness are less attractive for those who believe that foreign policy reflects incremental adaptations to initiatives and responses in the field. On a short-term basis, or from a local perspective, it is usually much harder to see patterns. Studies of Soviet relations with particular countries or in particular regions often emphasize the reactive nature of Soviet behavior and the limits set by local circumstances. Moreover, once certain actions have been taken, these can inhibit or predetermine the kinds of policies subsequently pursued. Goals themselves may derive from actual experiences in attempting to manage relationships with other countries.

Foreign policy may also represent the outcome of factional or bureaucratic strife within governments. This entails focusing on decision-making bodies as well as on the actors themselves. We can look as well at the process by which individuals may guide or direct Soviet foreign policy—even if this has to be largely a speculative overview. A focus on actors permits attention to a variety of influences on choice and behavior, including values, perceptions, needs, priorities, and resources. The specific environmental context of action is also important. Perceptions of the situation and available options, as well as expectations about other actors and their probable responses must be included. Makers of foreign policy can be assumed to be sensitive to calculations of possible risks, prospects for success, and considerations about the effects of foreign policy on the USSR's image and credibility.

It is possible, then, to explain any given instance of Soviet foreign policy behavior in a number of ways, each of which can appear valid. The same action could be explained as part of a grand strategy for world conquest, a logical response to U.S. policy, a victory of Soviet "hawks," an action required by alliance commitments, a Marxist-Leninist impulse, a clever attempt to maximize influence, a reluctant response to the demands of a client regime, or a lucky blunder. In reality, none of these approaches is mutually exclusive. Foreign policy is undoubtedly a product of multiple causes. A thorough job of accounting for Soviet–Third World relations should ideally be sensitive to this complexity, and attempt to be comprehensive. In what follows, we will identify Soviet goals and preferences, insofar as they may be inferred from the USSR's behavior in the Third World. We will also consider the ways in which the dynamics of domestic and international politics may interact with these preferences to affect Soviet state behavior.

OBJECTIVES

Discerning purpose in Soviet–Third World relations is a matter of emphasis and perspective. It is possible to discuss Soviet objectives in a number of ways. The record we have examined does not permit generalizations about the importance of specific Soviet activities in the Third World relative to activities elsewhere. Nor can we be certain of overall Soviet foreign policy goals. However, several conclusions about the apparent aims of Soviet–Third World relations, about Soviet role conceptions, geopolitical concerns, and political preoccupations can be drawn.

Reflection upon the record of Soviet activity in the Third World suggests that status and image considerations may have a powerful influence. That is, in a general sense, Soviet behavior reflects the character of the Soviet political system and its leaders' conceptions of their appropriate international role. These conceptions blend Marxist-Leninist values with changing perceptions of the international political balance and increased Soviet capabilities.

As we have seen in Chapter 1, Soviet ideology stresses common interests of the Soviet Union and the states of the Third World. The effort to make common cause with Third World countries against a mutual enemy may be considered a congenial imperative of the Soviet belief system. The very appearance of the new states, their aspirations toward socialism, their attempts to assert their independence and autonomy, and their efforts to develop their economies are welcomed as contributing to human progress. In this scenario, the Soviets present themselves as a kind of global guardian angel, indirectly responsible for the independence of these states, and motivated by altruism and high principle. In 1963, Khrushchev described the Soviet attitude toward the Third World in glowing terms:

> In respect to the liberated countries, the Soviet Union and other
> socialist countries do not pursue any aims contrary to the interests

of the peoples of those countries. We do not seek any advantage for
ourselves. We have no bases on the territories of the liberated
countries and do not want any. Unlike the imperialists, we do not
seek to draw those countires into military blocs. A striving to
enslave or exploit other peoples is alien to the socialist states, by the
very nature of their social system.[1]

Brezhnev made a very similar statement in 1976 at the Twenty-Fifth
Communist Party Congress. He declared that the Soviet Union would
not interfere in the internal affairs of other countries, despite its bias
in favor of progressive forces: "Our Party supports and will continue
to support peoples who are fighting for their freedom. In doing so, the
Soviet Union seeks no advantages for itself, is not hunting for concessions,
does not seek political domination, does not ask for military bases. We
act as we are bidden by our revolutionary conscience and our communist
convictions."[2] This heroic role combines a Marxist-Leninist analysis of
world politics with Soviet superpower ambitions: The USSR becomes
supersocialist, a kind of global Robin Hood. In this role the USSR has
offered its services as protector of the weak, ally in local struggles, and
United Nations cheerleader. It has practiced gunboat diplomacy and
become major armorer to the Third World. To the extent that cooperating
with Third World states promotes increased independence and reduction
of Western influence, such activities can nicely benefit both ideological
and national security concerns. But this proclaimed selflessness must be
matched against the record of Soviet pursuit of political advantage. The
tenacity with which the USSR has attempted to serve its own interests
in its Third World relations suggests that the heroic role is a pose.

Since the Bolshevik Revolution in 1917, the Soviet party has served
as guide and mentor to generations of revolutionaries, and the USSR
has assumed the role of patron and protector of communist political
groups around the world. But the role of political champion of challengers
of the West sometimes comes into conflict with the role of revolutionary
headquarters. The Soviets have been sensitive to the situation of Third
World communists, and have sometimes attempted to secure better
treatment for them. However, the USSR has generally been willing to
overlook the plight of local communists in favor of correct relations
with ruling groups and has recommended communist tactics that would
not unduly offend sitting governments. Exceptions appear in the case
of some clearly anti-Soviet regimes such as that of Augusto Pinochet
in Chile, or José Napoleón Duarte in El Salvador. Moreover, the USSR
has abandoned support of liberation groups when this conflicted with
ties with existing governments. Examples include the Eritreans, Kurds,
and Pushtus.

Despite their willingness, on occasion, to abandon local communist parties, the Soviets are extremely interested in maintaining their ideological authority over international communism. The Third World has been the setting for two challenges to Soviet authority: one from the Cubans, and one from the Chinese. Polemics and heated debate with both of these ideological adversaries have affected Soviet policy in a number of countries. It is quite clear that in the sixties the Soviets regarded Castro's plans to foment rural guerrilla struggle to be at odds with their own attempts to improve their diplomatic and commercial relationships with Latin American countries. The Soviets also resented the fact that in South America the Cubans sponsored groups that challenged established, pro-Soviet communist parties. The Soviets worked hard to obtain ideological control over Castro and to safeguard their own authority over revolutionary movements in Latin America.

The Chinese communists presented Soviet authority a direct challenge that proved more difficult to manage. In the public polemics of the sixties, the Chinese charged that the USSR was not truly revolutionary but had itself become an imperial power. The Soviets vehemently denied this and argued that the Chinese were attempting to separate the Third World countries from their natural allies. In 1964 the Chinese began to split the international movement by setting up pro-Chinese communist parties in Third World countries. The Soviets reacted vigorously by attacking Maoist ideas as "adventurist" and damaging to socialist prospects. In several instances Soviet relations were affected by the activities of pro-Beijing communist parties. In Indonesia, the PKI adopted a Maoist posture with the apparent approval of Sukarno, a recipient of considerable Soviet aid. The USSR kept discreetly distant from the Indonesian communists' attempted coup in 1965 but was never able to establish really good relations with the successor military government. The Chinese affiliations of the Khmer Rouge in Kampuchea no doubt encouraged the Soviet official stance in favor of a neutral regime during international negotiations about Indochina in 1961 and 1962. Maoism has been a persistent phenomenon in the Indian communist movement, where a breakaway pro-Chinese party has complicated the electoral position of the dominant Moscow-oriented group. The Communist Party of India has sometimes been embarrassed by its reluctance to criticize its own government, which is generally pro-Soviet in its foreign policy, but often highly authoritarian in its domestic policy.

Competition with the Chinese for the loyalties of ruling groups and movements is a factor that has also affected Soviet behavior. In 1964 and 1965, the USSR tried hard to win support among Third World states for an invitation to the second Afro-Asian conference in Algiers— an invitation the Chinese energetically opposed. Soviets have also lobbied for adoption of their own formulations over those of the Chinese at meetings and conferences such as the Tricontinental Conference in Havana in 1969 and conferences of the Nonaligned Movement. Soviet scholars and ideologues have frequently needed to address serious Chinese criticism of their behavior: for example, for the Cuban missile crisis, their policy of détente, and arms control agreements with the United States.

At several points, Soviet actions have responded to Chinese presence or activity. In fact, Moscow's involvement in the Third World has sometimes appeared designed to offset potential Chinese gains and to rebuff China as a rival champion of national liberation causes. Soviet efforts to improve their relations with Pakistan in 1968 and to consolidate their alliance with Vietnam during its war with the United States were at least partly a response to Chinese ties with Pakistan and Vietnam. Maneuvers in Southeast Asia in the late seventies, when Soviet-backed Vietnam challenged China's position in the region, reflect the continuation of this Sino-Soviet competition. Although support for Vietnamese control of Indochina has many drawbacks, it would appear the Soviets feel compelled to maintain this alliance in order to contain China. In Africa, the Soviets found themselves in competition for influence with the Chinese among the liberation movements in Angola (where they backed the winner), and in Zimbabwe (where the Soviet-supported candidate group lost). Aid policies and programs in East Africa seem to be sensitive to comparisons with the terms of Chinese assistance projects in that region. More recently, the Soviets have charged Beijing with attempting to expand its influence in the Gulf, and Moscow has reacted to this apparent challenge by stepping up its own involvement in the area. An African tour by the Chinese premier in 1982–1983 drew cynical Soviet commentary.

The net effect of Chinese ideological criticism has probably been to fortify the Soviet preference for a moderate and evolutionary tactical posture. The Soviets insist that their policy of support for noncommunist radicals and anti-American regimes is more truly Leninist and more likely to produce positive political results in the long run. The Soviets have become much less defensive about this role for several reasons. On the one hand, the Chinese no longer present an active leftist challenge; instead, the Chinese themselves can be criticized for their "active collaboration" with the United States. On the other hand, the emergence of Marxist-Leninist radicals in a number of Third World countries has provided client states that permit the USSR to demonstrate its revolutionary character and associations. At the same time, Soviet doctrine has come to represent a more patient world outlook in which considerable weight is given to the presence and activity of the USSR as a global power, with less concern about challenges to the validity of its revolutionary credentials.

While it remains difficult to be precise about the impact of role conceptions on Soviet–Third World relations, it does seem fair to say that the Soviets have been constrained by overall considerations about the propriety of their own behavior and that role conceptions have changed to adjust to Third World realities.

Many students of Soviet foreign policy begin with the premise that all states are subject to similar pressures created by the semianarchical nature of the international system. It thus seems axiomatic for the Soviet Union to be involved in the competition for security and influence, which is understood to be the essence of world politics. From this standpoint, the basic revolutionary ideology that may incline the USSR toward a challenging orientation is not necessarily central. It can be argued that most of the USSR's actions can be understood as efforts to secure its position in a competitive environment. Thus the Third World can be seen as an area of political fluidity and changing alignments that became a logical object of Soviet attention.

The overall pattern of Soviet–Third World relations suggests that they have been guided by geopolitical considerations. These include efforts to deny access or position to potential adversaries, to improve their own position and capabilities relative to such adversaries, or to acquire clients and allies. Geopolitical or strategic concerns are reflected, for instance, in the importance attached to good relations with neighboring states, such as Iran and Afghanistan. Despite all the attention that has been accorded Soviet relations with radical nationalists or prominent neutralists in the Third World, the most enduring Soviet investments have been in neighboring states. And until the 1978 coup in Afghanistan, Soviet relationships with nearby countries have stressed stability and neutrality, cemented by "neighborly" aid, assistance, and commercial exchange.

Attention to the strategic value of relations with Third World countries can be understood as the reason for the rapid development of Soviet ties with the PDRY, the Cuban-Soviet intervention in Angola, Soviet interest in the Horn of Africa, and the invasion of Afghanistan. In the PDRY, Somalia, and later in Ethiopia, the Soviets have spent large sums of money developing port facilities and naval installations to accommodate their fleet. Indeed, in its relations with African states, the Kremlin has followed the traditional dictates of the pursuit of safe harbors, supply depots, refueling stops for ships and aircraft, overflight rights, and semipermanent bases. Such access rights enhance its capability to assist or participate in local conflicts.

The concern for strategic positioning has paralleled the growth of Soviet naval strength. The increased presence and patrol activity of the Soviet navy is an aspect of Soviet–Third World behavior most troublesome to Western analysts. Some argue that this reflects a long-term interest in open sea lanes. Others fear that the Soviet presence in places such as Ethiopia and the PDRY may be part of a general plan to acquire the potential to interdict military and nonmilitary traffic. The USSR has persistently requested calling privileges in the ports of friendly Middle Eastern and African regimes, including Algeria, Syria, Iraq, Egypt, Guinea, Ethiopia, Mozambique, and Angola. In a related vein, the intensity of Soviet interest in concluding fisheries agreements and acquiring calling rights for its trawlers wherever possible has been regarded by some as ominous, in view of the familiar Soviet use of its fishing vessels for espionage purposes. The regime now in power in Vietnam began as an embattled liberation movement, eager for Soviet aid. Now Vietnam is an important potential proxy in Southeast Asia, and a base for Soviet naval operations in the region.

Judging from the record of Soviet policy in the Third World, it seems clear that Moscow has consistently sought to challenge the West and to counter Western influence. Praise for defiance of Western military plans and for removal of foreign military bases was an important aspect of initial postwar Soviet enthusiasm for Third World nationalism, and continues to be a prominent reason for Soviet attention to a particular state or political movement.

India was an early object of Soviet attention, and good relations were cemented by a willingness to offer aid projects on terms unavailable from Western countries and by shipments of military goods to support India against Pakistan and China. Thus the Soviets preempted U.S. efforts to win India as an ally and secured friendship with the dominant power in South Asia. Similar efforts during the Khrushchev era to establish a lasting military assistance relationship with the Indonesian government in Southeast Asia were successful for a time but came to naught with Sukarno's fall in 1965. The Middle East has been an important center of Soviet activity for nearly forty years. Not only have Soviet activities had the effect of reducing the Western presence and installing the USSR as major arms supplier to Israel's antagonists, but they have also enhanced perceptions of the necessity for Soviet involvement in any settlement of the region's problems.

This policy of making friends with important regional powers and establishing footholds in new regions also applies to Southern Africa. Soviet efforts to install themselves as suppliers and supporters of the liberation movement in Angola were successful in helping to establish a pro-Soviet, Marxist-Leninist government there. The USSR was not able to displace Western powers or become recognized as a major actor in the diplomatic process surrounding the independence of Zimbabwe or in Namibia, although efforts to that end continued within limits. By 1984 it could be argued that the Soviets have opted not to become involved in major military challenges to the South Africans, at least for the time being.

In many cases, the acceptance of Soviet military aid was the foundation for a much fuller relationship; in other cases, this was not possible. Many of the military supply relationships were obviously intended to outflank the West and undermine plans for military security pacts. At a minimum, all of them had the effect of reducing dependence on Western states. Offers of arms to Israel, Guatemala, Egypt, Syria, and Iraq were among the first friendly overtures to the new states. They were all designed to encourage opponents of Western policies to enlarge their freedom of action by diversifying arms suppliers. Offers of assistance to Cuba in 1961, India in 1962, Yemen in 1967, Peru in 1973, Angola in 1975, Ethiopia in 1977, Iran in 1980, and Argentina in 1982 may all be considered motivated by a desire for potential strategic gain at the expense of the West.

The presence and activity of Eastern European, Cuban, Vietnamese, and North Korean military advisors, instructors, or combatants is widely taken to constitute an addition to the net Soviet presence as measured by its own personnel. The increasing scope of this military presence in the Third World must be noted in any effort to assess Soviet objectives. It is apparent that the Soviets are quite aware that such a presence may provide protection for friendly regimes, a base for potential intervention in nearby nations, and a possible deterrent to Western involvement. As a Soviet military writer recently observed: "In some situations, the very knowledge of a Soviet military presence in an area in which a conflict situation is developing may serve to restrain the imperialists and local reaction."[3]

The geopolitical impact of the Soviet-Cuban alliance is of course potentially enormous. However, the sensitivity of the United States to Soviet efforts to capitalize on it has so far been inhibiting. The Soviets have regularly made efforts to test U.S. tolerance for strategic military uses of Cuban facilities and have made use of airport and naval access in Guyana and Nicaragua. So far, however, it is clear that they wish to avoid provoking forceful U.S. reactions to acquisition of strategic advantages in the Western hemisphere, particularly since the 1983 invasion of Grenada and military pressures against the Sandinista regime in Nicaragua.

Whether or not the Soviets are in fact orchestrating their world involvement to outflank the West strategically and politically is a matter of some debate.[4] Most analysts deny that the Soviets have a master plan or any deliberate long-range strategy that guides all their efforts. Nonetheless, despite the fits and starts in Soviet–Third World relations, the sudden setbacks and surprising gains, the scope of the Soviet presence in the Third World has certainly enlarged tremendously. It seems logical at this point to look back and conclude that the USSR must have been pursuing superpower status from the beginning. It could even be suggested that Soviet leaders must have been seeking to accumulate allies in the Third World to contain the United States and/or to outflank the West from the South.

The acquisition of allies, clients, and friends has a logic of its own. Foreign Minister Andrei Gromyko's 1971 statement that "there is no question of significance which can be resolved without the Soviet Union, or in opposition to the Soviet Union" became a popular theme of foreign policy commentary in the seventies. The agreements that comprised détente incorporated a recognition of Soviet-U.S. strategic equality, taken by the Soviets as recognition of their superpower status. They attribute this both to military might and to the "sweep of history" that has caused the balance of forces to shift in favor of the socialist camp. The scope of Soviet foreign policy in the Third World, and the effort devoted to establishing normal diplomatic and commercial relations with nearly all countries can be seen as reflecting an urge to be globally established.

Beyond this question of status and recognition, the interest in acquiring clients, dependencies, or allies also reflects the pursuit of influence and control over regimes and their assets. While it is fairly easy to notice those relationships where the USSR has attempted to exert control and to guide events to its benefit, it is somewhat more difficult to be sure of the magnitude of Soviet efforts to acquire potential for control. Should Third World states truly internalize Soviet values, they would view Moscow as their authority and would adapt their behavior to Soviet cues without being coerced, because they would perceive this to be in their own interests. All Soviet activity directed at fostering or rewarding political radicalism in the Third World can be seen as serving this end. Short of this ideal situation, Soviets appear to aim for relationships in which they can reasonably hope to secure cooperation with their projects and plans and through which they can increase the probability of successfully thwarting the projects and plans of their adversaries.

It is difficult to measure influence or to be sure when the Soviets have sought to exercise it.[5] Signs of frustration by patrons or statements by leaders who complain of pressure can sometimes provide clues to incidents of attempted influence. It is of course exceedingly difficult to discern whether a dependent state or ally is acting in ways beneficial to the USSR because its leaders believe that they should do so or because they share Soviet perceptions or have congruent interests. Sometimes the USSR has carefully and publicly outlined its preferences. In the Middle East, the Soviets have sought to advise and guide their friends and associates to base political solutions to the Arab-Israeli confrontation on Arab unity. In Africa, they have sought to coordinate liberation movements around anti-Western confrontational themes. Soviet statements about regional cooperation and the nonaligned conferences regularly remind Third World countries that their aims can best be achieved through "consistent anti-imperialism." Many inducements have been used in the attempt to persuade states to accede to Soviet wishes or, at the least, to convince leaders that Soviet interests deserve attention.

Soviet commentators have been enthusiastic about the popularity of the "socialist orientation." Efforts to cultivate party ties, cultural exchanges, and formal treaty links with its allies as well as a military presence appear to reflect aspirations to multiply the potential for control. Sometimes this is very direct, as in cases where security assistance is provided to protect heads of state. Other aspects of this interest in control are reflected indirectly in political and economic advice that would have the effect of institutionalizing a pro-Soviet policy. A number of friendship and cooperation treaties, which formalize alliance relationships and give them an air of permanence, have been signed.

Political changes and Soviet action in the Third World have helped to produce several new members of the socialist camp: Cuba, Vietnam, Laos, and Afghanistan. Kampuchea may be counted in this number, while Marxist-Leninist regimes such as PDRY, Congo, Angola, Mozambique, Ethiopia, and Benin can be considered close affiliates. Soviet penetration of the political systems of the camp members is extensive; control is less well-established in the latter group. The majority of Soviet relationships with Third World countries are less intensive and therefore less predictable.

The creation of various types of dependencies is obviously expected to serve control objectives. Presence and influence are not the same thing; in fact, the pursuit of influence may interfere with the maintenance of a presence. Soviet military equipment deliveries to Middle Eastern clients have often been intended to guide behavior by limiting capabilities. Soviet refusal to supply certain kinds of offensive weapons was a major complaint of both Nasir and Sadat. In Syria, Soviet personnel currently man antiaircraft defenses—perhaps as a safeguard to prevent Syrian belligerence from triggering a war with Israel. Conflicts with its allies have sometimes centered on Soviet attempts to retain control. In 1968, oil shipments to Cuba were cut off as part of a coercive effort to convince Castro to adopt more moderate domestic and foreign policies in line with Soviet wishes. Egyptian President Nasir is reported to have threatened to resign in favor of a pro-American leadership in 1970, in order to convince the Soviets to commit combat pilots to the defense of Egyptian air space.[6] India's leadership has had numerous disagreements with the Soviet Union over military aid. In one instance, the Soviets agreed to an Indian request that the USSR furnish a plant in India for the production of MiG jet engines, but only if the plant were dependent on Czechoslovakian metal products. Moscow has evidently not been pleased with the manner in which Vietnam has used its economic assistance, nor with the costs and consequences of the 1978 invasion of Kampuchea.

Soviet clients are expected to provide diplomatic support for the USSR at the United Nations and other international gatherings. A Soviet author has stated that "solidarity with the Soviet Union and the world socialist community is the internationalist revolutionary duty" of all "consistent fighters against imperialism."[7] Thus the network of Soviet relations with Third World states not only ends Soviet diplomatic isolation, but also helps to advance specific goals or projects, such as the Indian Ocean Zone of Peace, the Non-Proliferation Treaty, or the campaign to oust the United States from Diego Garcia.

It can be argued that various domestic needs and national interests are relevant to Soviet–Third World relations. Although it would be misleading to identify the pursuit of economic benefits as a motive for Soviet–Third World policy, it is still apparent that advantages accrue in many instances. Financing of assistance projects often includes commitments to deliver products of equivalent value, frequently at preferential prices. In this way the Soviet economy has obtained Egyptian cotton, Guyanese bauxite, Ethiopian coffee, Iraqi oil, and Iranian natural gas. Some relationships with Third World countries can be seen as motivated almost entirely by Soviet needs, so that diplomacy adjusts to economics. For instance, Soviet-Moroccan relations have been guided by a need to preserve the arrangement by which the USSR obtains a large share of Morocco's production of phosphate, an important fertilizer. Cordial relations with Argentina have been a major facilitator of regular grain purchases.

The persistent Soviet shortage of foreign exchange has undoubtedly been a factor behind the expansion of Soviet arms sales to oil-rich Arab states, particularly to Libya. While Libya, in turn, dispenses arms to radical associates in Africa and the Middle East, it is not clear that the Soviets are able to exercise control over these transfers. The USSR has also attempted to multiply its opportunities to benefit from export sales of oil. This has included arrangements with Venezuela to supply oil to Cuba, thus freeing some Soviet stocks for open market sales.

It has sometimes been argued that the Soviet political system needs successes and that evidence of foreign policy gains enhances its legitimacy. Thus the expansion of the Soviet presence in the Third World can be seen as serving domestic Soviet political stability by confirming its ideological rationale. It is difficult to accept this argument in view of the fact that the appearance or claim of foreign successes should suffice for this purpose. Given the controlled nature of Soviet media, it is hard to see why this impulse would be necessary to account for Third World activism. Nonetheless, it may be true that such gains may be perceived by particular leadership groups as useful and enhancing of their own position. This certainly seemed to be true of Khrushchev, who more than any other leader personally associated himself with the effort to broaden Soviet foreign contacts. An overall impression that the USSR is active and respected as a superpower may have indirect social control benefits. Global responsibilities, while intensifying patriotism, may be recalled to justify sacrifices at home.

THE DECISION-MAKING CONTEXT

Explanations of foreign policy that focus on decision makers and their operational environment can enrich our understanding of the dynamics of Soviet–Third World relations. The operational environment refers to the internal and external context in which calculations, judgments, choices, and perceptions occur. Decision makers are understood to be subject to considerations that can include factional or bureaucratic politics; sources and nature of information and interpretive advice; resources available; and determinations about the needs and priorities inherent in the situation. Additionally, those who formulate policy do so with reference to what they perceive to be the political economic and military situation in the countries with which they are concerned; the potential impact of their actions on relationships elsewhere; and their estimates of costs involved and the chances for success.

Studies of the internal determinants of Soviet foreign policy–making rely on indirect evidence, and occasional testimony from participants. Nonetheless, the detailed studies available suggest that fully satisfactory explanations of Soviet external behavior must consider the weight of the internal decision-making context. Careful scrutiny of speeches and writings of the leadership group will often show differences among individuals on foreign policy questions. Inside information has supported rumors that officials like Pyotr Shelest and Mikhail Podgorny were demoted at least in part because of differences over foreign policy questions. Mikhail Suslov, until his death in 1981 the chief Soviet ideologue and liaison with foreign communist parties, appeared to be more militant in spirit and interested in demonstrable progress toward advancement of communist causes in the Third World. Certainly some parts of the Soviet leadership elite were less enthusiastic about détente than others, and the policy had to be defended vigorously as in harmony with Marxist-Leninist ideology and Soviet national interest. Such assessments must be made with care, however, since some officials seem to shift their positions over time.

A belief also persists that factional struggle in the Soviet political system can affect policy choice. For instance, it has been argued that in 1955 Georgy Malenkov opposed Khrushchev's plan to become involved in the Middle East by supplying military aid to the Arabs. Similar criticisms were directed at Khrushchev's defeated rivals during the Twenty-First CPSU Congress in 1959. Several highly placed members of the Soviet leadership were demoted after the 1967 Middle East war, amid evidence they had criticized policy decisions made at the time. In 1969, a dispute arose over the most appropriate assistance for Egypt during the War of Attrition. Statements relating to Soviet aid policies intimate that domestic economic planners have objected to lavish credits to Third World countries or warned not to pledge more than the Soviet economy could bear to poor developing states.

The overall mood or orientation of the Soviet leadership can be important too. When Khrushchev was ousted in October 1964, his successors criticized his "harebrained schemes," which included his sometimes incautious involvement in the Third World. Leonid Brezhnev and Aleksei Kosygin brought to their leadership roles a cautious and managerial approach. A number of signals indicated reduced tolerance for ideological diversity and a greater stress on explicitly communist values. By the last years of the Brezhnev era, it was clear that a conservative mood, which would discourage any policy that could be described as "adventurist," had set in.

Soviet academic specialists on the Third World seem to have a policy relevant role as advisors and consultants to policy makers. While we cannot always link the views of specific academics with those of particular Soviet leaders, we can infer that the debates that occur in Soviet scholarly journals reflect alternative viewpoints on unresolved policy issues or problems. Most observers agree that general research tasks are set at the higher levels and assigned to the several institutes of the Academy of Sciences dealing with contemporary issues. Specialists are also regularly asked to contribute opinions or analyses on specific topics, which circulate as background and position papers and are expected to be sources of basic information. It seems fair to say that most of the information and analysis supplied by the Soviet academic specialists to foreign policy decision–makers has supported pragmatic adaptation to local events and tolerance of ideological diversities. However, published works of highly placed specialists also contain elements of a "principled critique," which must create some pressure on the leadership to demonstrate successes and benefits from their foreign policy.

A great deal of speculation exists about the relative importance of various social and economic groups on the foreign policy decision-making process. Given extensive evidence of debate among analysts about important choices, it is frequently argued that functionally distinct members of the Soviet elite will represent views that reflect particular perspectives or interests. It is often suggested that the Soviet military must be responsible for acquisitive or boldly aggressive moves in the Third World—or the military buttressed by party bureaucrats and ideological specialists. Diplomats, academics, and economic planners interested in modernizing the Soviet system are often presumed to favor accommodative foreign policy tactics. The tendency of high-level military officers to stress the need to keep the Soviet military well-equipped is often interpreted to mean that the military will be more confrontational in its own interests; that is, the military is presumed to have a vested interest in a foreign policy posture that emphasizes external dangers, justifying a continuing military build-up. Although the military might be an advocate or supporter of activist and interventionist Third World policies, various parts of the military are differentially affected by both the general tone and specific policies of Soviet foreign policy. Thus it seems the navy has been most likely to benefit from and therefore to support expansion of the Soviet presence in the Third World. Arms transfer decisions are made, at least partially, within the military hierarchy. It is possible to speculate that military planners will want to protect their resources for their own first use and may, therefore, add a conservationist pressure to the process of foreign policy making. Moreover, it can be claimed that military representatives are less willing to take risks than their civilian counterparts. Attempts to weigh the influence of the military generally acknowledge that the Defense Council of the USSR is a major actor in foreign policy decision making. This group brings together key political and party leaders, including the general secretary of the CPSU, the prime minister, the chairman of the presidium, the party secretary for military affairs, and the minister of defense. The composition of this body suggests firm civilian control of the military.[8]

The difficulties in discovering how clustered differences in attitude or policy preference actually affect the process of policy choice go beyond simple problems of evidence. Association of benefits with advocacy is logical but may not prove that parties that benefit from a policy helped to produce it. That is, we could assume that somehow the Soviet navy must have been in favor of establishing a Soviet presence in the PDRY (since doing so acquired access to a deep water port), but was against abandoning Somalia (since that meant losing port access). Similarly, we might presume that the party *apparatchiki* were in favor of developing close relations with Marxist-Leninist Third World regimes, but less tolerant of nonsocialist allies. However, a correlation or presumed correlation between a particular foreign policy and the needs or attitudes of a segment of the leadership elite is not sufficient to prove that the policy represented a political victory of some kind for that group.

Identifying groups or tendencies within the Soviet political system that may differ in their position on foreign policy questions adds a considerable burden to the task of accounting for Soviet behavior. Even if we are unable to be certain about the relative role of various groups, we should at least be sensitive to the possibility that contention among such groupings can be part of the decision-making process, and thus that foreign policy may represent the outcome of bargaining or joint decision-making processes.

The external operational environment is also an important determinant of Soviet–Third World policy. Attempts to explain Soviet behavior that concentrate on goals or the policy-making process can create an impression that the USSR is in control of its own behavior or is pursuing coherent plans. But detailed case studies suggest that Soviet actions evolve in response to rapidly unfolding events and the behavior and attitudes of other international actors. That is, Soviet policy is easily shown to be reactive, developing incrementally to cope with actual or anticipated consequences on any number of levels. This does not mean that goals, values, or preferences are not important; however, it does suggest that foreign policy is actually a dynamic process, wherein Soviet actions will reflect concerns about the impact of their policies on events.[9]

Soviet behavior is affected first of all by the nature of specific Third World events. This is certainly true of those cases where the Soviets had to adapt quickly to a coup or local war involving a client state. On the one hand, there are the temptations of political opportunities, particularly when a leadership group requests Soviet assistance—as in Ethiopia, Egypt, Syria, and Angola. On the other hand, the terms of Soviet participation in political events in the Third World are also set by local leaders, who often effectively restrict Soviet options. The reluctance of most Third World states to permit Soviet bases on their territory is one example of the limits on Soviet policy. In Southern Africa, the frontline states have not only monopolized political decision making about policy toward the Republic of South Africa but have insisted on controlling the flow of international aid to liberation groups and often imposed their own ideas about preferred leaders and strategies on guerrilla groups. In the Middle East, the USSR has often had to follow the lead of its clients and adapt to shifts of policy or sudden quarrels. Syrian conflicts with Jordan and the decision by Assad's government to boycott the Arab summit in 1980 thwarted Soviet efforts to associate themselves with a united Arab front. Thus, in a general sense, Soviet activity is always affected by "what the traffic will bear."

Yet, as the record shows, the Soviets also seem to take into consideration the costs and benefits of seizing an opportunity to become involved. On the benefit side of the ledger would be the chance to gain a new anti-Western or anti-Chinese client or a new facility. Fear of anticipated loss can also be a powerful motivator, and it has been argued that Soviet interventions in both Ethiopia and Angola resulted from a perception that a useful, or potentially useful client was in grave danger of removal.[10] More problematic is the matter of anticipated probability of success. While the Soviet leadership would probably view any opportunity more favorably if it appeared that victory would be swift, it is difficult to be certain afterward what judgments preceded any action.

Another factor that the Soviet leadership is likely to consider is the regional ramifications of its activities. Several determinations may be involved: Will that involvement damage ties between Moscow and other potential allies or clients? This consideration acquires additional significance if the dispute in question is between Soviet allies. The Soviets, as we have seen, are fully cognizant of the costs of having to choose between friends. Could the Soviet Union be drawn into wider fighting as a result of its activities? The risks are multiplied in an area such as the Middle East, where many states could easily be mobilized in common cause against Israel, or in an instance where the potential client is a national liberation movement. Should that national liberation movement have bases in a neighboring country, a cycle of retaliation and counterattack could develop with target states. It is of course possible that the Soviets will expect regional reactions to be positive. If other regional powers welcome the Soviet involvement, as was the case in Angola, this can provide an added inducement to intervention.

The Soviets, while wishing to weaken Chinese and U.S. positions, certainly act with an eye to Chinese and Western reactions. More interesting is the question of Soviet sensitivity to the risks of a U.S. reaction. The Soviets have been cautious about involvement in situations where the West already had a firmly established presence or might be expected to respond.[11] In those situations where U.S. interests appeared to be more concretely engaged, the Soviet leadership have been careful to advertise their intentions and to attempt to allay possible anxieties about their behavior. (This kind of signaling and careful communication was present during the Vietnam conflict, the Middle East war of 1973, and in the Ethiopia-Somalia war of 1978.) Recently, Soviet aid recipients such as Mozambique, Angola, and Nicaragua have found the USSR reluctant to become committed to their defense against possible external threats. Protective pledges even to Cuba remain untested.

In general, lack of Soviet control over events and the policy choices they present sometimes seems to be the result of the actions of allied countries and the consequent pressures on the superpower as patron to go along, or lose credibility. The Soviets have been dragged into a number of conflicts, such as the Indian war with Pakistan over the secession of Bangladesh in 1971, the Vietnamese invasion of Kampuchea in 1978, and the Syrian assault on the established leadership of the Palestine Liberation Organization in 1983. Soviet relations with African states and with conservative Arab states have been compromised by the perception that the USSR is responsible for disruptive Libyan activities.

An environmental emphasis also stresses the effects other actors have on Soviet policy. As superpower, bloc leader, and alleged champion of the forces of political change, the USSR simultaneously manages a large number of relationships of various kinds. Inevitably, actions directed at modifying one relationship will have an effect on others. To the extent that Soviet leaders are actively guiding the USSR's foreign behavior, we may assume that they will normally attempt to assess the probable risks, costs, and gains of possible actions—not only with respect to particular goals but also for their possible effect on the quality or durability of important bilateral relationships.

Taken together, these factors present a persuasive picture of the reactive nature of Soviet policy. With overall political objectives and considerations in mind, the Soviets necessarily behave within the parameters of the local situation. In sum, consideration of the complexity of the processes and factors that can affect Soviet–Third World behavior suggests not only that care should be taken in explaining Soviet policy but that caution is also advisable in predicting Soviet action even when the pattern of past actions seems clear.

NOTES

1. *Pravda*, December 22, 1963; in *Current Digest of the Soviet Press* [hereafter CDSP], vol. 15, no. 51, p. 11.

2. Report to the 25th Congress of the CPSU, *Pravda*, Feburary 25, 1976, in CDSP, vol. 28, no. 8, p. 3.

3. V. M. Kulish, *Military Force and International Relations* (Moscow: International Relations, 1972), Joint Publications Research Service 58947 (May 8, 1973), p. 103.

4. It is impossible to say for certain, for instance, whether the increase in Soviet naval capabilities animates Soviet attempts to win friends in the Third World, or whether successes in the Third World have elicited the expansion of the navy. Ultimately, it may be that the capabilities and the presence grow together.

5. See Alvin Z. Rubinstein, "Assessing Influence as a Problem in Foreign Policy Analysis," in his *Soviet and Chinese Influence in the Third World* (New York: Praeger Publishers, 1975), pp. 1–22.

6. See George W. Breslauer, "Soviet Policy in the Middle East, 1967–72: Unalterable Antagonism or Collaborative Competition?" in Alexander George, ed., *Managing U.S.-Soviet Rivalry: Problems of Crisis Prevention* (Boulder, Colo.: Westview Press, 1983), pp. 65–106.

7. B. G. Gafurov, introduction to *Lenin and National Liberation in the East*, ed. by B. G. Gafurov and G. F. Kim (Moscow: Progress Publishers, 1978), p. 17.

8. See Morton Schwartz, *The Foreign Policy of the USSR: Domestic Factors* (Encino, Calif.: Dickenson Press, 1975); Michael MccGwire et al., eds., *Soviet Naval Policy* (New York: Praeger Publishers, 1975); Hannes Adomeit and Robert Boardman, eds., *Foreign Policy Making in Communist Countries: A Comparative Approach* (New York: Praeger Publishers, 1979); Timothy J. Colton, "The Impact of the Military on Soviet Society," in Seweryn Bialer, ed., *The Domestic Context of Soviet Foreign Policy* (Boulder, Colo.: Westview Press, 1981), pp. 119–138.

9. Arthur J. Klinghoffer, *The Angolan War: A Study in Soviet Policy in the Third World* (Boulder, Colo.: Westview Press, 1980), pp. 2–5; 304–306.

10. Jiri Valenta, "Soviet-Cuban Intervention in the Horn of Africa: Impact and Lessons," *Journal of International Affairs*, vol. 34, no. 2 (Fall/Winter 1980/81), pp. 353–367.

11. Stephen Hosmer and Thomas Wolfe, *Soviet Policy and Practice Toward Third World Conflicts* (Lexington, Mass.: Lexington Books, 1983), Chapters 14 and 15.

Chapter Seven

Soviet– Third World Relations: Trends and Prospects

Our analysis of Soviet–Third World relations has examined the ideological prism through which Soviet leaders look at the LDCs and surveyed chronologically Soviet activities there. We have investigated the openings and obstacles that the USSR has encountered, reviewed tools of the trade, and considered sources and explanations for Soviet policy. Having explored all these issues in Soviet–Third World relations, it is left for us to pull together all the strands of Soviet policy in the Third World. Our overall assessment of Soviet–Third World relations will include an evaluation of the trends in Soviet behavior to ascertain how successful Moscow has been in its Third World policy. Lastly, we will speculate on prospects for the future, based on our understanding of the political dynamics of the Third World, probable developments in the Soviet Union's attitude and outlook, and the lessons of the past.

TRENDS AND LESSONS

Since the earliest days of the Soviet state, what we call the Third World attracted, in one way or another, the attention of the Soviet leadership. Lenin and the other Bolsheviks emphatically declared their interest in the fate of peoples and nations in the "Orient."[1] Although the Bolsheviks were politically active in some of the colonies through Comintern agents, this did not have a lasting impact. Diplomatically, the Bolshevik leadership proclaimed itself in favor of equal relations among states and set out to negotiate treaties with the Soviet Union's immediate neighbors.[2] Yet, it was not until after World War II, as the colonial era drew to a close, that Moscow began a serious effort to become a factor in Third World politics. We have seen how, in the fifties, the USSR startled the West by stepping forward as an economic aid donor and arms supplier to receptive ex-colonial governments. Soviet rhetoric offered "aid without strings," pledged support to independence movements, and denounced "neocolonialism." In the decade after Stalin's death in 1953, the Soviet Union sought increasingly to associate itself with the emergence of Third

World states as active international actors and to encourage these states to adopt positions and roles congruent with Soviet interests. For some new Third World states, relations with the Soviet Union offered a welcome opportunity to assert their independence and to diversify their foreign affiliations. In certain instances, the USSR settled for a minimal role as an unobtrusive commercial customer. Elsewhere, the USSR has acted as external guarantor of a regime's anti-Western orientation or strategic independence. In still other cases, Moscow became a particular government's patron in local disputes.

In the sixties and seventies, the circles of Soviet contacts with the Third World states were widened. Friendly relationships were established with regimes that expressed their defiance of the West with socialist and anti-imperialist rhetoric and whose policies echoed Soviet foreign policy positions. Alliance relations have varied from those with the new members of the socialist camp to a more traditional type, such as that with India, which appears to be based on reciprocal need or coincident long-term interests. In between, there is a spectrum of Soviet supporters ranging from pro-Soviet yet independently minded Algeria to the socialist-oriented states of the Congo, PDRY, Ethiopia, Angola, and Mozambique. The scope of Soviet commitments, particularly in the military sphere, changed as well. In addition to its Arab customers, the Soviets provided significant lifesaving assistance to radical regimes in Angola and Ethiopia. And the USSR, of course, acted with its own troops to prop up the communist regime in Afghanistan.

The trail of Soviet involvement in the Third World is by no means a straight line. Setbacks occurred from time to time, while the thrust of policy varied regionally. Overall, an examination of the USSR's Third World policy reveals a major enlargement of the range and scope of Moscow's activity. Several trends that will help us to assess Soviet–Third World relations emerge from the analysis. First, ideology has blended with pragmatism to affect Soviet approaches to all states. Second, there is a trend toward the militarization of some types of involvement in the LDCs. Third, perhaps in view of the reverses they have suffered at the hands of erstwhile allies, the Soviets seem to be devoting more effort to perpetuating friendships. Today we can see them employing a blend of techniques, all aimed at ensuring continuity and predictability in relationships. And fourth, in a related development, there is a marked tendency to avoid overcommitment.

From their first tentative ventures into the tumultuous Third World up to the present, the Soviets have demonstrated their ideological relativism. This includes sacrifice of local communists and diplomatic pragmatism. Although revolutionary mythology lives on, the Soviets seem to have learned that in many cases expediency dictates an emphasis on state-to-state relations, rather than on the promotion of socialism. Soviet foreign policy has, in reality, always been dualistic. Even Lenin, as noted in Chapter 1, sacrificed Iranian communists in return for the 1921 treaty of neutrality. The competing priorities exist as well in the era under consideration in this book. The USSR wavered at first between condemning the "fictitious" independence of ex-colonial successor states and dealing cordially with them as welcome additions to the "anti-imperialist" camp.

But several forces have combined to make ideological relativism more prevalent today. For the Soviets, acceptance as a superpower is expressed at least partially by the maintenance of diplomatic ties with nearly all states. Longstanding Soviet relations with Mexico and Ethiopia typify the pursuit of diplomatic relations and acceptance. Moscow maintained diplomatic ties with Ethiopian Emperor Haile Selassie until his ouster in 1974. In the case of Mexico, ties with the USSR include a cooperative agreement between Mexico and COMECON. Even among the more "progressive" states, there are sharp gradations of ideologies. Over the years, many radical, although obviously not Marxist-Leninist states, also merited Soviet approbation. A tolerant and accepting attitude toward the home-grown socialisms and radical nationalisms of those in power has been profitable. For a long time, the Soviets enjoyed a major presence in Egypt and they somewhat successfully cultivated the Ba'ath socialist governments in Iraq and Syria. Moreover, they continue to maintain relatively close political and military ties with Algeria.

Another force impelling the Soviets to their current approach would seem to be the desire to deal with Third World states in ways that are economically beneficial to Moscow. This has translated into dealing quite profitably with regimes that can hardly be called progressive. Two striking examples from opposite ends of the Middle East are Iran and Morocco. As we noted, Soviet relations with neighboring Iran produced mutual economic benefit in the form of a major long-term agreement under which Iran was expected to export approximately 1.3 billion cubic feet of natural gas to the USSR for transshipment to Germany. Despite disputes over pricing and over the shah's pro-Western orientation, economic ties remained strong until Iran's Islamic revolution. In Morocco, King Hassan is far from radical, yet the Soviet Union has made its largest Third World investment in this Middle East monarchy. This joint venture assists Moroccan industrial development and provides the phosphates sorely needed for Soviet agriculture. The war in the Western Sahara delayed but did not prevent the signing of the agreement, and King Hassan's military agreements with the Reagan administration have thus far not prevented either side from going ahead with the project. And the Soviets have assiduously pursued political and economic relations with Argentina. Not only did the USSR support Argentina during the Falklands/Malvinas crisis, but after the imposition of the U.S. grain embargo, the Soviet Union bought millions of dollars worth of wheat from Argentina.

Their diplomatic pragmatism has meant that the Soviets have not generally encouraged the political ambitions of local communists. Although in some isolated instances the Kremlin has tried to use local communists, the USSR clearly prefers to deal with ruling groups. Of course, in certain cases, Moscow has pursued a double-edged policy of using the local communists to keep an "iron in the fire" while dealing quite cordially with ruling cliques. Where they deemed it expedient, the Soviets sacrificed local communist members both figuratively and literally to facilitate state-to-state relations. Local communist parties frequently are a hindrance to Soviet policy objectives. This has been a troubling and recurrent problem in the Middle East, at times causing sharp deteriorations in bilateral relations with the states in the region. In Latin America, ties between the USSR and local communists seem at best a force that tends to isolate Moscow. Nicaragua and El Salvador are illustrative examples. In both, Moscow had maintained ties to local communist parties that were slow to join the revolutionary and progressive tide.

There is another dimension to Moscow's increasing ideological relativism. Soviet policy obviously benefits from the popularity of socialism and the proliferation of radical regimes across the globe. Since the mid-seventies, a new brand of progressiveness seems to have taken hold. According to Soviet observers and orientalists, the newer self-proclaimed Marxist-Leninists are even more progressive than their predecessors, Ghana's Nkrumah, Mali's Keita, and Egypt's Nasir. Yet while these states and their domestic and foreign policies are welcomed by the Kremlin, the Soviets have been sensitive about the boundaries of the socialist camp. Of the several radical states, most of which have signed friendship and cooperation treaties with Moscow, only three are considered full-fledged members of the group. The PDRY, Angola, Mozambique, Congo, Nicaragua, Benin, and Guinea-Bissau have never been identified as members of the socialist camp. It is also quite interesting that Soviet statements about the socialist community do not include Kampuchea, whose Vietnamese-controlled regime is not widely recognized as the legitimate government. The Soviets are apparently not eager to take on economic and political responsibility for these regimes.

A second trend that emerges from our survey is that over the years the pattern of Soviet expansion into the Third World displays a shift in instrumentalities. Diplomacy is the obvious currency of international relations and the Soviets seem, as noted above, increasingly interested in the fruits of diplomatic activity. But diplomacy is complemented by other tools of cultivation, especially economic and military assistance. The current data, as analyzed in Chapter 5, reveal that although Moscow never distributed economic assistance on the scale of the United States, the amount and number of new economic credits and related items has declined. The Soviets, at first, emphasized economic rationality—that is, the most productive and well-managed use of their aid. Subsequently, military transfers appear to have become the preferred tool. This seems a logical choice on the part of the Kremlin in light of the major economic difficulties Moscow is experiencing and because widespread and recurring Third World conflicts create a steady demand for such aid. The change to arms transfers represents a measure of the effectiveness of military assistance as a tool; in addition, the value of arms sales are a welcome source of income for the hard-pressed Soviet economy. The USSR has become a major provider, both directly and indirectly, of military hardware and is currently the principal military supplier for several combatants.

Arms transfers are but one aspect of the trend toward increasing militarization of Soviet involvement in the Third World. In retrospect, the seventies ushered in a decade of particularly dramatic Soviet military activity. The decade began with Moscow sending Soviet pilots to fly intercept missions from Egypt across the Suez Canal during Nasir's War of Attrition. During the 1973 Middle East war, Brezhnev threatened to introduce troops unilaterally into the war zone if the United States would not agree to joint intervention to protect Egypt from Israeli truce violations. The Soviets transported and supplied Cuban troops in cooperative interventions in Angola in 1975–1976, and in Ethiopia in 1977. Finally, as the decade closed, the Soviets sent their own troops into Afghanistan.

This tendency toward active participation in Third World politics has been coupled with the marked expansion of Soviet military and naval capabilities. Although no country has granted the USSR a permanent base, the Soviets do have access to a number of military and naval facilities around the world. The Soviets themselves suggest that this military presence will enable them to support allies who may be threatened by either foreign or domestic enemies. For example, the arrival of Soviet ships in Guinean ports apparently was enough to deter the Portuguese from repeating their attack on Conakry. In other cases, the provision of massive arms transfers, the stationing of military personnel, and even vociferous Soviet expressions of support have not had the desired effect. Whether or not the demonstrations of force (including gunboat diplomacy) are effective, it is the very willingness to use force, coupled with the new naval and military capabilities, that makes this trend so significant.

The December 1979 invasion of Afghanistan seems to be a watershed in the record of Soviet–Third World relations. In some senses, the Soviet invasion was nothing new. It was not even the first time Soviet troops entered a neighboring Asian state. Soviet troops had moved into Afghanistan in early 1929 and occupied Northern Iran in 1945. And Soviet troops were used twice in Eastern Europe to prevent the desertion of a Marxist-Leninist ally. However, the invasion elicited international condemnation precisely because it was so blatant and because Afghanistan was not previously a Soviet satellite. Clearly, the use of military force to protect a friendly Third World regime, as in Angola and Ethiopia, was not wholly new. But the use of Soviet troops in the Third World was an innovation.

A debate currently rages among commentators on Soviet international behavior as to whether the Soviet invasion of Afghanistan was the culmination of the trend toward militarization or an emerging pattern of future Soviet interventions around the world. As we have already noted, the Soviet stake in Afghanistan increased substantially in the period between the overthrow of the Afghan monarchy and the April 1978 coup bringing the communist party to power. That is not to say that relations between the two Central Asian neighbors had been entirely smooth. When Daoud attempted to expand Afghanistan's ties to the West, Moscow could not help but be alarmed. His simultaneous crackdown on local communist activity precipitated the coup, which the Soviets probably did not plan, but which Soviet personnel helped carry out. Once a Marxist-Leninist government came to power immediately next door, the Soviets stepped up their levels of assistance and intensified diplomatic relations. A friendship and cooperation treaty was signed in late 1978. However, by the fall of 1979, the communist party was weakened by political infighting and was under increasing attack by insurgent Islamic tribes. This presented Moscow with a dilemma: Could the Kremlin afford to let this Marxist regime on its borders fall to anticommunist Islamic forces without hurting its stature as a "super-socialist"?

When seen in this light, it can be argued that Soviet policy makers in reality had exceptionally limited options. Afghanistan represents the coalescence of particular factors that precipitated the intervention. One was Soviet prestige; a second was the proximity of Afghanistan and its traditional neutral status; a third, probably less important, was the Islamic character of the insurgents. Many Westerners argue that the Soviets feared the contagion of the Islamic revival sweeping areas contiguous to the Soviet Union. They base their assessments on the view that Moscow has never successfully incorporated the Muslims of Central Asia into the Soviet regime. Furthermore, this school of thought concludes that revolt in Central Asia is inevitable. This picture appears to be overdrawn. While there is some evidence that the Soviet leadership was concerned about infiltration in the period after the Iranian revolution, Moscow has generally tried to use Central Asia as a showplace of Islam to further its contacts with the Muslim Middle East. In addition, Central Asian religious leaders frequently meet with their coreligionists from Middle Eastern countries as part of the Soviet cultivation effort. All of this indicates that even though Central Asia is not about to explode and in fact may contain certain pluses for the Soviet Union, there is nonetheless an edge of defensiveness in Soviet attitudes. By the same token, the Islamic factor alone would not have been sufficient to prompt the Soviet invasion.

Since Afghanistan, there have been no new interventions of this type. However, the Soviets continue to develop their military and naval capabilities, as befits their superpower status. Thus it would seem fair to conclude that the trend toward militarism continues, but on a lower scale. Arms still are big business for Moscow, and the potential for direct military intervention remains.

A third trend has been the growing skill and energy of the Soviet effort to consolidate and perpetuate their Third World ties. This has several aspects: It includes ties between ruling parties and the CPSU, intensified state-to-state ties as embodied in friendship and cooperation treaties, and a concern for the internal structure and politics of the more radical Soviet friends.

In the early sixties, Moscow was, to quote Stalin, "dizzy from success." It had acquired friends in the Middle East and Asia, and many of these proved to be radical and anti-Western in their policies. The Soviets of course wanted both to maintain those ties and to convince certain of these states to proceed even further in their progressive and what was then labeled "noncapitalist" development. To that end, the USSR attempted to establish party-to-party relations, which were clearly considered to be of a higher order than routine state-to-state formal diplomatic ties. But none of the ruling parties was actually in organization or ideology akin to the CPSU. Generally, they were highly personalized and could not be relied on to preserve a pro-Soviet foreign policy orientation after a leadership change. The Soviet leadership also employed other types of incentives to win the continuing favor of these early radical states. For a while, they lavished attention and honors on Third World leaders: They handed out Orders of Lenin and Lenin Peace Prizes to visiting dignitaries such as Sukarno, Ben Bella, Nasir, Keita, Nkrumah, and Castro. But by 1968 only one of these leaders was still in power.

In the seventies, Moscow began to use a new technique, the friendship and cooperation treaty, in the ongoing political struggle to maintain its ties with and presence in a select number of Third World countries. As our discussion of the treaties revealed, the states with which these agreements have been signed vary in the extent to which their foreign policies parallel Moscow's, in the nature of the ruling groups, and in their domestic structures. Despite these differences, the treaties represent a serious try at managing the USSR's allies. They formalize Soviet bilateral relations with the signatories and emphasize the congruity of viewpoints on a number of issues. Yet they are sufficiently vague to allow each side room for maneuverability. The treaties imply some sort of Soviet military commitment, but they do not specify just what that commitment is. In fact, a review of the behavior of treaty partners does not really establish a common pattern with regard to security matters. If there is a pattern it may be in the hope or expectation that the treaty relationship will deter potential aggression. Perhaps the key element lies in the pledge of mutual consultations in the event of threats, thus ensuring policy coordination.

Clearly, this tool has been used selectively. There exist other likely treaty partners that as of this writing are not signatories. One such country is Nicaragua. Although this regime is self-proclaimed Marxist-Leninist and has since 1979 enjoyed close relations with Cuba, the USSR has kept its distance. In this case, signing a friendship treaty would be provocative to Washington. Another seemingly likely candidate is Libya. Although not Marxist-Leninist, it is Islamic socialist, supportive of Soviet foreign policy positions, and a major Soviet arms customer. In fact, in April 1983, the two publicized an "agreement in principle" to sign a friendship and cooperation treaty. Here too Moscow may be the reluctant party. It would seem that the ambitious Qaddafi is probably too unmanageable for Soviet tastes. Also given the Reagan administration's antipathy to the Libyan leader, the Soviets may well be wary of being put in a position where they might be called upon to back Qaddafi in a showdown (like the Gulf of Sidra incident) with the United States.

Soviet interaction with Third World countries has thus involved several types of relationships and levels of commitment. The inner circle of states, which maintain extremely close relations with the USSR, includes Cuba, Vietnam, and Afghanistan. The absence of a formal treaty with Cuba is a reminder that the character of the relationship must be assessed apart from the question of explicit public agreements. The next grouping, that is, the next wider circle, includes socialist-oriented states which have signed friendship and cooperation treaties, i.e., Angola, Mozambique, Ethiopia, PDRY, and the Congo. From that point on the picture becomes more complex. India, one of the first states to sign a treaty, may be considered to have a traditional relationship with Moscow. It reflects mutual needs and noninterference. Syria and

Iraq are treaty partners in a very limited sense; neither could be considered a docile client. Both are ruled by offshoots of the Ba'ath party, and neither supports the kinds of domestic political change that would be expected to please Moscow. The three are friends of the Soviet Union. Algeria, Libya, and Nicaragua are considered Soviet friends, yet none is a treaty signatory. Benin, another self-proclaimed Marxist state, might also be included in this category. All of this means that treaty management works where the Third World state is willing, where Moscow deems it necessary and advisable, and regardless of the domestic orientation.

This is not to say that domestic considerations are unimportant. On the contrary, wherever possible, Moscow has urged construction of domestic political structures to support and maintain the pro-Soviet orientations of many of these states. Soviet scholars who have studied the Third World states note that highly personalized rule inhibits political development. Extrapolating from their own experiences, they urged Third World elites to concentrate their efforts on mass mobilization and party building. Basically what they were suggesting was a two-tiered strategy: First, Third World radical elites were to campaign among the people to increase their popularity. A corollary to this was Soviet-style ideological training and indoctrination to ensure the people's loyalty not only to the leader but also to the system he installed. Second, sympathetic regimes were advised to establish Leninist vanguard political organizations. These tightly controlled hierarchical organizations could ensure the country's political direction, even if the leader were to be deposed or die in office. Clearly none of the Third World states possesses an organization exactly parallel to that of the USSR; several, however, are considered to have established acceptable institutions. Among the vanguard parties with which the CPSU deals directly are the People's Democratic Party of Afghanistan, MPLA (Angola), Benin People's Revolutionary Party, Congolese Labor Party, Ethiopian Workers' Party, FRELIMO (Mozambique), and the Yemen Socialist Party (PDRY).

Party building has not been the only concern of the Soviet leadership and the community of Soviet experts on Third World developments. They urge the progressive regimes to cooperate with local communists and, presumably, vice versa. In addition, in the aftermath of the near collapse of the Afghan regime in late 1979, Soviet recommendations are emphatic about the need to proceed at a snail's pace with the restructuring of local societies so as to avoid alienating large segments of the population that might otherwise be disposed toward supporting the ruling socialist-oriented regime.

The general thrust of Soviet development literature and of Soviet advice to ruling elites has shifted from how to achieve socialist development to how to maintain progressive elements in power. The directives are clearly aimed at avoiding reversals. Nodari Simoniia, a prominent Soviet scholar, offered the following practices as guarantees against counterrevolution: (1) the dissociation from adventurist leftist factions; (2) the struggle against bureaucratic entrenchment within the leadership; (3) the adherence to Marxism-Leninism and alliance with local communists; (4) the creation of a vanguard party; (5) the reconciliation of ethnic groups within a centralized state structure; and (6) the establishment of military and political ties with the socialist bloc.[3]

Despite this interest in policies aimed at depersonalizing politics and at establishing stable political structures, the USSR implicitly recognizes that in certain cases a political orientation is only as deeply embedded as the top-level leadership. It is, therefore, in Moscow's interest to keep these pro-Soviet and prosocialist individuals in power. Measures to increase citizens' support and to augment a leader's popularity are one means, and insuring the leader's physical safety is another. The Soviets have employed Cuban and East German troops as palace guards in, for example, Ghana, the PDRY, Mozambique, and Ethiopia. Additionally, the East Germans are also actively involved in setting up security services and training the secret police in many friendly countries. Taken together, these approaches and policies demonstrate a significant Soviet commitment to consolidate their Third World gains, to ensure against losses, and to give permanence to Soviet relations with a select client list.

A fourth and parallel trend seems to be a tendency to avoid overcommitment. Particularly since 1979, Soviet actions and public pronouncements all indicate an unwillingness to expand the range of active military and economic commitments. For example, Yuri Andropov said in June 1983:

> In the former colonial world, the countries that are the closest to us are those that have chosen a socialist orientation. We and they are united not only by common anti-imperialist and peaceable goals in foreign policy but also by common ideals of social justice and progress. We also see, of course the complexity of their situation and the difficulties of the revolutionary development. After all, it's one thing to proclaim socialism as a goal and another thing to build it. . . . The socialist countries are in sympathy with these progressive states, provide them with assistance in the spheres of politics and culture, and help to strengthen their defenses. We are also helping their economic development to the extent of our possibilities. But in the main this, like all social progress in these countries, can, of course be only the result of their peoples' labor and a correct policy on the part of their leaders.[4]

Caution seems to be the watchword. For the moment, Soviet Third World activities appear to have peaked. This is not to say that the leadership of the USSR would not seize new opportunities, should they occur.

In the first place, as we noted in our discussions of "Soviet handicaps" above, there appears to be an economically determined cap on Soviet ambitions. The slowdown in the Soviet economy (despite the 4 percent growth rate registered in 1983) means a very real limitation on the ability of the Soviet Union to dispense development assistance. Credits have been less generous and repayment agreements much stiffer. The Soviets have also been less willing to reschedule debt repayments. Third World countries, even the socialist-oriented ones, are no longer urged to decrease their ties to the West. Indeed, many of them have recently opened up their economies to foreign investment and increased economic relations with the United States and Western Europe, even with the former metropolitan powers. Gulf Oil continues to operate in Angola; Mozambique recently negotiated several new agreements with the Portuguese; and the People's Republic of the Congo has been courting Western investors since the beginning of the decade. Additionally, the oil-producing Middle East "radicals" do not hesitate to sell their product to the West and Japan.

The Soviets would clearly prefer to be involved in those states and regions in which gains can be made without many costs. They would like to maintain their list of friends without having to underwrite the local economies. As they learned in Cuba and Vietnam, such extensive involvements are extremely costly. Cuba is estimated to cost Moscow between US\$8 and \$10 million a day and Vietnam approximately US\$2 million per day. It has been reported that one of the major reasons for strains in Soviet-Vietnamese relations is Moscow's pressure on Hanoi to utilize Soviet economic aid more efficiently so as to reduce Soviet costs.[5] Of course, there are obvious payoffs: Havana, it can be argued, has repaid at least some of the Soviet investment by sending combat troops to Angola and Ethiopia as well as civilian and military advisors to Nicaragua. Nonetheless, for an economy in trouble an additional US\$10–12 million daily expenditure is a significant economic drain.

Despite the evidence indicating the militarization of Soviet–Third World relations, active military involvement (i.e., Cuban troops in Angola and Ethiopia and the Soviet invasion of Afghanistan) seems to have run its course. The Soviets have displayed considerable caution since then and, with the possible exception of Syria, do not seem anxious to take up new active military commitments. We have previously noted and analyzed the nature of the Soviet-Syrian relationship: In their efforts to remain a factor in the Middle East, the Soviets have provided Syrian

President Hafez al Assad with sophisticated arms, including SA-6 missiles and reportedly SS-21s, but have also clearly indicated to Assad that the Soviet commitment does not extend beyond the international borders of Syria. Presumably, this indicates that the USSR will not become involved in the battles in Lebanon.

SUCCESSES AND FAILURES

No analysis of Soviet–Third World relations would be complete without an assessment of Moscow's successes and failures. Overall, a review of the record shows a reasonable degree of success, coupled with several notable failures. Making this kind of assessment is always subjective since it involves speculation about Soviet objectives and about Soviet decision-making calculations. In Chapter 6 we discussed Soviet objectives and concluded that, among other things, the Soviet leaders seek to probe Western and Chinese weaknesses, to expand the presence and influence of the USSR in the Third World, and to be accepted as a superpower. At the optimum, the Kremlin hoped to achieve these goals without risking a direct Soviet-U.S. confrontation and without damaging its international prestige.

1. Has the USSR, in fact, managed to supplant the United States or at least to counter the West through its activities in the Third World? The Soviet Union has, over the years, added to its list of friends at the West's expense. Using anti-imperialism, Moscow has managed to seize opportunities created by decolonization and Western missteps. In the Middle East, when Nasir sought alternative arms sources, the Soviets transformed the opening into a major bridgehead into this volatile and strategic region. From meager beginnings in 1955, the Soviet Union became the major arms supplier to the Arab states. Because of continuing U.S. support for Israel and persisting Arab opposition to Israel, the Soviets' position as champion of the Arabs was strengthened at the expense of the Western powers and particularly of the United States. However, the Soviet Union has been unable to displace the United States as the dominant outside power in the region. Moscow, lacking diplomatic relations with Israel (since 1967) and without leverage over Israel, could not deliver to Egypt anything comparable to Henry Kissinger's successes in negotiating the disengagement agreements and to the Carter administration–sponsored Camp David Accords. The Soviets suffered a major loss in the region when Egypt became a U.S. friend.

In the Gulf, the overthrow of the shah of Iran seemed to create a major opening for Moscow—and one that would be utilized at Washington's expense. The Ayatollah Khomeini's anti-Americanism seemed tailor-made for the USSR. However, Khomeini's suspicions of outside powers extended to the Soviet Union as well. In addition, as we saw above, the USSR's policies at the outset of the Iran-Iraq war served to attenuate the already weakened ties between Moscow and Baghdad, without winning over Iran. Thus at present the Soviet Union is in a fairly weak position vis-à-vis the United States in the Gulf.

Nonetheless, Moscow has not been totally eliminated from the Middle East. Ties with Syria are retained, although they are tenuous at times. And Soviet-backed Syria has scored a major success in Lebanon with the pullout of the multinational force. In 1984, the Soviet Union exercised its veto in the United Nations Security Council to prevent the deployment of UN troops in Lebanon. Even Jordan, frustrated with U.S. backing of Israel and Washington's inability to moderate Israeli policies on the West Bank and in Lebanon, claims that the USSR *cannot* be excluded from the Middle East.

In Asia, the end of the Vietnam war and the subsequent unification of Vietnam by the communists clearly represented a Soviet gain and seemed to end the U.S.-Soviet competition for the present. The ASEAN states profess nonalignment, and although Moscow alleges that they are "tools of imperialism," it has sought to increase trade ties with them. In general, Soviet policy in this region appears directed at containing China (see below) and much less obviously at the United States.

Soviet policy in Africa has aimed at supporting decolonization, a concept that in the Soviet view means weakening Western positions. However, the USSR, despite its long history of vocal support for national liberation, has not been entirely successful in capturing the decolonization struggles on the continent. Although Moscow provided military and verbal support for the Zimbabwe African People's Union (ZAPU) during the struggle for Zimbabwe's independence, it was Western diplomatic intervention that proved successful in bringing independence to Salisbury in 1980. Just as at Camp David, the Soviets were effectively excluded from the diplomatic process. The Soviets continue to aid SWAPO, but Western-sponsored negotiations with South Africa probably hold the best chances for resolving the Namibian question. Elsewhere on the continent, the French have been actively involved on both a military and economic level. Even a radical state and treaty signatory such as the Congo has significant economic ties to France.

And finally, in Central and Latin America the Soviet Union has been the beneficiary of anti-Yankee sentiments and the trend toward the radicalization of several states in the region. Since Moscow's first tentative probe, in Guatemala in 1954, was successfully parried by a CIA-sponsored coup, the USSR's first major gain in the region was

Cuba. Although the Soviets have been cautious not to appear to violate the pledges made in the settlement of the Cuban missile crisis of 1962, Havana is the base from which they exert influence on the rest of the hemisphere. Political change, particularly in Central America, has offered tempting opportunities to the Soviets in the past five years. The revolution in Nicaragua and the political turmoil in El Salvador have benefited Moscow, albeit indirectly. The Sandinista government in Nicaragua immediately sought an alliance with both Cuba and the Soviet Union. Cubans play an active role there, assisting in medical, educational, and in military affairs, while Moscow has been cautious. The USSR praised the rising revolutionary tide in Central America as represented by the Sandinista victory but also signaled that no direct military support was forthcoming. The warning is particularly significant in light of U.S.-sponsored guerrilla activity that has troubled the Sandinista regime since 1981. El Salvador continues to simmer, and Cuban military assistance flows to antigovernment rebels there. Despite Reagan administration claims, the United States has been at a loss to detail direct Soviet involvement. Should the Salvadoran leftist rebels ultimately be successful, it would be a major blow to Washington and a major opportunity for Moscow.

Yet, Moscow's gains have been undone by local politics, and by U.S. activity. The U.S.-led invasion of Marxist Grenada held major implications for Moscow's future in the region: Fears were aroused that Nicaragua was next. The Sandinista government moved to decrease the number of Cuban advisors in Nicaragua, announced a date for elections, and proclaimed an easing of the pressures on opposition forces.

None of the preceding is meant to imply that Soviet concern with probing Western weaknesses is necessarily a zero-sum game. Across the globe, states that conduct close diplomatic and party ties with the USSR also manage to maintain ties with the West. Even friendship and cooperation treaties with Moscow do not preclude close economic ties with Western states. We have already noted the economic constraints on Soviet ambitions. It can be argued that economic ties with the West, participation in the franc zone, ties to the European Economic Community, and so forth, counterbalance Soviet ties. Generally, the Soviet role in Africa is also limited by the determination of the various liberation movements and their local supporters to avoid outside involvement. In Latin America, although Soviet economic relations have expanded greatly in the last ten years, ties with the West will continue because Western goods and technology are more attractive than comparable Soviet items.

2. Has the USSR "contained" China? Sino-Soviet competition has occurred primarily in Africa and Asia. On the African continent, China proved to be a factor in Mozambique, Angola, and in East Africa.

FRELIMO, at first a recipient of Chinese aid, has since independence turned toward the Soviet Union. And in Angola, the Soviet- and Cuban-backed MPLA won political and military power from its rivals, including the Beijing-supported FNLA. However, in East Africa, a significant Chinese presence remains.

Asia presents a different and contrasting story. In 1965, despite the extensive military aid provided to the Sukarno government, the USSR suffered a significant reversal in Indonesia. When (probably at Chinese instigation) the PKI attempted to overthrow Sukarno, the Soviet-supplied military staged a countercoup, installing a far more conservative government. Thus in a sense Moscow lost its position due to Chinese activity.

Also in Southeast Asia, the Moscow-Beijing rivalry is the driving force behind Soviet-Vietnamese-Kampuchean relations. Hanoi, with at least the acquiescence of Moscow, overthrew the pro-Chinese Pol Pot regime in Kampuchea. The regime change, while a relief to most of the world because of the bloodthirstiness of Pol Pot, was an embarrassment to Beijing, which responded by invading Vietnam. Although China was routed, the simmering animosities and continuing occupation of Kampuchea could involve the Soviet Union in future regional conflicts. Moreover, the issue of the international recognition of the pro-Soviet Heng Samrin government continues to trouble the region and Soviet relations with it.

The record thus indicates moderate success, but the possibility remains that it will be short-lived. Even India, which has fought wars with China and with Chinese-backed Pakistan, has reopened diplomatic relations with China.

3. To what extent has the USSR expanded its presence and influence? If, as we have suggested, the Soviet Union has been involved in the Third World with a view to cultivating Third World regimes, then on balance Moscow has been successful. Indeed, one of the recurring themes of this exploration of Soviet–Third World relations has been the expansion in the range and scope of ties. At the broadest level, the fact that the USSR maintains diplomatic ties with some ninety-two countries indicates its global acceptance. Still not welcome everywhere—the Soviets are trying to change that—the days are past when Moscow was regarded as insufficiently bound by conventional rules to be trusted in normal state-to-state relations.

Yet clearly trade alone, and/or exchanges of ambassadors, do not denote significant presence or influence. On a narrower level, the proliferation of new radical states, particularly in the seventies, has benefited Moscow. The quasi-orthodoxy of many of these fosters a congruence of interests that translates into support for pro-Soviet policies.

Where this congruence occurs on more than one specific issue, there seems to be greater likelihood of longer-term relations. This helps to explain the trend discussed above that urges specific domestic politics to insure a radical regime's stability.

Longevity, stability, and assistance can be converted into presence. Soviet credits, arms, even military advisors and combat troops have been distributed to many countries. There is a Soviet presence in a good number, for example, Algeria, Libya, Ethiopia, Mozambique, Angola, PDRY, Cuba, Vietnam, and Syria. In some cases, this is a strategic presence and in others, a political one.

Over the years, Soviet requests for basing rights and port access have been reported, and much has been made of the vastly expanded strategic presence. Yet, the very platform of anti-imperialism and opposition to foreign military bases on which the Soviets have sought to create commonalities has worked against them: Third World states of all types have been extremely reluctant to offer bases unless directly threatened. In fact, it is the United States that has recently increased its strategic access in the wake of the apprehension caused by the invasion of Afghanistan. At this point, the Soviets probably can reliably count on access rights within their Marxist-Leninist clients, although specific requests for strategic facilities have been publicly rejected by African coastal states. Several close Soviet associates, such as India, have taken great care to advertise their strategic impartiality and opposition to all foreign military bases. In 1980 before the outbreak of the Gulf war, Iraq proposed an Arab Charter that would prohibit Arab countries from permitting foreign bases or from granting military facilities. In addition, Saddam Hussein even called for a boycott of any Arab country that did not abide by the charter.

The strategic access that the Soviets do enjoy in many cases infuses a Soviet political presence into areas as well. The availability of Soviet combat vessels or aircraft could help to bolster the position of particular client regimes, or act as a deterrent to Western intervention. The mere fact of the availability of small numbers of advisors, troops, or weaponry can be crucial to the outcome of a Third World struggle. Yet even this kind of aid may be self-limiting. Partisanship, in reality the entrée through which the Soviet Union has found friends, often makes it difficult to expand a presence in one country to greater positions in the region as a whole.

Despite its diplomatic support, its aid, its military assistance, and its treaties, Moscow has been virtually unable to transform presence into influence. In bilateral relations with even its closest Third World allies, control has proven elusive. The details of Soviet-Cuban and Soviet-Vietnamese relations have been discussed above: Neither is a wholly compliant client. Despite the considerable overlap of Soviet and Cuban objectives in Africa and probably Nicaragua and El Salvador, and despite extensive Soviet underwriting of the Cuban economy, the possibility of divergent goals, as in the past, remains. And Vietnam's continuing occupation of Kampuchea, token pullouts notwithstanding, may not be in Moscow's best interests. In the Middle East, the Soviet Union has been particularly pushed to the sidelines. Here, of course, the most striking example is Egypt. Despite massive economic and military assistance and even Soviet combat troops, President Sadat moved first in 1972 to expel Soviet advisors and then in 1976 to abrogate the treaty. The sole remaining Soviet-linked confrontation state, Syria, has waged war in Lebanon apparently against Moscow's better judgment and virtually decimated the Arafat branch of the PLO, also a Soviet client. Elsewhere, for example in Asia, India has given at least tepid support to most Soviet diplomatic positions, including Afghanistan and Kampuchea. Yet, it has resumed diplomatic relations with China, is currently negotiating a nonaggression treaty with Pakistan, and has begun diversifying its arms supplies. And in Southern Africa, Mozambique and South Africa have signed a major accord by which Mozambique will halt assistance to the African National Congress, and South Africa will cease support for anti-Maputo guerrillas.

4. What are the costs of success? That the Soviet Union is a major factor in Third World politics today is unquestioned, but that status has been achieved with not insignificant costs. While it is difficult to put a dollar value on Soviet investment in the Third World, current estimates run upwards of US$90 billion in total economic assistance and military transfers. But the overall return is of questionable value. We have seen the limits to influence and speculated on the limits of presence. Expenditures for development assistance and arms went for naught in Somalia, Indonesia, Egypt, and Grenada. And while these are dramatic examples, in other locales regimes accepted Soviet assistance and then proceeded to distance themselves politically from Moscow.

There are political costs as well. The Soviets may have gained in international prestige, but they have lost some stature. Their reputation is no longer untarnished. As we have previously noted, partisanship has its costs. Once a conflict or dispute has been resolved with Soviet arms and/or diplomatic support, the need for Soviet assistance passes. The regime that made use of Soviet support may or may not be grateful for the assistance, while the opponent generally remains hostile. Of particular significance in this regard was Soviet behavior on the Horn of Africa. The abandonment of Somalia in favor of Ethiopia created doubts about Soviet reliability. Islamic countries that had supported Somalia criticized Moscow for its choice, and other African states, when they considered the switch on the Horn, coupled with Soviet involvement in Angola, became wary. In 1978 a Nigerian delegate to the OAU warned Moscow not to become the new imperial presence on the continent.

A great many of the nonaligned countries are sympathetic to the Soviet version of anti-imperialism and are more than willing to echo radical criticism of U.S. policy; however, many are also suspicious of Soviet claims to be disinterested. They are equally quick to associate the USSR with imperial aspirations and intentions in the Third World. As long as the Soviets themselves can be seen to behave in domineering ways, to seek control over Third World clients, or to shape political outcomes to favor their allies, they will be vulnerable to the very anti-imperialist nationalisms they have sought to foster against the West.

Finally, we would be remiss if we concluded this assessment of successes, failures, and costs without discussing Afghanistan. However one explains the Soviet invasion, it is clear that it resulted in benefits and costs to the USSR. First and most obviously, the invasion forestalled Afghanistan's defection from the Soviet camp, a goal that we assume was the top priority. Although the current situation is tenuous, the People's Democratic Party of Afghanistan remains in power at least nominally. Second, whether or not the invasion was motivated by designs on the Gulf, 115,000 Soviet troops have moved closer to the oil fields. (One must add, however, that there is exceptionally difficult terrain between those Soviet soldiers and the Gulf.) Third, an unexpected plus has been the invaluable counterinsurgency training and experience Soviet troops have received while "on the job." Recent Soviet military journals contain detailed examinations of U.S. experiences in Vietnam, including such topics as the use of helicopter gunships.

On the cost side of the balance sheet, there are both military and political consequences of the Soviet invasion. First, evidence has reached the West of discontent among Soviet troops. There have been reports of low morale and drug problems—reminiscent of the experiences of U.S. troops during the long Indochina war. In early 1983, it was announced that some Soviet officers were executed for smuggling, a fact that may indicate a breakdown of discipline. Second, the collapse of the monarchy in Iran, the seizure of U.S. hostages there and the Afghan invasion prompted the United States to increase its military presence in the Gulf area. The American Rapid Deployment Force has conducted joint maneuvers with several Middle East countries and the U.S. naval presence in the Gulf has been increased significantly. This major step-up in U.S. military presence in the region can hardly please the Soviet Union.

Third, the political repercussions of the invasion have been significant. The use of Soviet troops altered international perceptions of the Soviet Union. Several Third World allies of the USSR refused to vote against the UN resolution condemning the invasion. The Islamic Conference, to which many of the Soviet's Middle East friends belong, overwhelmingly condemned Soviet actions and suspended Afghanistan in January 1980. Even Castro was reportedly discomfited by the invasion because it weakened his position within the Nonaligned Movement. When Castro hosted the Sixth Nonaligned Summit in 1979 in Havana, he set a sharply anti-American and pro-Soviet tone, declaring the USSR the "natural ally" of the movement. He also parroted the Soviet line that true anti-imperialism should not be just neutralism, but something more positive. After Afghanistan such pro-Soviet statements are less tenable. In 1983, Indira Ghandi was hostess to the Nonaligned Summit. She specifically denied that the Nonaligned Movement had either natural allies or natural adversaries and called for a condemnation of all foreign interventions. The final declarations of the conference incorporated far less enthusiastic endorsements of Soviet positions than previous conferences.

On balance, the Soviet record is mixed. Many of their objectives have been at least partially met, but at considerable costs. Of course this is a moment-by-moment tally. The fluidity and volatility of Third World politics could facilitate new successes and new failures. One can also question at what point the costs could potentially become too great. The Soviets seem willing to run risks, to incur costs, to stay in Afghanistan, to keep Assad in line, to continue their presence in the Americas via Cuba, and to maintain their presence in sub-Saharan Africa. Thus far, the Soviets seem to feel that history is on their side. They have consistently sought to interpret political changes in the LDCs as proof that the correlation of forces and the world balance of power are shifting in their favor. Indeed, they can point with pride to the very considerable gains made in the last thirty years.

PROSPECTS

Having examined the record of Soviet–Third World relations, including the successes the USSR has enjoyed and the failures Moscow has been forced to endure, and having examined the apparent trends in Soviet behavior, we turn to speculating on the future of Soviet relations with the LDCs. Speculation is by its very nature dangerous. Unanticipated events occur with surprising regularity; one cannot predict the assassination of a leader, nor can anyone lay out the exact course of events in a regional conflict. Only the volatility of Third World politics remains unchanged.

Our exploration of this record indicates that Moscow has assets and liabilities in each geographic area. In the Middle East, despite the apparent success of Syrian President Assad in forcing the withdrawal of U.S. Marines from Lebanon and in dictating the abrogation of the Israeli-Lebanese treaty, communal fighting within Lebanon continues. There are thus still many problems to be overcome if Syrian control is to be established and extended. From the Soviet perspective, Syria, over which the Soviets seem to exercise very little control, has become stronger and has even challenged Moscow's authority. Although the USSR has tried to limit its commitment, it has also pumped military equipment into Damascus. The Soviets may find this increasingly risky because the situation changes from day to day. In general, the volatility of the region seems to limit Soviet endurance, and the persistent intra-Arab disputes multiply Soviet vulnerabilities.

The Soviet situation in Asia continues to be complicated by the Vietnamese occupation of Kampuchea and the presence of 115,000 Soviet troops in Afghanistan. Nevertheless, there are no signs that either occupation is about to end. Continuing international pressure apparently prompted a token pullout from Kampuchea in 1983, but the Khmer resistance remains and shows signs of becoming more active. In other parts of the region, while relations with India remain generally close—including a new major arms deal concluded in March 1984—there are increasing signs that India is seeking its own solution to regional problems. Nineteen eighty-three saw the creation of a joint Indo-Pakistani commission aimed at ameliorating relations between these two longtime rivals. Should the Indian-Pakistani negotiations prove fruitful, then one of the major rationales for India's substantial arms purchases from the Soviet Union would disappear. It is, therefore, not surprising that the USSR tried to dampen enthusiasm for the significant step toward ending tensions in the area. In their broadcasts to India, the Soviets claim that Pakistan is insincere in its desire to negotiate with India.[6] It seems on balance that the Soviet Union is highly vulnerable in this region despite the establishment of pro-Soviet communist regimes in Indochina and Afghanistan.

The Southern African terrain is currently undergoing major changes. The two Soviet allies there, Mozambique and Angola, have each concluded agreements with South Africa in 1984. Mozambique's nonaggression pact with Pretoria was signed with much fanfare and amid Western reports that Machel was dissatisfied with the levels of Soviet economic and military aid. Mozambique was clearly unable to sustain continuing South African military attacks and apparently decided that revived trade with Pretoria was in its best interests. The Angolan situation reflects several factors, including the question of Namibian self-determination.

At issue are the South African occupation of Angolan territory, the presence of Cuban troops in Angola, Luanda's support for SWAPO, and South Africa's backing of UNITA. It seems clear that South African military activities convinced the Angolans to make a deal. South Africa has disengaged its troops from Angola, and the two signed a cease-fire agreement. Then in March 1984, Angolan President José Eduardo dos Santos visited Cuba to discuss the withdrawal of Cuban troops. According to Western accounts of the joint communiqué, several preconditions for the withdrawal were set, including the unilateral withdrawal of all South African troops from Angolan territory, South African withdrawal from Namibia, and the cessation of all aid to UNITA. In the Mozambican case, Pretoria did agree to end its support of antigovernment rebels, but thus far it has not withdrawn its backing of UNITA. It remains to be seen how long-lived these new regional security arrangements are, but a future role for Moscow cannot be ruled out. Should either accord collapse, Mozambique and especially Angola would certainly invite Moscow and/or Havana to stay.

On the whole, Central and Latin America are difficult regions for the Soviet Union. Until October 1983, the Soviets appeared to have made major gains in the area. But following the U.S.-led invasion of Grenada, Soviet policy there appears to be on hold. Particularly in Central America, anti-Americanism is widespread. Yet, although anti-Americanism has been used successfully in other locales, the Soviets seem to realize that the region's proximity to the United States dictates that Moscow proceed cautiously. The late Soviet President Yuri Andropov explicitly compared Afghanistan with Central America in an interview in April 1983. He said:

> It is, however, far from being a matter of indifference to us what is happening directly on our southern border. Washington even goes as far as arrogating for itself the right to judge what government must be there in Nicaragua since this allegedly affects U.S. vital interests. . . .
>
> But Nicaragua is over a thousand kilometers away from the U.S.A. and we have a rather long common border with Afghanistan.[7]

Despite the sarcasm in the comment, Andropov, by making the comparison, acknowledged U.S. interests in the region.

Given the current tendency toward conservation, it seems likely that the USSR will move to shore up its allies and to limit its liabilities. Hence Soviet policy in the Middle East will be characterized by the clear determination to remain a factor in the region and to regain its status as a major player. Moscow's Asian policy will be geared to minimizing the detrimental effects of the ongoing occupations of Kampuchea and Afghanistan, continuing to contain China, maintaining good relations with India, and expanding formal relations with the ASEAN countries. As the momentum toward Mozambican and Angolan accommodation with South Africa builds, the Soviets are apt to try to cut their losses by putting the best façade they can on the South African political (if not military) victories. Elsewhere, the consolidationist trend means further enhancing the military and political ties to Ethiopia. Central America is the most problematic. Following the invasion of Grenada (probably not by itself a major loss), the Soviets have very cautiously proceeded to renew their political support to Nicaragua and their "sympathies" with the Salvadoran people.[8] Moreover, they are working hard to continue the expansion of trade relations with Latin America.

Of course, any one of the characteristics could change overnight. Instability and volatility could produce additional setbacks and openings. The key question would, therefore, seem to be: How will Moscow respond to future challenges?

We have seen several signals that the USSR has set priorities among the erstwhile clients and among the regions. Foreign Minister Andrei Gromyko, writing in *Kommunist,* the theoretical journal of the CPSU, offered a roster of Soviet concerns. Implicit in his list was a set of priorities: (1) maintenance of ties with those countries that are treaty partners; (2) support for the Arab cause; (3) continuing "assistance" to Afghanistan until alleged international interference is eliminated; (4) "sympathy" for Nicaraguans and Salvadorans; (5) solidarity with the people of Namibia.[9] Several features should be noted about this formulation. First, these are very limited commitments in the sense that each is a specific country or issue—not, for example, assistance to national liberation movements in the abstract. Second, the priority for the Middle East should not be surprising, given the long history of Soviet involvement and of Soviet military and economic investment in the region. And third, even though the article was written before the U.S.-led invasion of Grenada, the Soviets expressed *sympathy,* not *support,* for the Central American radicals.

In general, any Soviet response would be cautious. As our analysis of Soviet–Third World relations indicates, caution is dictated both by internal Soviet factors and the Third World terrain. In early 1984, Yuri Andropov died, after only fifteen months in office. His successor, Konstantin Chernenko, is seventy-two and reportedly suffering from emphysema. What this clearly means is that the succession struggle is not over. Until the leadership and attendant generational disputes are resolved, it seems highly unlikely that the Soviet Union will embark on a new, adventurous course. Furthermore, Chernenko's successors must necessarily grapple with the same problems as he. Given the poor performance of the Soviet economy, the trend to avoid overcommitment will continue.

The Soviet Union's economic problems affect its foreign policy in a basic way. The USSR cannot afford any new Cubas or Vietnams. A related issue is Soviet ability to continue to supply arms. At a time of significant U.S. military build-up, the Soviet defense budget is likely to reflect the rubles going to the USSR's immediate security and not to increasing the stockpile of new weapons for export. Thus, weapons exports may compete with other Soviet needs, could potentially limit Soviet behavior, and specifically may affect the decision of whether or not to get involved and how to get involved.

The Soviets are increasingly constrained by their past history. Nowhere is this clearer than in the Middle East. Moscow has found it difficult to mend relations with Egypt, and it will have similar problems repairing the damage to relations with Iraq caused by its tilt toward Iran at the outset of the Gulf war. Moreover, the USSR is less free than previously to take sides in regional disputes. Indeed, the lessons of the Iran-Iraq war, as previously noted, or of the situation on the Horn of Africa are that when potential allies fight each other not only does Moscow have to choose, but the residue of resentment and the ramifications of the choice are long-lived. The instability in the Third World also induces caution. As we have noted, Moscow has frequently been the victim of coups and interstate, as well as intrastate, turmoil. It would appear that when the Soviet leaders have debated foreign policy inside the Kremlin, they have adapted their behavior to the constraints of the local situations.

On a global scale, it would seem fair to speculate that other international issues take priority over Third World politics. Moscow appears preoccupied with the strategic relationship in Europe and the general deterioration of Soviet-U.S. relations. The Soviet leadership has also devoted considerable attention to Sino-Soviet relations. Joint commissions have been meeting, but thus far only minor issues have been resolved. Of course, these issues are not truly separable. The Soviets still see the Chinese as a major factor in the Asian calculations, and Moscow would have to take into consideration Western responses to any activity. President Reagan's harsh rhetoric and the invasion of Grenada seem to have made the USSR wary of new provocative adventures.

None of this, however, means that given the right circumstances, the Soviets would hesitate to intervene. On the contrary, their opportunism pervades the record. One cannot rule out the future use of Cuban troops or cooperative intervention involving Vietnamese or North Korean troops or, for that matter, direct Soviet military intervention. However, the circumstances would have to be propitious. It would seem that four conditions would have to coexist for cooperative intervention to occur: (1) if there were a clear-cut choice of sides—it is simpler to intervene if the choice of client is easy; (2) if there is a great likelihood of regional acceptance of Soviet activity—as in Angola, the initial Cuban-Soviet intervention was, as we have noted, practically legitimized by the South African incursion; (3) if it is not likely to provoke the United States— this would seem to rule out active Soviet intervention in the Middle East or Latin America; (4) if it appears that success will be quick—a long fight as in Angola militates against involvement because the costs incurred would be too great.

The question of a repeat use of Soviet troops is difficult to gauge. It seems highly unlikely that Soviet troops would fight in the Third World except in areas contiguous to the Soviet Union. The security of Soviet borders is clearly of top priority. Even so, only very specific circumstances would permit direct Soviet intervention. There would have to be a socialist-oriented or communist regime threatened by imminent collapse, as in Afghanistan. Such a regime's call for help would legitimize Soviet action. However, other contiguous areas present greater hazards than Afghanistan in the form of potential U.S. reaction. It is difficult to imagine that the United States would not respond in a major military way to the Soviet invasion of, for example, Iran or Turkey.

Over the long run, Soviet–Third World relations are likely to be characterized by an "oozing" into future openings. Yet, the openings of the future are likely to be of a different order. The era of decolonization is over. The USSR will be less and less able to use anti-imperialism and anti-Westernism as the rallying cry in the Third World. And, as we have seen, there are limits to what weapons can buy. The convergent interests that facilitate weapons transfers and in turn are facilitated by them are increasingly short-lived. Economic development, not independence, is the current priority of most of the Third World. The needs and problems of the LDCs cannot be met with increasingly restricted economic assistance and rhetoric. The time has passed when Moscow could get away with this.

The changes in the Third World presage a lessening of Moscow's appeal. Although, in the abstract, the ideal of socialism continues to have its admirers, the model of the Soviet Union's economic system can no longer be held up as *the* example to follow. In addition, the Soviet Union no longer commands the superior moral power it once did. The

Kremlin has once too often abandoned an ally or behaved in a imperial manner.

All these factors would appear to limit the attractiveness of the USSR to potential friends in the Third World. Once that appeal is lost, Moscow will behave like any other great power, playing great power games. The one factor that has not changed is the availability of the Soviet Union as an alternative arms supplier. As long as there are conflicts in the Third World, local militaries will need weapons (with all the limitations implicit in that sort of relationship).

One might conclude that, since Afghanistan, the Soviets have found that their global presence restrict and moderates foreign policy options and that Soviet economic interest in trade and commerce with certain Third World countries has acted as a disincentive to the sponsorship of political change. The heady success of ten to fifteen years ago is not likely to recur.

NOTES

1. The Russians and now the Soviets use the term "Orient," *vostok* in Russian, to refer to what we call the Middle East and Asia. The discipline of studying these countries is known as oriental studies or *vostokovedenie*.

2. In 1921, the Soviet government signed treaties with both Iran and Afghanistan.

3. Nodari Simoniia, "Present Stage of the Liberation Struggle," *Asia and Africa Today* (Moscow), no. 3 (March 1981), p. 4.

4. *Pravda* and *Izvestiia*, June 16, 1983, pp. 1–2 in *Current Digest of the Soviet Press*, vol. 35, no. 25 (July 20, 1983), p. 8.

5. See the details in Leif Rosenberger, "The Soviet-Vietnamese Alliance and Kampuchea," *Survey*, no. 118/119 (Autumn/Winter 1983), pp. 207–231.

6. Moscow in English to Southeast Asia, May 19, 1983, *Foreign Broadcast Information Service* [hereafter FBIS-SOV] 83-099 (May 20, 1983), p. D1–2.

7. Interview with Yuri Andropov, TASS, April 24, 1983, in FBIS-SOV 83-080 (April 25, 1983), pp. AA9–10.

8. Andrei Gromyko, "V. I. Lenin i vneshnaia politika sovetskogo gosudarstvo," *Kommunist*, no. 6 (April 1983), p. 24.

9. Ibid.

Maps

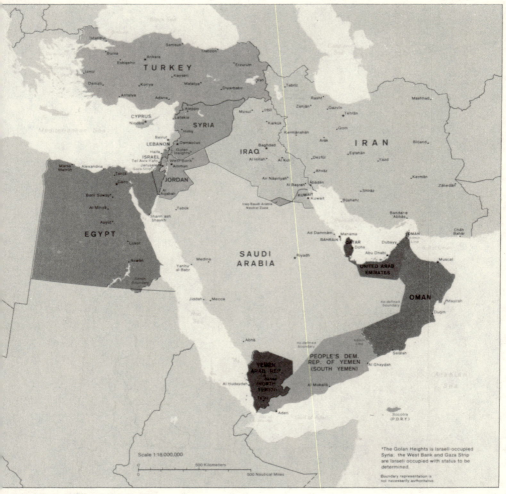

Map 1 The Middle East

220

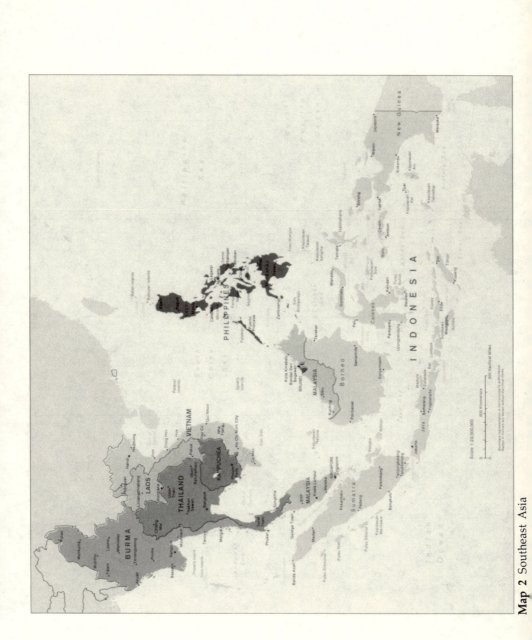

Map 2 Southeast Asia

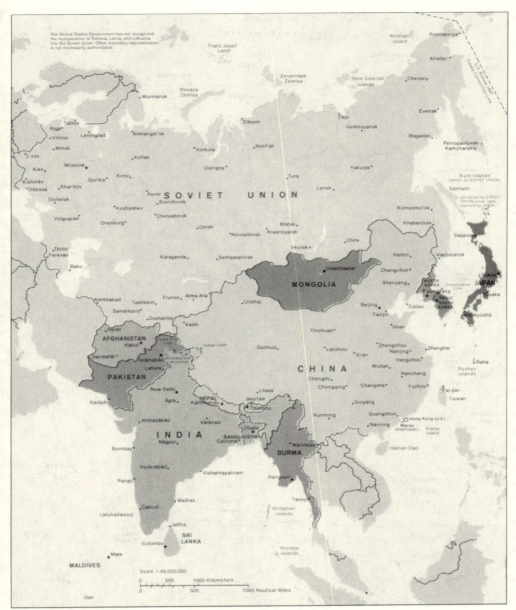

Map 3 The Soviet Union, East Asia, and South Asia

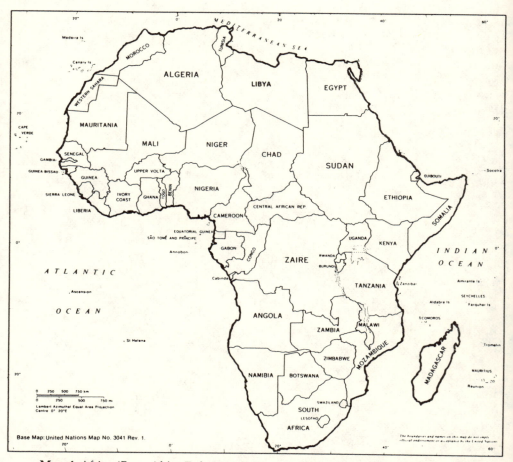

Map 4 Africa (*From Africa Today: An Atlas of Reproducible Pages,* © 1983, World Eagle, Inc. Reprinted by permission.)

Map 5 Central America and the Caribbean

224

Map 6 South America

Bibliography

WESTERN SOURCES

Books

Adomeit, Hannes, and Robert Boardman, eds., *Foreign Policy Making in Communist Countries: A Comparative Approach*. New York: Praeger Publishers, 1979.

Albright, David. *Communism in Africa*. Bloomington: Indiana University Press, 1980.

Arlinghaus, Bruce E. *Arms for Africa*. Lexington, Mass.: Lexington Books, 1983.

Arnson, Cynthia. *El Salvador, A Revolution That Confronts the United States*. Washington, D.C.: Institute for Policy Studies, 1982.

Bialer, Seweryn, ed., *The Domestic Context of Soviet Foreign Policy*. Boulder, Colo.: Westview Press, 1981.

Blasier, Cole. *The Giant's Rival, The USSR and Latin America*. Pittsburgh: University of Pittsburgh Press, 1983.

Clissold, Stephen, ed. *Soviet Relations with Latin America, 1918–1968: A Documentary Survey*. New York: Oxford University Press, 1970.

Degras, Jane, ed. *Soviet Documents on Foreign Policy*. Vol. 1. London: Oxford University Press, 1951.

Donaldson, Robert H., ed. *The Soviet Union in the Third World: Successes and Failures*. Boulder, Colo.: Westview Press, 1981.

Duncan, W. Raymond, ed. *Soviet Policy in Developing Countries*. Waltham, Mass.: Ginn-Blaisdell, 1970.

Eran, Oded. *The Mezhdunarodniki, An Assessment of Professional Expertise in the Making of Soviet Foreign Policy*. Ramat Gan, Israel: Turtle Dove Press, 1979.

Fahmy, Ismail. *Negotiating for Peace in the Middle East*. Baltimore: Johns Hopkins University Press, 1983.

Freedman, Robert O. *Soviet Policy Toward the Middle East*. New York: Praeger Publishers, 1975.

―――― . *Soviet Policy Toward the Middle East Since 1970*. Rev. ed. New York: Praeger Publishers, 1978.

George, Alexander, ed. *Managing U.S.-Soviet Rivalry: Problems of Crisis Prevention*. Boulder, Colo.: Westview Press, 1983.

Golan, Galia. *The Soviet Union and the Palestine Liberation Organization*. New York: Praeger Publishers, 1980.

Herman, Donald L., ed. *The Communist Tide in Latin America*. Austin: University of Texas Press, 1973.

Hersh, Seymour. *The Price of Power: Kissinger in the Nixon White House.* New York: Spectrum Books, 1983.

Hosmer, Stephen T., and Thomas W. Wolfe. *Soviet Policy and Practice Toward Third World Conflicts.* Lexington, Mass.: Lexington Books, 1983.

Kalb, Marvin and Bernard. *Kissinger.* Boston: Little, Brown and Company, 1974.

Kaplan, Stephen S., ed. *Diplomacy of Power: Soviet Armed Forces as a Political Instrument.* Washington, D.C.: Brookings Institution, 1981.

Klinghoffer, Arthur J. *The Angolan War: A Study in Soviet Policy in the Third World.* Boulder, Colo.: Westview Press, 1980.

MccGwire, Michael et al., eds. *Soviet Naval Policy.* New York: Praeger Publishers, 1975.

Mesa-Lago, Carmelo. *Cuba in the Seventies: Pragmatism and Institutionalization.* Albuquerque: University of New Mexico Press, 1974.

Nogee, Joseph L., and Robert H. Donaldson. *Soviet Foreign Policy Since World War II.* New York: Pergamon Press, 1981.

Rothenberg, Morris. *The USSR and Africa: New Dimensions of Soviet Global Power.* Miami: University of Miami Press, 1980.

Rubinstein, Alvin Z. *Red Star on the Nile: The Soviet-Egyptian Influence Relationship Since the June War.* Princeton: Princeton University Press, 1977.

Rubinstein, Alvin Z., ed. *Soviet and Chinese Influence in the Third World.* New York: Praeger Publishers, 1975.

Schwartz, Morton. *The Foreign Policy of the USSR: Domestic Factors.* Encino, Calif.: Dickenson Press, 1975.

Ulam, Adam. *Dangerous Relations: The Soviet Union in World Politics, 1970–1982.* New York: Oxford University Press, 1983.

———. *Expansion and Coexistence: Soviet Foreign Policy, 1917–1973.* 2d edition. New York: Praeger Publishers, 1974.

Valkenier, Elizabeth K. *The Soviet Union and the Third World, An Economic Bind.* New York: Praeger Publishers, 1983.

Voth, Alden. *Moscow Abandons Israel for the Arabs: Ten Crucial Years in the Middle East.* Washington, D.C.: University Press of America, 1980.

Articles

Chubin, Shahram. "The Soviet Union and Iran." *Foreign Affairs,* vol. 61, no. 4 (Spring 1983), pp. 921–949.

Edgington, Sylvia Woodby. "The State of Socialist Orientation: A Soviet Model for Political Development." *Soviet Union,* no. 8, pt. 2 (1981), pp. 223–251.

Golan, Galia. "The Soviet Union and Israeli Action in Lebanon." *International Affairs,* vol. 59, no. 1 (Winter 1982/1983).

Legum, Colin. "The Soviet Union, China and the West in Southern Africa." *Foreign Affairs,* vol. 54, no. 4 (July 1976), pp. 745–764.

Morison, David. "Soviet and Chinese Policies in Africa." *Africa Contemporary Record,* vol. 10 (1977–1978), pp. A94–A101.

———. "Soviet and Chinese Policies in Africa in 1978." *Africa Contemporary Record,* vol. 11 (1978–1979), pp. A73–A78.

Rosenberger, Leif. "The Soviet-Vietnamese Alliance and Kampuchea." *Survey*, no. 118/119 (Autumn/Winter 1983), pp. 207–230.

Rothenberg, Morris. "Latin America in Soviet Eyes." *Problems of Communism*, vol. 32 (September-October 1983), pp. 1–18.

Spaulding, Wallace. "Checklist of 'National Liberation Movements.'" *Problems of Communism*, vol. 31 (March-April 1982), pp. 77–82.

Valenta, Jiri. "Soviet-Cuban Intervention in the Horn of Africa: Impact and Lessons." *Journal of International Affairs*, vol. 34, no. 2 (Fall/Winter 1980/81), pp. 353–367.

Wesson, Robert. "Checklist of Communist Parties, 1982." *Problems of Communism*, vol. 32 (March-April 1983), pp. 94–102.

U.S. Government Documents

C.I.A. Foreign Assessment Center. *Communist Aid Activities in Non-Communist Less Developed Countries, 1979 and 1954–1979*. ER80-10318U, October 1980.

U.S. Arms Control and Disarmament Agency. *World Military Expenditures and Arms Transfers, 1970–1979*. ACDA Publication 112 (released March 1982).

U.S. Department of State. *Conventional Arms Transfers in the Third World, 1971–1981*. Special report 102. August 1982.

——— . *Soviet and East European Aid to the Third World, 1981*. February 1983.

Unpublished Sources

Edgington, Sylvia Woodby. "Leninism for the Third World: Recent Trends and Tensions." Paper presented at the American Association for the Advancement of Slavic Studies. Kansas City, Mo., October 1983.

Fain, Sylvia Woodby. "Evolution of Soviet Attitudes Toward Colonial Nationalism, 1946–1953: South and Southeast Asia." Ph.D. dissertation, Columbia University, 1971.

Porter, Bruce. "Soviet Military Intervention: Russian Arms and Diplomacy in Third World Conflicts." Ph.D. dissertation, Harvard University, 1979.

Saivetz, Carol R. "Periphery and Center: The Western Sahara Dispute and Soviet Policy Toward the Middle East." Paper presented at the American Association for the Advancement of Slavic Studies. Kansas City, Mo., October 1983.

——— . "Soviet Policy Toward Iran and the Persian Gulf: Legacies of the Brezhnev Era." Paper presented at the Midwest Slavics Conference. Chicago, Ill., May 1983.

Singleton, Seth. "Soviet Opportunities and Vulnerabilities in Africa." Paper presented at the American Association for the Advancement of Slavic Studies. Kansas City, Mo., October 1983.

Woodby, Sylvia. "Leninism Revisited: The Fate of the Lenin-Roy Debate." Unpublished manuscript.

Other Periodicals

Current Digest of the Soviet Press.
The Financial Gazette (Salisbury).

Foreign Broadcast Information Service. Soviet Union: Daily Report.
Ha'aretz.
New York Times.

SOVIET SOURCES

Books

Dolgopolov, E. I. *Natsional'no-osvoboditel'nye voiny na sovremennom etape.* Moscow: Voennoe izdatel'stvo ministerstva oborony SSSR, 1977.
Gafurov, B. G., and G. F. Kim, eds. *Lenin and National Liberation in the East.* Moscow: Progress Publishers, 1978.
Kulish, V. M. *Military Force and International Relations.* Moscow: International Relations, 1972. Joint Publications Research Service 58947. May 8, 1973.
Pavlenko, A. *The World Revolutionary Process.* Moscow: Progress Publishers, 1983.
Primakov, E. M. *Anatomy of the Middle East Conflict.* Moscow: iz. Mysl', 1978.
_____. *Vostok posle krakha kolonial'noi sistemy.* Moscow: iz. Nauka, 1982.
Stalin, I. V. "Ob osnovakh Leninizma" (1924), in *Sochineniia,* vol. 6. Moscow: Gospolitazdat, 1947.
Trotsky, Leon. *The First Five Years of the Comintern,* vol. 1. New York: Pioneer Press, 1945.
Ul'ianovskii, R. A. *National Liberation.* Moscow: Progress Publishers, 1978.
_____. *Sotsializm i osvobodivshiesia strany.* Moscow: iz. Nauka, 1972.
Ushakova, N. A. *Arabskaia Respublika Egipta: Sotrudnichestvo so stranami sotsializma i ekonomikcheskoe razvitie.* Moscow: iz. Nauka, 1974.

Articles

Akopian, G. "O natsional'no-osvoboditel'noi dvizhenii na blizhnem i srednem Vostoke." *Voprosy Ekonomiki,* no. 1 (January 31, 1953), pp. 58–75.
"Andropov Interview." FBIS-SOV 83-080. April 25, 1983, pp. AA1–AA10.
Brezhnev Speech at 25th CPSU Congress. *Current Digest of the Soviet Press,* vol. 28, no. 8 (1976), pp. 3–15.
Brezhnev Speech at 26th CPSU Congress. *Current Digest of the Soviet Press,* vol. 33, no. 8 (March 25, 1981), pp. 3–32.
Diakov, A. "Sovremennaia India." *Bol'shevik,* no. 3 (February 1946), pp. 38–53.
Dolgopolov, E. "Armiia razvivaiushchikhsia stran i politika." *Kommunist Vooruzhennykh Sil,* no. 6 (March 1975), pp. 76–81.
Frantsev, Iu. "Natsionalizm, oruzhie imperialisticheskoi reaktsii." *Bol'shevik,* no. 15 (July 1948), pp. 45–55.
Frolov, A. V. "Vashington i Arabskie strany Afriki." *SShA,* no. 10 (1983), pp. 34–42.
Gromyko, Andrei. "V. I. Lenin i vneshnaia politika sovetskogo gosudarstvo." *Kommunist,* no. 6 (April 1983), pp. 11–32.

Guber, A. "Situation in Indonesia." *New Times*, no. 4 (February 15, 1946), pp. 6–10.

_____. "What's Happening in Indonesia and Indochina?" *New Times*, no. 11 [21] (November 1, 1945), pp. 10–13.

Irkhin, Iu. V. "Avangardnye revoliutsionnye partii trudiashchikhsia v osvobod-ishikhsia stranakh." *Voprosy Istorii*, no. 4 (1982), pp. 55–67.

Kulykov, Iliodor. "Economic and Technical Cooperation of the USSR with Asian Countries." *Asia and Africa Today* (Moscow), no. 6 (November/December 1982), pp. 23–26.

Manchka, P. I. "Communists, Revolutionary Democrats and the Noncapitalist Path." *Voprosy Istorii KPSS*, no. 10 (October 1975), pp. 57–69 in *Current Digest of the Soviet Press*, vol. 27, no. 51 (January 21, 1976), pp. 2–5.

Novopashin, Iu. S. "Vozdeistvie real'nogo sotsializma na mirovoi revoliutsionnyi vopros: metologicheskie aspekty." *Voprosy Filosofii*, no. 8 (August 1982), pp. 3–16.

Serezhin, K. "Events in Egypt." *New Times*, no. 5. (March 1, 1946), pp. 7–10.

Simoniia, Nodari. "Present Stage of the Liberation Struggle." *Asia and Africa Today* (Moscow), no. 3 (March 1981), pp. 2–5.

Vasil'eva, V. "Sobytia v Indoneizii." *Mezhdunarodnoe Khoziaistvo i Mirovaia Politika*, no. 1-2 (January-February 1946), pp. 85–93.

Vieira, Sergio. "Viability of Scientific Socialism." *World Marxist Review*, March 1979, pp. 58–60.

Zhdanov, Andrei. "The International Situation." *For a Lasting Peace, for a People's Democracy*, November 10, 1947, pp. 1–6.

Zhukov, E. "Obostrenie krizisa kolonial'noi sistemy." *Bol'shevik*, no. 23 (December 1947), pp. 51–64.

_____. "Porazhenie iaponskogo imperializma i natsional'no-osvoboditel'naia bor'ba narodov vostochnoi Azii." *Bol'shevik*, no. 23-24 (December 1945), pp. 79–87.

_____. "Velikaia oktiabrskaia sotsialisticheskaia revoliutsia i kolonial'nyi vos-tok." *Bol'shevik*, no. 20 (November 1946), pp. 38–47.

Periodicals

Aziia i Afrika Segodnia.
Izvestiia.
Kommunist.
Latinskaia Amerika.
Literaturnaia Gazeta.
Mirovaia Ekonomika i Mezhdunarodnye Otnosheniia.
Narody Azii i Afriki.
New Times.
Pravda.
World Marxist Review.

Recommended Reading

IDEOLOGY

Kelley, Donald R. "Developments in Ideology." In *Soviet Politics in the Brezhnev Era*. Edited by Donald R. Kelley. New York: Praeger Publishers, 1980.

Meyer, Alfred G. *Leninism*. Cambridge: Harvard University Press, 1957.

Valkenier, Elizabeth Kriedl. *The Soviet Union and the Third World: An Economic Bind*. New York: Praeger Publishers, 1983.

GENERAL STUDIES

Dallin, David J. *Soviet Foreign Policy after Stalin*. Philadelphia: J. B. Lippincott, 1961.

Donaldson, Robert H., ed. *The Soviet Union in the Third World: Successes and Failures*. Boulder, Colo.: Westview Press, 1981.

Duncan, Raymond W., ed. *Soviet Policy in the Third World*. New York: Pergamon Press, 1980.

Feuchtwanger, E. J., and Peter Nailor, eds. *The Soviet Union and the Third World*. New York: St. Martin's Press, 1981.

Hosmer, Stephen T., and Thomas W. Wolfe, eds. *Soviet Policy and Practice Toward Third World Conflicts*. Lexington, Mass.: Lexington Books, 1983.

Kanet, Roger E., ed. *Soviet Foreign Policy in the 1980s*. New York: Praeger Publishers, 1982.

_____. *The Soviet Union and the Developing Nations*. Baltimore: Johns Hopkins University Press, 1975.

Rubinstein, Alvin Z., ed. *Soviet and Chinese Influence in the Third World*. New York: Praeger Publishers, 1975.

Ulam, Adam. *Dangerous Relations: The Soviet Union in World Politics, 1970–1982*. New York: Oxford University Press, 1983.

_____. *Expansion and Coexistence: Soviet Foreign Policy, 1917–1973*. 2d ed. New York: Praeger Publishers, 1974.

REGIONAL STUDIES

Asia

Bradsher, Henry S. *Afghanistan and the Soviet Union*. Durham, N.C.: Duke University Press, 1983.

Donaldson, Robert H. *The Soviet-Indian Alignment: Quest for Influence*. University of Denver Monograph Series in World Affairs, vol. 16, Books 3 and 4, 1979.

Hammond, Thomas T. *Red Star Over Afghanistan: The Communist Coup, the Soviet Invasion, and their Consequences*. Boulder, Colo.: Westview Press, 1983.

MacLane, Charles B. *Soviet-Asian Relations*. New York: Columbia University Press, 1973.

————. *Soviet Strategies in Southeast Asia*. Princeton: Princeton University Press, 1966.

Van der Kroef, Justus M. *Communism in South-East Asia*. Berkeley: University of California Press, 1980.

Zagoria, Donald S. *Vietnam Triangle: Moscow/Peking/Hanoi*. New York: Pegasus, 1967.

Zagoria, Donald S., ed. *Soviet Policy in East Asia*. New Haven: Yale University Press, 1982.

The Middle East

Dawisha, Karen. *Soviet Foreign Policy Toward Egypt*. New York: St. Martin's Press, 1979.

Freedman, Robert O. *Soviet Policy in the Middle East Since 1970*. 3d ed. New York: Praeger Publishers, 1982.

Kass, Ilana. *Soviet Involvement in the Middle East: Policy Formulation, 1966–1973*. Boulder, Colo.: Westview Press, 1978.

Kauppi, Mark V., and R. Craig Nation. *The Soviet Union and the Middle East in the 1980s*. Lexington Mass.: Lexington Books, 1983.

MacLane, Charles B. *Soviet-Mideast Relations*. New York: Columbia University Press, 1973.

Roi, Ya'acov. *The Limits of Power: Soviet Policy in the Middle East*. London: Croom Helm, 1979.

Rubinstein, Alvin Z. *Red Star on the Nile: The Soviet-Egyptian Influence Relationship Since the June War*. Princeton: Princeton University Press, 1977.

Africa

Albright, David E., ed. *Communism in Africa*. Bloomington: Indiana University Press, 1980.

Brzezinski, Zbigniew, ed. *Africa and the Communist World*. Stanford: Stanford University Press, 1963.

Klinghoffer, Arthur Jay. *The Angolan War: A Study in Soviet Policy in the Third World*. Boulder, Colo.: Westview Press, 1980.

MacLane, Charles B. *Soviet African Relations*. New York: Columbia University Press, 1973.

Ottaway, Marina S. *Soviet and American Influence in the Horn of Africa*. New York: Praeger Publishers, 1982.

Schatten, Fritz. *Communism in Africa*. New York: Praeger Publishers, 1966.

Latin America

Alexander, Robert J. *Communism in Latin America*. New Brunswick, N.J.: Rutgers University Press, 1957.

Blasier, Cole. *The Giant's Rival: The USSR and Latin America*. Pittsburgh: University of Pittsburgh Press, 1983.

Clissold, Stephen, ed. *Soviet Relations with Latin America, 1918–1968: A Documentary Survey*. New York: Oxford University Press, 1970.

Herman, Donald L., ed. *The Communist Tide in Latin America: A Selected Treatment*. Austin: University of Texas Press, 1973.

Poppino, Rollie. *International Communism in Latin America: A History of the Movement, 1917–1963*. Glencoe, Ill.: Free Press, 1964.

Ratliff, William E. *Castroism and Communism in Latin America, 1959–1976: The Varieties of Marxist-Leninist Experience*. Stanford: Hoover Institution Press, 1976.

Wesson, Robert, ed. *Communism in Central America and the Caribbean*. Stanford: Hoover Institution Press, 1982.

ANALYSES OF SOVIET BEHAVIOR

Adomeit, Hannes J. *Soviet Risk Taking and Crisis Behavior: A Theoretical and Empirical Analysis*. London: Allen and Unwin, 1982.

Adomeit, Hannes J., and Robert Boardman, eds. *Foreign Policy Making in Communist Countries: A Comparative Approach*. New York: Praeger Publishers, 1979.

Aspaturian, Vernon V. *Process and Power in Soviet Foreign Policy*. Boston: Little, Brown and Company, 1971.

Bialer, Seweryn, ed. *The Domestic Context of Soviet Foreign Policy*. Boulder, Colo.: Westview Press, 1981.

Byrnes, Robert F., ed. *After Brezhnev*. Bloomington: Indiana University Press, 1983.

Dismukes, Bradford, and James McConnell, eds. *Soviet Naval Diplomacy*. New York: Pergamon Press, 1979.

George, Alexander L., ed. *Managing U.S.-Soviet Rivalry: Problems of Crisis Prevention*. Boulder, Colo.: Westview Press, 1983.

Harkavy, Robert E. *Great Power Competition for Overseas Bases: The Geopolitics of Access Diplomacy.* New York: Pergamon Press, 1982.

Hoffmann, Erik P., and Frederic J. Fleron, Jr., eds. *The Conduct of Soviet Foreign Policy.* 2d ed., expanded. New York: Aldine Publishing Co., 1980.

Kaplan, Stephen S., ed. *Diplomacy of Power: Soviet Armed Forces as a Political Instrument.* Washington, D.C.: Brookings Institution, 1981.

Schwartz, Morton. *The Foreign Policy of the USSR: Domestic Factors.* Encino, Calif.: Dickenson Press, 1975.

Abbreviations and Acronyms

ANC	African National Congress
ASEAN	Association of Southeast Asian Nations
ASU	Arab Socialist Union
CAR	Central African Republic
CENTO	Central Treaty Organization
CMEA	See COMECON
COMECON	Council of Mutual Economic Assistance (also known as CMEA)
COPWE	Commission for Organizing the Party of the Working People of Ethiopia
CPI	Communist Party of India
CPSU	Communist Party of the Soviet Union
FLN	National Liberation Front (Algeria)
FNLA	National Front for the Liberation of Angola
FRELIMO	Front for the Liberation of Mozambique
FSLN	Sandinista National Liberation Front
GCC	Gulf Cooperation Council
GDR	German Democratic Republic
MPLA	Popular Movement for the Liberation of Angola
NCP	Noncapitalist Path
NDS	National Democratic State
LDC	less-developed country
NIEO	New International Economic Order

NATO	North Atlantic Treaty Organization
OAS	Organization of American States
OAU	Organization of African Unity
PAICG	Party for the Independence of Guinea-Bissau and Cape Verde
PDG	Democratic Party of Guinea
PDRY	People's Democratic Republic of Yemen (South Yemen, formerly known as Aden)
PFLO	Popular Front for the Liberation of Oman
PFLOAG	Popular Front for the Liberation of Oman and the Arabian Gulf
PLO	Palestine Liberation Organization
POLISARIO	Popular Front for the Liberation of Saquia-el-Hamra and Rio de Oro
PRC	People's Republic of China
SADR	Sahwari Arab Democratic Republic
SALT I	Strategic Arms Limitation Treaty
SWAPO	South West Africa People's Organization
UAR	United Arab Republic (1958–1961, union of Egypt and Syria)
UNITA	National Union for the Total Independence of Angola
WTO	Warsaw Treaty Organization (also known as Warsaw Pact)
ZANU	Zimbabwe African National Union
ZAPU	Zimbabwe African People's Union

About the Book and Authors

Soviet–Third World Relations
Carol R. Saivetz and Sylvia Woodby

Soviet–Third World Relations presents an overview of Soviet policy toward the less-developed countries and considers the determinants of that policy and its reflection in action. The authors first examine the theoretical underpinnings of Soviet–Third World policy, including Leninism and Soviet developmental models, and explore the tensions between prescribed "progressive" development strategies and the realities of Third World political processes. Next, the authors present a detailed look at the record of Soviet activities in the Third World. This is a chronological and regional account, which describes Soviet policy in the Middle East, Africa, Latin America, and Asia.

This part also provides a discussion of the openings (such as local conflicts, "liberationist" movements, and socialist causes) and the obstacles (nationalism, anti-imperialism, the volatility of Third World politics) to Soviet policy in the Third World. It closes with an analysis of Soviet foreign policy tools, and asks whether chosen policy instruments achieve their desired objectives.

In the final section of the book, the authors look at the decision-making context for Soviet–Third World relations, including an analysis of Soviet objectives, decision-making variables, and the participants in the decision-making process. They conclude by assessing trends in Soviet–Third World relations, the successes and failures of Soviet activities in the nonindustrial world, and analyzing the current situation. Here they address as well the lessons learned from the past and the prospects for the post-Brezhnev, post-Andropov era.

Carol R. Saivetz is a visiting associate professor at Simmons College and a fellow at Harvard University's Russian Research Center. **Sylvia Woodby** is associate professor and chairman of the International Relations Program at Goucher College.

Index

Israel and, 26
Korean intervention, 27
Laos and, 38
Latin America policies, 86, 88, 177, 211
Lebanese civil war and, 80–81, 106
Middle East and, 97, 202–203
Moroccan civil war and, 35, 193
Namibia policy, 85
Nicaragua and, 177, 211
Nigerian civil war and, 56
Pakistan and, 83
policy-making decisions and, 184
Rapid Deployment Force, 80, 130, 208
recent policies, 78, 79–80
South Africa and, 101
South Atlantic Conflict and, 88–89
Soviet-Cuban relations and, 177
strategic access, 206
Suez Canal crisis and, 32
Truman Doctrine, 26
Turkey and, 26
Vietnam War, 27–28, 37, 45, 54, 65, 104–105, 203, 204, 208
Uruguay, 58, 59, 88

"Vanguard" parties, 13. See also Communist parties
Velasco, Juan, 111
Venezuela, 44, 58, 59, 180
Vieira, Sergio, 136
Vietminh, 104
Vietnam, 24, 179, 198, 206
ASEAN and, 122
Cuban support of, 59
in détente era, 65–67
diplomatic relations, 104–105, 162–163, 164, 198
economic assistance to, 83, 180
expansionism, 66, 82–83
Kampuchea and, 62, 66, 82–83, 124–125, 134, 180, 186, 194, 205, 207, 210, 212
Laos and, 66

military assistance to, 104
national interest, 207
overcommitment in, 201
peace treaty, 65
post-Stalin relations with, 37–38
PRC and, 27, 54, 67, 104, 124, 174, 205
Thailand and, 124–125
troop utilizations, 214
war in, 27–28, 37, 45, 54, 65, 104–105, 203, 208
Volatility. See Political stability
Voroshilov, Kliment, 102
Vostok, 215(n1)
Vostokovedenie, 215(n1)

Warsaw Treaty Organization (WTO), 22
West Germany. See German Federal Republic
WTO. See Warsaw Treaty Organization

YAR. See Yemen Arab Republic
Yemen
civil war, 51
economic assistance to, 35
Egypt and, 99
military assistance to, 177
See also People's Democratic Republic of Yemen; Yemen Arab Republic
Yemen Arab Republic (YAR), 51, 99–100
Yepishev, A. A., 17(n11)
Yom Kippur War. See Arab-Israeli conflict
Yugoslavia, 22, 23, 26

Zahir (King), 53
Zaire, 55–56, 70, 71, 75
Zambia, 57, 58, 70, 75, 85, 154
ZANU. See Zimbabwe African National Union
Zanzibar, 43
ZAPU. See Zimbabwe African People's Union